'A VERY FINE COMMANDER'

'A VERY FINE COMMANDER'

The memoirs of General Sir Horatius Murray
GCB, KBE, DSO
(Commander of Legion of Honour and Grand
Knight of the Sword Sweden)

edited by

John Donovan

Pen & Sword
MILITARY

To the dear memory of Marjorie Florence,
younger sister of 'Nap' Murray

First published in Great Britain in 2010 by
Pen & Sword Military
an imprint of
Pen & Sword Books Ltd
47 Church Street
Barnsley
South Yorkshire
S70 2AS

Copyright © John Donovan, 2010

ISBN 978 1 84884 337 0

The right of John Donovan to be identified as Author of this Work
has been asserted by him in accordance with the Copyright,
Designs and Patents Act 1988.

A CIP catalogue record for this book is
available from the British Library.

Typeset in Sabon by
Phoenix Typesetting, Auldgirth, Dumfriesshire

Printed and bound in England by
CPI UK

Pen & Sword Books Ltd incorporates the imprints of Pen & Sword Aviation,
Pen & Sword Maritime, Pen & Sword Military, Wharncliffe Local History,
Pen & Sword Select, Pen & Sword Military Classics and Leo Cooper.

For a complete list of Pen & Sword titles please contact
PEN & SWORD BOOKS LIMITED
47 Church Street, Barnsley, South Yorkshire, S70 2AS, England
E-mail: enquiries@pen-and-sword.co.uk
Website: www.pen-and-sword.co.uk

Contents

Introduction

My uncle, General Murray, personally typed these memoirs in the mid-1970s with a view to having them published 'later'. Around that time, he wrote in 1974 to a former officer under his command, Colonel Rose Price: 'My so-called memoirs amount to 250,000 words written from memory. Their pruning and editing for someone else, much later on . . . I'm afraid I get bored when gazing too long into the past.' For many years his memoirs gathered dust in old metal military boxes and if he made any attempt to get them published, it is not recorded. He certainly mentioned the fact that he had written them to his old friend and mentor Field Marshal Montgomery, whose comment was typically unsentimental: '<u>Your</u> memoirs? Nap, whoever do you think is going to read them?'

Many years have since passed and it is hoped that they will now be read as an historic personal account of a forty-year distinguished military career, starting at Sandhurst in 1922 and ending as NAATO northern C-in-C in 1961; written by a very special man, self-deprecatory with a wicked sense of humour and a prodigious recall to the end of his long life. When one met him, one always felt better for having done so. If there is such a thing as an 'X-factor' in human nature, my uncle had it in spades. He was a most careful keeper of possessions which had significance in his life, from a bundle of correspondence with his splendid mother, a description of whom is vividly penned in the first chapter, to correspondence from Montgomery, Harding, Mark Clark and other World War Two Generals.

Curiously enough his hero was not a soldier, but Admiral Lord Nelson, whom he quoted from time to time, in particular his message to his fleet before battle: 'In Victory, Humanity.' A statement which he followed himself, both in the small and the big events of his life. Apart from a glittering military career, his handicap of five in golf and playing football for the Army, he had wide interests including the wish to read Goethe in the original, which led to his becoming an Army interpreter in German.

He considered his greatest achievement was being a Divisional Commander in four separate commands, namely the 6th Armoured Division in Italy; 1st Division in Palestine; 50th Division in Catterick; and the Commonwealth Division in Korea when Montgomery described him as being 'the best Divisional Commander that I have come across for some time, and I see a good many in my travels'. These four commands are well described in the memoirs, together with fascinating accounts of his time training with the German Army in 1937; Edward VIII (when he was King) at Staff College; the pre-war life of an Army officer in the Empire serving in India, China and Egypt; his first meeting with Montgomery in England as staff officer in the 3rd Division during the threatened invasion by Germany; his graphic accounts of battle in the Desert, Sicily, Normandy and Italy between 1942 and 1945; and his subsequent military career, ending as Commander-in-Chief, Northern Europe in the 1960s.

After retirement he turned his energies to helping others; in particular the Royal Hospital for Incurables at Putney, of which he was Chairman, and a settlement in the East End in which he sometimes lived to help the young and destitute.

John Donovan
17 May, 2010

19. January, 1953.

My dear John

   I have just returned from a visit to 50 Div in the Newcastle and Durham area. I had two objects :-

  1. To renew my contacts with that Division, which I know so well.

  2. To gain some information as to the efficiency of a Division in the Reserve Army of the U.K.

I fulfilled both objects. It was a very great pleasure to meet again the units I used to know so well; representative parties were brought in from every unit. And I checked up on what one can expect from a T.A. Division on mobilisation. 50 Div is without doubt a very fine Division. I spent nearly three days with Nap Murray. I would like to let you know that I was much impressed with him.

He has the Division completely in hand and he is liked and respected by everyone. He is without doubt a very high class Commander; he knows what he wants and he has the character and determination to see it through. I would commend him to you as being very well worthy of promotion to a Lieut-General's Command. He is the best Divisional General I have come across for some time, and I see a good many in my travels.

      Yours ever

        Montgomery of Alamein

General Sir John Harding,
  G.C.B., A.D.C.,
 C.I.G.S.
   War Office,
    London, S.W.1.

Acknowledgements

This book would not have been possible without the assistance of a number of people, and my thanks must go to the following: first and foremost Wendy, my good secretary without whom this book would never have seen the light of day; the three Cameron Highlanders ADCs, Colonels Douglas Miers, Andrew Duncan and Johnny Langlands; Major Neil Wimberley; Lieutenant General John MacMillan; Dr Alex Powers-Jones, Archivist Cameron Barracks, Inverness; Colonels J N D Lucas and McKay OBE, IC & Covenanter Cameronian Association; the Estate of Bill McFarlan MC; Brigadier Henry Wilson and the late Bobby Gainher of Pen & Sword; my brother Hugh for reproducing all the photographs; Ian McCorquodale; Broo Doherty; and Dr Yellowlees, MO 5th Cameron Highlanders, Normandy 1944.

Part 1

The Early Years 1903–1939

Chapter One

Childhood

I was the third of five children, having a brother and sister who were older than I was, and a brother and sister who were younger. My mother was a Yorkshire woman from Leeds, and my father an Irishman from Glasgow. On my mother's side, her father was a gifted engineer but he died when my mother was quite a small girl, leaving his wife with a large family and little else. The family name was Batty and they were a very well-known family in Leeds for a considerable number of years.

I do not know what the circumstances were which led to them meeting and the mutual attraction that followed. My mother was a very striking woman with rich auburn hair which fell to her waist and could only be secured by being piled up in an enormous 'bun' on the top of her head. She had the clear skin which went with it, but radiated vitality and was a veritable Yorkshire dynamo. She was slightly above medium height, had a good figure and was a dominating personality. She was very fond of music and had a good contralto voice, but had little or no opportunity of getting her voice trained when she was young. She did everything she could to encourage us to play a musical instrument, which would be either the violin or the piano. My father was definitely quite different from the ordinary kind of Yorkshireman. As a father he was a firm believer that the rod should, in no circumstances, be spared for the education of his children, a painful experience that was perhaps too frequently repeated.

My parents were married in Leeds in 1899 before settling in London where my elder sister was born in 1900. My father suffered a great deal from arthritis and twice had rheumatic fever, as a result of which he was transferred to the Winchester branch of Boots. And so it came about that the family settled in that city, where it remained through three generations for nearly seventy years.

I do not know why, but whereas my brothers and sisters were given family and conventional names, I was singled out for special treatment. My mother took a keen interest in politics and very much admired Benjamin Disraeli, although he had died when she was quite a small girl. She thereupon decided that I should be christened Benjamin Disraeli. I do not know what the reaction of my father was to this suggestion, but Grandma Batty, when she heard of this, wrote at once and told my mother 'Not to be daft'. That scotched this idea as my mother had a very wholesome respect for her own mother. At about this time my father was reading Macaulay's *Lays of Ancient Rome* and chanced upon a brave Horatius 'who kept the bridge in the brave days of old'. There was something romantic about this name which my mother was prepared to accept and so I emerged with an unusual Christian name, and as it stood also, in solitary grandeur, led inevitably to a life of abbreviations and nicknames. However, it was unique and as time went on I was pleased with the thought that, anyway, in respect of my name I was different.

Above the shop was the drawing room where there was a piano without which no household in those days could be regarded as in any way complete, and which was put to considerable use. My mother had a very pleasant contralto voice, and the piano came into its own when we had company on Sunday evenings. My elder sister and I were given piano lessons and I found this a source of considerable pleasure as the years went by. In fact, this drawing room, with its piano, were the beginnings of a great love for music for me, which remained with me for the rest of my life.

During the years preceding the First World War my mother decided that we should all become vegetarians. This meant the elaborate preparation of complicated dishes, which took so long to serve that we sometimes despaired of having anything to eat at all. This particularly applied to Sunday lunch. But no matter how much trouble was taken, and no matter how excellent the meals might have been from the point of view of quality, they always left us ravenously hungry. It came as something of a relief when the advent of the War made a strictly vegetarian diet out of the question and we could have other food which seemed to be more sustaining. My mother also had strong views on the clothes we should wear. It was normal for the boys to wear only a pair of blue shorts, a blue pullover, a pair of sandals and nothing else. We never wore hats and I do not remember that in those early days we possessed such a thing as an overcoat. The girls wore gym slips and whatever went with them. None of us seemed to get more than a fair share of colds so it proved very effective.

There were no buses in Winchester, but plenty of bicycles and tricycles. The penny-farthing had gone out of fashion before our time and we seldom saw them. The car was just coming in but was still in a very early stage of its evolution. We saw so few of them in Winchester that the appearance of one of them was an event. They had relatively little power and often had difficulty in mounting slopes which could not be considered steep by any standards. The roads for motor traffic were undeveloped and as Winchester was in the middle of a chalk belt a car would rapidly become engulfed in a swirling cloud of thick dust. I saw an aeroplane for the first time in 1914 when Gustav Hamel 'looped the loop' from the Downs just outside of the city.

Most Sundays we would go off to Sunday school, move on to church and then return home before the sermon. On arrival we would settle down to our vegetarian lunch and after a suitable interval would troop out for the Sunday walk. It was almost a route march of interminable length, made to feel so as we reckoned we were marching on an empty stomach. We walked for miles and miles. Had any of us known anything about trees or flowers or plants, or the rudiments of botany, we might have derived interest and pleasure from these walks, but as it was, they constituted a real physical ordeal, which I, for one, dreaded. I have never really got over the revulsion I felt for them. Later on, when I became a soldier, the Army was still on a horse-drawn basis and we naturally did a great deal of marching, but these never bothered me as much as the aimless wanderings in those pre-war years. We were rescued in an unexpected manner. A friend was an organist at the Garrison Church and this led to my older brother and I becoming choristers there. I think we were paid a penny for each attendance, which was very acceptable at the time. There were two services on Sunday, including one in the evening, which saw the end of the route marches.

The Barracks in Winchester included the Regimental Depots of the Green Jackets and the Hampshire Regiment. Both depots went to early morning service in Winchester Cathedral. We never seemed to get up in time so it meant that we had to race to the Garrison Church in Southgate Street, seize a surplice and cassock and dart down a short cut to get to the Cathedral ahead of the troops. The Hampshires moved out of their barracks with slow and measured tread as if they had all the time in the world and were prepared to spend it in this particular way indefinitely. They slowly wound their way down the High Street and gradually disappeared from view; as regards time and space we had nothing to fear from them. The Riflemen, however, presented an altogether different picture. Their barracks were on the upper level and they moved down past a side road past the Garrison Church and over Southgate Street into St Swithins Street. There would be a warning blast of bugles and the race was on. They simply cascaded down the hill, roared across Southgate Street, shot down St Swithins Street and round the corner at the bottom, thereafter vanishing as if the ground swallowed them up. Travelling like a train, and with the bugles firing on all cylinders, they swept up to the West Door of the Cathedral and through into the Nave like an irresistible avalanche, leaving us all with a feeling of breathlessness. It was an experience that never palled and was made the more memorable by the fact that they wore Full Dress uniform with magnificent shakoes.

When the service was over we stripped off our surplices and cassocks and ran round again to the West Door where the troops paraded prior to returning to barracks. The Hampshire Regiment went first and took the route previously used by the Green Jackets. The machine of the County Regiment was duly put into gear and it picked its way carefully up the slope and slowly uncoiled into the street beyond. This stately performance was followed by an expectant hush. Then a sharp word of command and an explosion of feet and bugles, and again the Green Jackets vanished as if they had never been. One just got a fleeting glimpse of them as they raced up the High Street, and then silence except for the distant echoing of the bugles. It was no wonder that this treat never lost its freshness and excitement.

There was little organised sport during the week and we got out games on Saturday mornings or the long summer evenings. I cannot remember where the footballs or cricket gear came from, but there always seemed to be something to play with. Even at this early stage I seemed automatically to be selected as goalkeeper. My Christian name may have had something to do with it, but I also had a safe pair of hands. I was not very tall but this was offset by the fact that a lower crossbar could be fitted to the goals, although the width of the goal seemed enormous, even unfair. The fact remained that it was only in goal that I found my way into teams of any standing. (Later playing for both the Corinthians and the Army 1st XI.)

When the War broke out I went to Hyde School, whose Headmaster was Mr Seeviour. Both my younger sister and younger brother were there by then, but it seemed odd to find myself going as the senior representative of the family. One morning a messenger arrived at One City Road from the Hampshire Education Department and handed my father a letter in which he was informed that it had been decided to offer me a Free Scholarship into Peter Symonds School with immediate effect. I heard about this when I went back for lunch and it was all so completely unexpected that it took some time to grasp the full significance of it. I returned to Hyde School in the afternoon for the last time, but mainly to inform the Headmaster of this.

It always seemed to me that Mr Seeviour took a great interest in me, and this was reflected in his selection of me to be his sword-bearer in the *Mikado*, and I appreciated it very much. He was killed in 1917. The 1914–1918 War decimated his generation and he was one of the many who could ill be spared, but he left behind a splendid memory to those who had been privileged to know him. He was quiet and unassuming, with a marvellous sense of humour and great understanding of the young.

Chapter Two

Peter Symonds School

Peter Symonds was a Magnate of the City of London, and during the reign of Queen Elizabeth I, at the beginning of the seventeenth century, made a provision for the education of a few 'deserving boys'.

When I went to this school in September 1914 there were already 250 boys in it. There was the School House, which accommodated thirty so-called 'boarders', and the rest of us were 'day-boys'.

The school is situated on a hill, which looks onto the railway station and faces south. Needless to say it had its own cricket pitch, which being on a slope was a considerable advantage when playing visiting teams. The only games played were soccer in the winter and cricket in the summer.

The Headmaster was the Reverend Telford Varley, who was above medium height with a powerful figure. He was dressed as a parson and wore the inevitable mortarboard and gown. He had flashing brown eyes and wore a well-trimmed black beard. I have never met one who was so obviously a headmaster and it came as no surprise that he was known throughout the school as 'Boss'. I was to be at the school for some years and throughout that time he dominated all its affairs, great and small. He had been 8th Wrangler at Oxford and was a distinguished mathematician. He had been appointed Headmaster when the school was formed in 1897.

'Boss' had a singsong voice, but if something happened which roused his ire he would suddenly start to purr with rage, and this would be the prelude to a devastating explosion, which could be terrifying in its intensity. It was essential to avoid this final outburst if it was at all possible, but the first clash came when it was my turn to read the lesson at morning prayers.

It was my first attempt and I looked it up carefully beforehand, but in rendering it I was a bit nervous and stumbled once or twice. Not a particularly impressive performance, but I was not prepared for what followed. At the end of prayers 'Boss' said, 'I wish to see Murray Two in my study afterwards.' This was never a very encouraging start and I duly reported. He glared at me and said 'Murray, when you read the lesson you completely ruined one of the finest passages in the Bible. You will read the lesson for the remainder of this week and you had better ensure that you do not make another hash of it.'

If you were to be beaten for whatever reason he would move across to a corner of the study, open the door of a cupboard standing there and disclose an array of about six canes of varying lengths and thickness. 'Boss' would say 'Select your weapon, Sir,' and there you stood weighing up as best you could in the short time available whether it would be preferable to go for a short thick one, or a thin long one, or some combination of both. This very remarkable man was held in great respect and did a splendid job in keeping the school on an even keel during those difficult years of the First World War. The school has expanded considerably since those days and a second hall has been added. Appropriately enough this new hall is known as Varley Hall in his memory.

Then in 1918 the war was over. It was announced to the assembled school by the Headmaster, 'Boss' Varley and we were dismissed for the day. He was very moved and had some difficulty in making the necessary announcements. Its termination came as a great relief to him, but he could never forget the terrible price that had been paid in terms of a complete generation. Inevitably we poured out of school in a state of excitement and jubilation, moved down into the city and with linked arms marched abreast down all the main streets for hours.

In 1919 a new boy came to School House as a boarder. His name was E.C. Van der Kiste and he had come to the school from Cheltenham College. His father was a Lieutenant Colonel in the Royal Artillery and it was the ambition of 'Vandy', as we called him, to follow in his father's footsteps. It happened that we were in the same form and therefore we became friends. With his background as son of an officer in the Army, he was extremely well informed of Army matters and awoke in me a corresponding interest. The transition from war to peace was bound to be a slow process and this resulted in many highly educated and highly qualified men being temporarily out of work. It also led to a great number of men competing for far too few vacancies.

And so it was that I gradually came to the conclusion that I should run for a Commission in the Army. I think the possibilities that existed for sport may well have been the deciding factor.

By this time I had been made a subaltern in the School Cadet Force and was responsible for the Armoury. This was a sizeable room in the annexe to the school and there I was normally to be found working away during school hours. I naturally played a part in all other school activities and sport, and during my last year was successively Captain of Football, Captain of Cricket and Prefect of Hall. In 1921, I also succeeded in winning the School Sports for the third year in succession. But it has to be admitted that the work I had to do to get into the Army dwarfed all other considerations.

The Entrance Examination for Sandhurst was held in Winchester College in June 1921 and some thirty of us sat for a variety of Civil Service positions. The importance of the examination was not only to pass, but also to pass sufficiently well to qualify for Prize Cadetship, as it was so extremely valuable in the 1920s. The full payment was of £200 for each year of residence, and an extra £100 for uniforms and other 'kit'. A Prize Cadet was required to pay only £20 a year and, as the 'kit' was free, had a total commitment of £40. The burden on my parents had I gone as a Paying Cadet could well have been almost unsupportable, and I discussed with my father the risk entailed. He said that it was a risk which he was prepared to accept and could only hope that I would be successful in getting a Prize Cadetship.

With the examination behind me I relaxed for about the first time in twelve months. It was the marvellous summer of 1921 and the year that the Australian Cricket Team, under W.W. Armstrong was touring the country. I believe it was one of the best teams ever to tour here and we went down to Southampton to see Hampshire play them. The county bowlers, Kennedy and Newman, bowled well, though not well enough against this powerful team, but we were more than compensated with the batting of C.B. Fry, back from semi-retirement, and C.P. Mead. It was a wonderful match, which Hampshire managed to draw.

The summer term duly ended and with it my seven years as a scholar at Peter Symonds School. In retrospect much of what happened there has become somewhat blurred with the passage of time, but the debt I owed to it is immeasurable, with the figure of 'Boss' Varley towering above all.

We were still living at Three City Road in the summer of 1921 and it would be late July that the fateful letter from the Civil Service Commissioners arrived. I was in bed and my elder sister brought it up for me to open. I gazed at the long sheet which the envelope contained for some time without grasping exactly what the import of the mass of figures with which it was covered portended. Finally I got down to the bottom and read: 'Position: Sandhurst, 6th.' That was it. There were twelve Prize Cadetships for Sandhurst, so I had achieved my aim of getting into Sandhurst almost free.

I did not realise it at the time, but in September 1921 I was embarking on a career in which, for the next forty years, my life would be nomadic and I would not remain in any one place for more than three years at the most, usually much less, but the family retained a presence in Winchester for over sixty years. It was on a blazingly hot day in early September 1921 that I took the train to Camberley in order to start my career as a soldier.

Chapter Three

Sandhurst

Arriving at Camberley Station I found myself milling about amongst a great number of others of about my age, who were also obviously Cadets.

We remained in plain clothes for two or three weeks until such time as the whole platoon was fitted out, and we wore a patch on the sleeves of our jackets for purposes of identification, of red and white, the colours of the College. Our uniform was two suits of Service Dress, a jacket and plus fours, mess kit, which was blue with a high collar, riding breeches, leggings and boots. Everything, including the boots, was hand-made. The boots were the best I ever had. We were all provided with a Sandhurst blazer in red and white stripes, the whole thing being topped with a pillbox hat, which was small and round and was perched jauntily at the correct angle on the right side of the head, being secured by a piece of elastic at the back. The clothes I wore on arrival were what a Winchester tailor once called 'a little ultra'. I wore a blue suit, which possibly fitted just a bit too well and was, conceivably, classified as 'Gents Natty'. I think that might have passed notice but I also sported a large, fluffy, beige-coloured hat, which was actually too big for my head. The ensemble was completed by a pair of pale yellow silk socks with clocks on them and brown shoes. Of course nothing was said, but one sensed the creation of an atmosphere.

There were some personalities at Sandhurst, several of whom remain in the memory as if it were yesterday. The first was our company commander, Major M. Kemp-Welch. He had originated in the Queen's Regiment but had been promoted into a regiment in the Midlands, which was somewhat unkindly referred to in those days as one of the 'Points of the Compass regiments', as they were either south, north, east or west. He was tall, angular, liked his glass

12

of port, was a good golfer and remained a bachelor. We normally took violent evasive action when he put in an appearance, particularly in the morning, but that was not possible on an early morning parade. He would stalk out, select his target and reduce the individual concerned to a frazzle in no time at all, using remarkably few words in the process. He was a character and his bluffness and occasional rudeness did not succeed in hiding a warm nature that lay beneath. After he left Sandhurst he joined the Royal Tank Regiment and by the mid 1930s was a Brigadier. He would undoubtedly have gone further, but for an accident which incapacitated him and led to premature retirement. He had to be content with a Staff appointment on the outbreak of war. I met him for the last time in Northern Ireland in 1941; he had not changed a bit.

Another personality was Bob Relf. He was the cricket coach at Sandhurst and had played for England before the war. He was a most attractive person, and was always ready to give help and advice. He had many good stories to tell about his cricketing career, particularly playing in South Africa in the pre-war years. He would always be there and it was from him that I learned seam bowling, which stood me in good stead for the rest of my cricketing life. It was exciting to be coached by an All England Player. It enabled me to get into the Company eleven, but the College side was always well out of my reach.

The years after the First World War were the years of the horse, consequently we were all taught to ride. Our dummy horses, together with lectures and demonstrations, taught us a great deal about the horse and how to ride. By means of reins suspended from the walls we were taught how to hold them and use them. It was explained how the horse could be induced to trot, or canter with the near or off foreleg leading. In spite of the smugness we generated, we failed to impress sufficiently the Master of Equitation, Major Joe Dudgeon of the Royal Scots Greys, who decreed, in our third term, that from henceforth we would ride without stirrups. This proved to be a very painful experience and undoubtedly accelerated our progress as riders.

There were also rugger and soccer trials and at once I made an impact as a goalkeeper. After two trials I was selected to play for the College. This was flattering and to some extent surprising as the goalkeeper for the previous year was still available. I subsequently discovered that my predecessor was a keen shot and was happy to be retired.

I was unaware of the Public School technique in respect of work. The important thing was to sail out with full honours without, outwardly, doing a hand's turn. To start with I set about applying myself to the work in the way to which I was accustomed, but external pressures induced me to take it much easier. The result was that at the end of the first term I found myself in the sixties instead of the first dozen. The family was quite shocked and feared that I was slipping. Had the Commandant made his speech a little earlier I would probably not have fallen into this trap; on the other hand it was a lesson to be learnt earlier rather than later.

In the event, my passing-out position, poor as it was, did not affect my career in the slightest. In the first place I got the Regiment of my choice, the Cameronians (Scottish Rifles), and secondly of the three officers posted to the Regiment I was Number Two. It is worth recording that when I gave up command of Scottish Command in 1958 I was succeeded by Number Three, then Lieutenant General Sir George Collingwood. We were in turn the Colonel of the Regiment, and the Regimental Secretary throughout was Number One, Lieutenant Colonel J.E.B. Whitehead. It was extraordinary that the three of us remained in such close association together for nearly fifty years.

Until 1922 I had not thought much about the regiment I should join. I knew there were regiments which were somewhat exclusive and many which required officers to have private means of varying amounts. These considerations narrowed the field more than somewhat as there could be no question of a private allowance for me. Captain Stanley Clark came that year to command my Company, number 5, whose regiment was the Cameronians, a regiment I had never heard of before. He had been an Oxford Soccer Blue in pre-war years. This encounter proved to have a deciding effect on my career. I then discovered that an allowance would not be necessary for the Cameronians. This, combined with the great impression I got of Stanley Clark himself, decided me to seek a commission in this old regiment and in no other.

I went back to Sandhurst in September for the Third Term and the second football season there. It would be early October that Stanley Clark sent for me and told me that the Corinthians wanted me to play for them the following Saturday against Cambridge University. The Corinthians could hold their own against any side until well into the second half, but in a fast game often had few physical resources left in the last twenty minutes against the fitter professionals. But as an exhibition of football that game provided me with a standard which served me well in later years when I was concerned in raising a regimental team.

Going to Sandhurst so soon after the Great War ended ensured that we got caught up in the military thinking of the previous ten years and the decision by higher authority that the policy should be 'back in 1914'. We did not study the history of the First World War except for the opening two months which were mainly strategical. The tactical side was never touched upon. It was only later that we discovered the impact of the air power and the tank in the last two months of the war and were unaware that the thoughts of many serving soldiers and writers were directed towards a war of movement in which the horse would play little part and I only mention it in order to emphasise the narrow field in which my military education first commenced.

The day came for our final Passing Out Parade. We all left for home the same afternoon and the time at Sandhurst, and those with whom we shared it rapidly faded into history.

Chapter Four

Aldershot and the General Strike

I was posted in the summer of 1923 to the 1st Battalion the Cameronians, which was stationed at Aldershot and with whom I served for the next ten years.

On arrival I took a taxi to Ramillies Barracks where the Battalion was located. The taxi drew up outside the Officers' Mess and an officer, who turned out to be Lieutenant Cyril N. Barclay MC, came out to receive me.

My reception was warm but reserved. The only other officer I remember being present, although there were two or three others there, was a young gentleman of about my own age who had spread-eagled himself across the settee opposite the fireplace. He gave me an airy wave and said, 'I hope there's something left for you as I seem to have eaten pretty well everything.' This individual was Second Lieutenant George Collingwood who had arrived only half an hour before I did. It was a most impressive performance so soon after his arrival and clearly did not meet with the approval of the others, least of all the acting Commanding Officer.

I was posted to 'B' Company, then commanded by Captain Alexander Galloway, a dynamic Lowland Scot. His temper reached flash point at a relatively early stage in most encounters, but luckily faded very quickly and seldom left a wrack behind. George Collingwood went to 'A' Company commanded by Captain Ronald Brodie. This remarkable character was with the 2nd Battalion in Malta before the First World War, got into financial difficulties and got to loggerheads with some of the Maltese. He suddenly disappeared and was next heard of serving as a Legionnaire in the French Foreign Legion in North Africa. He did very well there and was promoted to the rank of Corporal 'sous Feu' for his services. However, when the War became imminent he

16

was transferred back to the British Army and was commissioned into the Middlesex Regiment with whom he fought the War, and only returned to us when the War was over.

It was getting on towards the end of November when we heard that at last a Commanding Officer had been appointed to take over command. He was Lieutenant Colonel E.B. Ferrers DSO, who had a powerful figure, was above medium height and normally wore an eyeglass. He had joined the Regiment in the South African War and was dedicated to everything the Regiment stood for. He fought throughout the War on the Western Front and it was said that he always wore his sword, and kept it with him at night. To his contemporaries he was known as 'Uncle' and by the soldiers as 'Joey', and this may help to convey the high respect in which he was held throughout his service. He had no interests outside the Regiment at all, except when he occasionally went off big game shooting. He had served most of his service with our 2nd Battalion, but when he was offered command of the 1st he decided to accept even though the then CO of the 2nd Battalion would have been prepared to exchange. The officers were assembled in the billiard room when he came and introduced himself, and he explained why he had taken the course he had, which had taken all his contemporaries by surprise. I can only say that it was very fortunate for us that he took this decision as I believe he did much to mould my generation in respect of regimental service. We all are very conscious of the great debt we owe to this great Cameronian and our four years under his command were to have lasting benefits.

In the years that followed the Colonel took great pains in the training and education of young officers, for which we were very grateful, and the experience gave us a grounding which lasted throughout our careers in the Army. The first lesson that we learnt was that it was necessary to look at the 'Boss' and the Officers' Mess before dealing with the rest of the unit. His next move was in the direction of the Sergeants' Mess and the first casualty was the Regimental Sergeant Major. Other changes followed. Those who were in higher authority may well have been dissatisfied with the slowness with which these changes were put into effect, but the Colonel, who had been educated at Peterhouse, Cambridge, never took short cuts in questions of policy. I think the presence of

Major Dick O'Connor [a fellow Cameronian, later to become the famous Desert War General], who was held in the highest regard by our superiors, did a splendid job in ensuring that there was no argument. Uncle was a most loveable character and it was a delight to serve him.

The Army of the 1920s seemed to retain a considerable number of characteristics ascribed to the pre-war Army, but there was a radical change in the attitude of the men and their habits. As regards senior officers we had as our Divisional Commander in the 2nd Division, Major General Sir Peter Strickland. He was known as 'Hungry Face', I suppose because he wore a lean and hungry look. He could be extremely unpleasant, even in public, to officers immediately subordinate to him.

In my first year of service, in the summer of 1924, I found myself commanding the Company and was the only officer available. We were given the task of defending the line of a canal and I decided to assemble the whole company under cover and explain the problem and the job we had to do. At that time of the year companies were short of men so this approach was not as reckless as it appeared. I was in the middle of my disclosure when there was a sort of bark over my shoulder, 'Who are you?' I turned around to find myself confronted by the Divisional Commander, who was accompanied by two or three staff officers. I explained who I was and what I was trying to do. His eyes strayed to my shoulder which sported the single pip of a Second Lieutenant.

'And where is your Company Commander?'

'He's umpiring elsewhere.'

'And the other officers?' They were also involved in other duties. He gave a sort of snort, made some remark to one of the staff officers to enquire into this situation, and then said, 'I will come forward with you. Now what is your plan?'

My orders were to line the canal with every man I had, but he did not seem to think this was a very good idea and we discussed the alternative of a defence in depth. That was the solution finally arrived at, and he stayed long enough to see how I put it into effect and then moved away. The Commanding Officer turned up later and I got one of the biggest 'rockets' of all time for disregarding his orders. The lesson I drew was that the solution to any given tactical solution in peacetime was in accordance with the views of the senior officer present.

The quality of the officers in the 1st Battalion in the 1920s was very uneven, but in the period 1923 to 1926 we had the services of three trained staff officers, who had had battle experience in the First World War and who had been in the Regiment a few years before the War broke out. Their knowledge and experience led, in due course of time, to the extraordinary situation whereby, within the period of 'Uncle's' command, he had serving under him eight future Generals*. All clearly had the ability and it is true that the outbreak of the Second World War about fifteen years later provided the opportunities they needed. But I feel that to have shared in the process of rehabilitating an indifferent battalion under a first-class Regimental Commanding Officer also played its part.

There were other lessons that we learnt from 'Uncle'. In the 1920s, other ranks could be posted at will, to the Regimental Depot, the 2nd Battalion, or elsewhere. 'Uncle' never posted his second-best. Only the so-called specialists were excused as long as they were so employed.

Although 'Uncle' had no military ambitions outside the Regiment, he gave us all every encouragement to widen our outlook. He had been educated at Cambridge and I believe this gave him a great advantage over those who had not been so fortunate. However, we profited from his attitude in this respect.

Uncle Ferrers introduced the custom of having a regimental lunch party after the Royal Review which included the wives. This was quite an occasion, as otherwise the wives never entered the Mess at all. The highest decoration we had amongst the officers in those days was the Distinguished Service Order, worn by at least three of them, including the Commanding Officer, but our Second-in-Command, Major Thorburn, wore a very ornate decoration round his neck which had been awarded to him by the Government of the Sudan for his services there. One of the wives asked Uncle Ferrers what this decoration was and, without a

---

* Three became full Generals (O'Connor, Murray and Riddell Webster), three Lieutenant Generals (Collingwood, Galloway and Evetts) and two Major Generals (Money and Graham).

moment's hesitation, he replied: 'A decoration awarded by the Sudanese Government entitling the wearer to be admitted to the harem on Thursdays only.'

The Field Force in the 1920s was entirely on a horse-drawn basis, except for the 11th Hussars and the 12th Lancers who converted into armoured car regiments, and the Royal Tank Regiment. It would be about this time that consideration was being given to the possibility of a mechanised army, but the cost made such a thing at the time completely impracticable, nor were the implications of it studied at unit level.

I had not appreciated it at the time, but there was no limit to the amount of leave one could take. This may have stemmed from the desire of higher authority to encourage travel to those who could afford it. We normally took three or four weeks of ordinary leave, but there was no difficulty in going off to shoot, fish or go on foot-ball tours, in addition. The only stipulation was that one could only draw allowances for twenty-eight days in the year. I heard of a Guards officer who normally spent the winter as a Master of Foxhounds. At the end of manoeuvres a Rolls-Royce crept up to Company Headquarters complete with driver and footman and awaited instructions. The Company Commander sent for the junior Ensign and said, 'Would you please take over command of the Company and take it back to Pirbright? I may be back before Christmas, but the probability is that I shall not return before the Spring Drills next year.' And on that note he made the most gracious of withdrawals for a period of about six months. We never quite achieved that standard.

The establishment allowed a fixed number of Captains and Majors for a regiment of two Battalions and its Regimental Depot. A vacancy only arose if somebody retired or was seconded. Often those returning balanced those going away. The promotion of a subaltern was therefore an event of the first magnitude as it so seldom ever happened. I was at the bottom of the list when I joined, but even twelve years later I was still 8th on the list of subalterns in the Regiment. Other regiments, particularly the Rifle Brigade, were even worse off and it was only the reforms of 1938 which put matters right. We were promoted, after two years service, to the rank of full Lieutenant and there we remained embedded for more years than I would care to think about. The presence of three officers who had actually passed through the Staff College and others who were working for it ensured that we had little time to vegetate. It was in these relatively unpromising conditions that the Regiment bred officers who were destined to go a long way in their careers and produced by the middle 1950s, thirteen generals in all. Of course the rise of Hitler, combined with the Second World War, led to increased opportunities, but at the time, we were merely concerned in learning our job.

Boxing was quite another matter. There were the inter-regimental boxing matches and from these there was no escape if you were reasonably fit and sufficiently junior. I was automatically qualified to fight for the Regiment by virtue of being a relatively junior officer and fit. I weighed in those days about 11 stone and normally fought as a middleweight. On one occasion we fought against the Middlesex Regiment, who were known to be very good and against whom it was essential to win at least one of the officer weights. The experts went in a huddle and decided that I should be sacrificed to the general 'good' by being elevated to heavyweight so as to enable our heavy to move down to middle and thereby gain that all-important extra point. The officers always fought first, I suppose on the principle that they should lead their men into action, however uninspiring this feat might be. We started off with the welterweight fight in which Eric Sixsmith fought against J.R.B. Worton, the English International scrum half, a fight that was quite tremendous in that they fought each other to a standstill. They got a standing ovation at the end when they themselves had difficulty in remaining on their feet, but unfortunately for us Worton won.

Then in went our middleweight, the hope of the team, and proceeded to get knocked out in the first round. And so it was that our stratagem came to nothing, at least it never occurred to me that I was likely to make up for these upsets, and I was not very far wrong. I stepped blithely forward to provide the next stage of the entertainment. I glanced across the ring and there I saw leaning in the corner opposite what at first sight appeared to be a gorilla. On closer examination it turned out, after all, to be a human being answering to the name of Jamie Clinch, the famous Irish international rugger forward who could hardly have weighed less than

14 stone. The prospect of taking on one that weighed approximately 3 stones more than I did was faintly ludicrous, had it not been so frightening. It was clear, however, that no useful purpose would be served by gyrating backwards performing a series of violent evasive movements for three whole rounds, so, at the bell I went straight into the attack with the object of impeding, so far as I was able to do so, his ability to see. I got away with it in the first round and did a certain amount of damage, but without in any way weakening him.

I fear I lost the fight in the end but somewhat surprisingly was still on my feet at the bell. At least I had earned one more precious point but it had been gained in one of the more painful ways because in the second round my opponent made real contact. I then found myself airborne and landed in the front row of the stalls amongst the senior officers who were there. They indicated I should resume the business in hand.

Soon after this the General Strike was declared and we made the final preparations for a long road move to the north from Aldershot. One evening the officers were assembled in the billiard room and the Commanding Officer gave out his orders; it then emerged that we were bound for Catterick.

The following morning a mass of buses and lorries turned up and by the early afternoon we were embussed and on the move. It was a three-day journey and the whole of the 5th Infantry Brigade were bound for the same place, moving at intervals. The staff of the 2nd Division saw us off and in doing so said goodbye to the Battalion for good, without realising it at the time. We ourselves also assumed that this was merely an interlude, but the circumstances changed as the year wore on.

It was astonishing that we finished this first day intact as a column, owing to the difficulty of control. The Adjutant was now Captain Alexander Galloway and he saw that although we had got away with it on the first day, our luck might not last, consequently many of the officers, including myself, were taken away from the companies and perched in front of the lorries containing important stores to ensure that they were not lost. I had the privilege of being installed on the front seat of the lorry containing the blankets. We went very slowly and Catterick seemed a long way off but the plan nevertheless worked. It may have been that our progress was unimpeded by strikers because we were a Scottish Regiment and apart from a few jeers we emerged unscathed at the other end. All of us were extremely vulnerable and I could not help wondering what the lorry driver and I would have done if the crowd, by any chance, became hostile. It was late evening when we ran past the Catterick racecourse and turned off to the camp. After several weeks of training in Catterick and acting as a force to deal with strikers, the Regiment returned to Aldershot when the general strike collapsed in the summer of 1929.

It was customary in those days when leaving a station to make regimental calls on higher Commanders. This duty I carried out, calling amongst others on the Divisional Commander, General Strickland. A few days later I ran into him and he said: 'I am very sorry indeed to have missed your Commanding Officer, and that your Regiment will be leaving my command and that I will not have the pleasure of saying goodbye personally to your Commanding Officer but I would be grateful if you would deliver this letter to him when you arrive at Catterick.' I was somewhat surprised by his affability, but the letter was duly brought around by his ADC and I put it amongst the other papers. On arrival I told 'Uncle' that I had a personal letter from General Strickland, which I then handed to him. 'Oh,' said Uncle Ferrers, who, without opening it, tore it into pieces and threw it into the waste paper basket. 'You may fall out, Mr Murray,' was all he said. I had no idea that 'Uncle' resented so deeply the treatment he had been accorded, and saluted and left. It went to show how little we knew about the affairs of our senior officers and the battles they had to fight on our behalf.

Chapter Five

China

We knew that China had been in a state of anarchy for some years, but it was only towards the end of 1926 that a real threat started to develop in the direction of Shanghai and the decision was taken to send a British Division there to protect it. The whole thing was planned in such a leisurely way that it was difficult to believe that we could possibly arrive at the other end in time. It emerged that troops were also being sent from India, which helped to make it all a little more convincing.

In those days all trooping to and from abroad was carried out by a fleet of troop carriers. The trooping season was confined to the period September to March as it was considered inadvisable to pass them through the Red Sea in the height of summer. The result was that no troopers could be made available for the move of the Shanghai Defence Force and the War Office was forced to hire such transport ships as they could collect in such a short time and convert them. The ship allotted to us was the *Herminius*, a freighter with practically no passenger accommodation at all. How, in the short space of a week they managed to convert the *Herminius* in order to accommodate us and a Field Regiment, Royal Artillery, complete with their horses and transport, bordered on the miraculous.

When we arrived on the quayside a horde of charwomen swept off the ship, which was deemed to be ready to sail, except for some carpenters who stayed on until we got as far as Dover. The men were embarked first and the officers followed them. We were packed pretty tightly and there were six of us in the cabin allotted to me. I had never been in a trooper before and therefore accepted the situation as unavoidable. Uncle Ferrers, however, was seething with rage. There is always an inspection of all ships sailing under

24

Government by the Board of Trade and the usual procession wended its way through all the various decks and quarters. As it went past us I heard the CO say, at the top of his voice, 'I was opposed when I joined this Regiment at the time of the South African War to travelling conditions such as these, and I am appalled to find the same state of affairs nearly thirty years later. It simply is not good enough.' But the Board of Trade officials obviously had orders to ensure that the ship sailed that day no matter what the conditions were. For one thing, there were about 2,000 officers and men in the ship and I doubt if the lifeboats and the improvised rafts would have held a third of that number.

In any case, never having travelled in a trooper before I was in no position to judge, except that when we went down to join the men on the mess decks I was quite shocked. The men had no beds, but slept in hammocks slung above the tables off which they ate and at which they sat throughout the day, there being nowhere else to go below deck. Going the rounds at night there was little headroom, the atmosphere could literally be cut with a knife and the presence of a great mass of human flesh was painfully apparent. At a later stage when we were all aboard and we tried to take stock we had an inspection of the mess decks. The men sat somewhat stonily on the trestles gazing to their front with completely expressionless faces; there was no need to ask them what they thought, and we shared their feeling of hopelessness. Our cabins were very elementary and there were no cupboards, only a few hooks.

It took nearly a week to round Ushant, sail through the Bay of Biscay and approach Gibraltar. It is difficult to describe the conditions during these first and most gruelling days as they were so bad, and we saw trooping at its very worst. The men stuck it out in the most admirable way, but I doubt if the troops of today would have been so forbearing. A canteen would have been something, but even that was lacking. There was a place where a glass of beer could be obtained, but you had to queue up for it and take it back to the mess deck to drink it.

All things come to an end and the day came when we sighted Cape St Vincent and changed course for Gibraltar and the Mediterranean. The sun was shining out of a cloudless sky, the sea was running high before a strong south-westerly wind, we had found our sea legs and suddenly we felt fit for anything.

So it is that the memory of the scene presented by Cape St Vincent had stayed in my memory ever since. I remember it for another reason, because it happened that I had temporarily lost my voice and speaking became almost impossible – all I could do was to produce a sort of whispered croak. I knew that there were considerable difficulties in getting a decent shave below deck, but there was one chap that morning who had appeared to do even less than the minimum in this respect.

'Why haven't you shaved?' whispered I.

'Somebody has taken my razor, and I cannot get a replacement,' whispered he in return. I glared at him, thinking he was merely imitating me.

'What are you going to do about it?' croaked I.

'Hope to borrow one later on,' croaked he in reply.

'Why did you not think of that before?'

'I wasn't feeling very well, Sir.'

'All right,' whispered I, 'but see that you are properly shaved tomorrow morning.'

For the next two or three days I made a point of having a word with him, to see whether his voice had really gone or not, but he won on points and never dropped his guard. It was, possibly, a coincidence that his voice recovered at much the same time as mine did.

When we arrived at Suez it was the first time many of us had been through the Suez Canal and it was fascinating. There were no convoys at this time and although it was possible for ships to pass one another when sailing through Lake Timsah, it was necessary for one or other of two ships meeting in the Canal itself to tie up and let the other through, which could be quite a lengthy business. It was a blazingly hot day and the whole of the Peninsula was shimmering in the heat. It was exactly the scene which we had expected to see and it was appropriate somehow that we should be going through on a Sunday.

We arrived at Singapore towards the end of February, stopped there long enough to take on extra water and then went straight on to Hong Kong where we dropped anchor on 7 March, over six weeks after leaving Tilbury.

*   *   *

Although we had few contacts with the Chinese we liked them enormously. They were very industrious, always courteous, always smiling and invariably obliging. It was a great help that their sense of humour was very similar to our own. We equipped ourselves with sufficient bamboo poles, hoisted our guns, ammunition boxes and other equipment onto them and set out. The Chinese did not know what it was in aid of, but turned out literally in their thousands and enjoyed the show enormously, particularly when one or more of the soldiers slipped on the cobbles and came crashing down with the whole of his load. The chatter and babble of the audience and their quick reactions amused us and they were very pleased to have had such an excellent show laid on specially for them. Soon after this we carried out one or two amphibious operations, one of which involved the 'invasion' of Stonecutters Island in the middle of the harbour. These were great fun and very instructive, and it was only later that we learned that plans had been prepared to attack the Chinese forts up the Canton River in certain eventualities. These, apparently, had had the 'effrontery' to impede or threaten traffic up the river. It amused me then and still does today to consider the arrogance with which we dominated affairs in those days as a result of our sea power.

It was in the late summer that year, 1927, that Colonel Ferrers' tenure of command came to an end. He had seen the Battalion through a very difficult period in its long history and the Regiment was deeply indebted to him for almost transforming the 1st Battalion. He made a farewell address, which was also conveyed to the Class 'A' Reservists, in which he recalled that he had joined the Regiment nearly thirty years before when it was on active service in South Africa and he was leaving it when it was again on active service in the Far East. The Regiment had been his life, and we all realised what it meant to him to find himself leaving it for good. My generation had particular reason for being grateful to our first Commanding Officer and one could not have had a more thorough and colourful introduction to our apprenticeship as soldiers.

It was now apparent that the Shanghai Defence Force had achieved the object for which it had been created because the arrival of a sizeable British force, which included naval and air support in the vicinity of Shanghai, caused the warring Chinese to move on elsewhere and the threat of January disappeared almost completely. The situation required a portion of the force to remain, but there was no reason why there should be any delay in releasing the Reservists.

[Editor's Note: It was at this time, according to one of his ADCs, that General Murray's nickname 'Nap' came about as a result of his being very 'self-opinionated' (Nap's words). He had been holding forth in the mess more than usual, and a fellow officer had said, 'For heaven's sake, who do you think you are? Napoleon or somebody?' And the nickname stuck.]

Chapter Six

Catterick and Egypt

Since the beginning of 1928 the Army had had to reconstitute the Army Football side owing to the number of players who had been ordered out to China. Therefore, as the season was already well under way, my services were no longer required.

It was all a little disappointing at the time but other things were beginning to move in. I had had four years' service by now and we were warned by the Adjutant that we would be required to sit for our promotion examination to Captain the following year; a course of instruction was planned to help us through. In the meantime we had lost Lieutenant Colonel Riddell Webster to a staff appointment, Major O'Connor as an instructor at the Staff College and Sandy Galloway as a student at the Staff College. The new Adjutant was Captain C.N. Barclay and the Company Commanders were now much younger and less experienced than their predecessors.

The year of 1928 was rather a year of transition. I went on a Chemical Warfare course at Winterbourne Gunner, which I found very interesting. Then came the autumn and I finally left the Machine Gun Platoon after four years in it and returned to a rifle company. This necessitated a course at the Small Arms School at Hythe in the autumn and by now I had had most of the education required of a regimental infantry officer. It was then that we heard that we should be going abroad the following winter on a long tour and in those days this meant twenty years!

The next hurdle was the Staff College Examination. The syllabus covered a very wide field and a considerable amount of preliminary work was desirable, particularly in the study of the May campaigns, which had to be covered. I was always better at German than any other language so I spent the New Year of 1929 in London cramming German. It resulted in my passing the Preliminary

Examination and I was thereby qualified for language leave abroad to enable me to become an interpreter. When the result of this examination was known I applied for and obtained leave of absence for three months in the autumn. I finally returned to Catterick during the first week of December and at once took over the duties of Adjutant.

Life in Catterick was entirely different from that in Aldershot. In the first place there was a very small garrison when we first arrived and competition was slight. The amenities were very poor and consisted of one cinema and the Soldiers' homes. Richmond was about 3 miles away down the hill and was really only a small market town. The 'bright lights' were no nearer than Darlington which was 12 or 15 miles to the north. The winters were harsh with high winds and driving rain and we could well imagine why the place got such an unfortunate reputation in the 1914–1918 War. The mud was glutinous and you carried it everywhere. It was here that I had my first experience of shooting.

The moors around Catterick were completely unspoilt at this time and a number of 'shoots' were organised. The Commanding Officer was a very keen shot and had always promised himself that when he got command he would present himself with a pair of Purdies. It was really rather fun to walk the moors with a gun under the arm and the fact that you were a beginner excused you from the stigma of missing 'sitters' which I was apt to do. Only occasionally did we have a drive and they were well out of my compass, as I had no idea where to aim.

In July I completed my preparations for a three-month stay in Germany. The arrangement was that I should go to Freiburg im Breisgau and stay with a Frau Maior Schaer. Apparently there was also a good German teacher there called Fraulein Rigaud and that clinched the matter. Just before I was due to leave, Captain Barclay, the Adjutant, passed into the Staff College and to my great delight the Commanding Officer invited me to replace him when he left. So it was a very buoyant subaltern who departed from Catterick on his way to Germany in that summer.

I had travelled in Europe before, but always as a member of some football team or another and this was the first time I had broken out on my own. The train journey seemed to be interminable as I felt I could not afford the luxury of a sleeper and sat up all night. I arrived in the early morning and went to my lodgings in the Schlierbergstrasse. The first requirement was to call on Fraulein Rigaud and fix up some lessons. Then I went on to the University to see if I could meet any students who would talk German to me if they wanted talks in English by way of return. This was called Sprach-austausch. I was fortunate enough to collect a couple of students for this purpose and we made a few arrangements for meeting. The University was still 'up' and it was possible to attend odd lectures without difficulty.

I hardly understood a word that was said, much of it being somewhat technical, but it helped to get the rhythm of the language. The Germans are great walkers and in order to get the required opportunities for speaking German I had to walk miles. After a few weeks I was beginning to think in German, after which progress was rapid.

In 1929 there was little evidence of what lay ahead. Field Marshal von Hindenburg was the President and Germany had an army of 100,000 men. All the people I met were very pleasant and easy to talk to. If I could have stayed a little longer my knowledge of German would have been deep, but as it was, three months had to suffice. We seemed to drink a lot of beer, but it was relatively light and produced no ill effects. The three months ended in the middle of October, I returned home and took a few weeks' leave before finally returning to Catterick. There was no Interpreter's Examination that year and I finally took it in Cairo the following spring. I was successful in becoming a Second-Class Interpreter and thereby had a strong optional subject when the time came to take the Staff College Examination.

At that time the Catterick garrison started to fill up with regiments from the Army of the Rhine, which made life a little more interesting. However, we were now looking forward to going abroad in the winter and we were delighted to hear that we were to go to Ismailia on the Suez Canal in Egypt.

We arrived at Southampton early in the morning on a day in the first week in January and the trains moved into a siding opposite to our ship, the *City of Marseilles*. I was now an Adjutant of exactly one month's standing and, perhaps not unnaturally, assumed that the task of embarking the Battalion complete with its baggage and equipment would provide me with my first big test, and I should be occupying a key position in this operation.

The men went aboard, stored their kitbags and greatcoats and also had lunch. Then the officers went aboard in their turn. It was a relief to discover that we had a separate lounge and that the dining room was properly set up. The cabins also were not quite so thickly populated, as had been the case before. In any case, being the Adjutant, I was a 'Very Important Person' and had a cabin to myself, even if it was on the small side. The visitors duly left the ship after lunch and the inspection by the Board of Trade followed. This was more or less formal as the ship was bound to be to specification having been in service for many years. We then went down to the mess decks. The conditions in which the men travelled were exactly the same as they had been in the *Herminius*, except that the men now had a place where they could get a drink. The scene on the mess deck therefore was much as before and the reaction of the men also was much the same and their expressionless faces hid their thoughts from us. Major General Kippenberger, the New Zealander, who wrote an excellent book on the war covering 1939 to 1943 called *Infantry Brigadier*, was appalled at the disparity between the accommodations provided for the other ranks compared with officers at the beginning of the War. The practice nevertheless continued throughout the War in British Troopers and was only rectified when the War was over.

The business of disembarkation commenced with little waste of time and the troops moved across the quayside and entrained on the far side. Two or three Cameronian officers of the 2nd Battalion put in an appearance asking permission to return to the United Kingdom forthwith, having stayed on the Canal with the turn-over draft.

Sand was everywhere; it crept onto the paths, it filtered into the barrack rooms, with little help from the wind, and it got into your hair, up your nose and into your ears. It was just something we had to get used to living with, but it took a little time to get used to sand in drink and food as well.

We were literally on the edge of the desert, which stretched away as far as the eye could reach, with only the bungalows providing any relief. The main road to Ismailia ran past the Officers' Mess and terminated 400 yards further on at the Brigadier's house. By an odd coincidence the King's Regiment was commanded by Colonel King, who was always known, for obvious reasons, as the King of Kings.

The organisation of the Battalion had been altered and we now had a complete Machine Gun Company. Command of this company was taken over by Major R.N. O'Connor who returned to us from being an instructor at the Staff College. Another 'character' that returned to the fold was Captain R.H. Brodie from an appointment in Iraq. The range and capabilities of the Company Commanders was fascinating and a great education in itself for any Adjutant.

In March the whole Battalion, including horses and transport, went up to Cairo by train and on to Polygon Camp out on the edge of the desert near Helmieh. We were less than 10 miles from the centre of Cairo and all that Cairo had to offer in whatever direction. This was my first introduction to a very sophisticated form of life, and we came to be aware of Gezira, the Surf Club and Shepheard's Hotel. We were in Polygon for at least three weeks before plodding off into the desert for the 'great manoeuvres'.

The first indication of the Battalion's approach was a wall of dust from the rear and gradually this disclosed the presence of more camels than I had ever seen in my life before. Even the Quartermaster could be discerned precariously perched on one of these slow-moving grunting beasts. On they came, agonisingly slowly, but with great dignity. The leaders, having arrived in the rear Battalion area, very slowly dropped to their knees and unloading thereafter commenced. It took hours for the operation to be completed and would have been much longer had ammunition been required. Then, in turn, the camels slowly heaved themselves to their feet and departed as slowly and gracefully as when they had arrived.

The exercise proceeded during the following day and we continued to make good progress northwards through terrain which had few physical features, and through sand of varying degrees of softness, when out of a cloud of dust burst two squadrons of tanks, which swept through the Battalion area and within the space of only a few minutes we were to all intents and purposes destroyed. We had practically no warning of the attack and it would have made very little difference if we had, because we had no anti-tank guns and no cover either from view or fire. This action brought the whole operation to a shuddering halt. The Chief Umpire, Brigadier George Lindsay, a great tank enthusiast, induced the Commanding Officer to re-deploy and stay put and there we remained for the rest of the day completely paralysed. It was a predicament in which the New Zealanders found themselves in the Western Desert eleven years later.

We were interested to note that there were a number of civilians present throughout the exercise. They were unobtrusive, and naturally we did not take exception to them, even when we discovered that they were all Germans. Hitler had yet to arrive on the European scene, but we were intrigued to find these people so interested in our affairs and put it down to curiosity regarding the problems confronting a 'modern' army in desert warfare. We shall never know what purpose they were serving at this time, but if they were regarding us as a potential enemy in such a setting it must have been quite encouraging for them.

In Colonel Hyde-Smith we had a just, but firm Commanding Officer, who meant what he said. I cannot recall a case in which he did not give the accused a chance to show that he could do better if he tried. If the man appeared for a second time he was dealt with otherwise, and if the case warranted it, he would ask the accused if he would take his award or whether he elected to take a trial by court martial. The fact remains that between April and August of 1930, as Adjutant I prosecuted at over forty courts martial, which included manslaughter at one end and simple drunkenness at the other. My knowledge of the Manual of Military Law became extensive and stood me in good stead in later years, but I would prefer to have acquired this knowledge in a more academic setting.

In the spring of 1930 Sandy Galloway managed to borrow a Vickers Vimy bomber from the Royal Air Force and he and Dick

O'Connor conducted a tour of the Palestine battlefields. Sandy had taken part in one or more of the battles of Gaza and therefore was more than averagely interested. One of the pilots was D'Arcy Grieg, who was famous at the time for having been a member of the Schneider Cup team for Great Britain. About eight of us took part in this expedition and we were away for about ten days. We tucked ourselves into some improvised seats in the bomber and flew out early one morning from the airfield at Abu Sueir, which was only about 10 miles away from Moascar. This was the first time I had ever flown in an aeroplane and as I have always had a bad head for heights I could not help wondering whether flying would not prove to be an ordeal. To my great relief the sense of detachment which an aeroplane provides made flying quite thrilling and I always entered an aeroplane thereafter with a feeling of excitement and pleasure. We flew straight over the Suez Canal and from the height at which we were travelling could see practically the whole of it, with Lake Timsah cut down to size, beneath us.

Thence on over the Sinai Peninsula, which looked deceptively flat, but which is actually a series of sand ridges of different heights and consistency. We were well on our way to Gaza when I noticed that D'Arcy Greig was leaning across the co-pilot and looking at something on the other side of him. Then they both leaned over and seemed to be inspecting the port side propeller. Then they passed a message back on a piece of paper and asked us to fasten our safety belts. We gradually lost height and after circling for a short space while inspecting the ground, they landed without further ado right in the middle of a relatively level piece of sand. The engines were turned off and we all got out. The two pilots examined the propeller and found that a long crack had developed in the propeller shaft some inches long and it was only a matter of time before the whole thing would fall off. This crack had caused a great deal of additional vibration, which they had been quick to spot, which was lucky for us. We spent two or three days studying the ground of the Gaza battles and the terrain could hardly have been less inviting from the point of view of an infantry soldier, with all the rawness of the desert combined with almost impenetrable cactus hedges. It was a relief to leave all this and go down to Beersheba where the cavalry had carried out a charge in 1918 which took the Turks almost completely by surprise.

In the following days we carried out a long walk along the lanes down which the troops marched in attacking Jerusalem. The only other tours we had were to the place where the cavalry charged to capture the villages of Katrah and El Mughar and on to the crossing of the River Auja. Our last visit was to the Nablus Gorse where the Royal Air Force virtually destroyed a column of retreating Turks. We paid a visit to the Sea of Galilee and then went back to Jaffa for a day off and a bathe. At this time there was no Jewish-Arab problem and the Royal Air Force in Rolls-Royce armoured cars policed the country. The days of Hitler were not yet bringing in its train the flood of Jewish refugees.

This was also the last year of Lieutenant Colonel Hyde-Smith's tenure of command, as he then completed four years. I think he enjoyed his four years as much as anything he had done during his long service, but he did a splendid job welding the 1st Battalion together during the first year of their overseas tour and its troubles were over when he stood down. The Battalion stayed on in India in a number of stations during the next few years and was still there when the Japanese launched their attacks in the Pacific ten years later. They first saw action in Burma.

I spent April, May and June in commencing to frame the plan for our departure, then handed over to Tom Binney and went home on two months' leave. It was a lovely trip in glorious weather and we landed at Tilbury ten days after sailing. I found the family in remarkably good order when I went down to see them.

I saw quite a lot of my brother-in-law, Terence Donovan, and it was clear that he was beginning to become a little restive. Within the year (1930) he went into chambers and embarked upon a legal career, which took him right to the top.* During my leave I played some qualifying matches for the Free Foresters, one at a country house near Guildford, which had its own cricket pitch and another against the Royal Engineers at Chatham. In those days, when playing against clubs, it was customary to wear a tailcoat with a little Free Forester ribbon in the buttonhole and we certainly looked very presentable. It was a very pleasant leave but two months was

* A High Court Judge in 1950, Law Lord 1964–71.

long enough and in early August I found myself on the train to Liverpool and the return to Egypt again in the 'Bibby' line.

Colonel Hyde-Smith had departed and the Battalion was being temporarily commanded by Major R.M.S. Baynes. The new Commanding Officer was Lieutenant Colonel R.C. Money. The Battalion came aboard and I think the new Commanding Officer was pleased with what he saw, but in the early morning the anchor was weighed and we moved out into the Gulf of Suez and set course for India.

Chapter Seven

India

Our route from Suez followed the usual course past Aden, and then we arrived at Bombay about ten days after our departure.

The customs at Bombay came as an unpleasant surprise. In the first place the Indian Government only allowed two bands into India duty free and at once we were in a dilemma because we had a Military Band, a Pipe Band and also a Bugle Band. Our Military Band and Pipe Band got through but not the Bugle Band, which is an integral part of all Rifle regiments. We used every possible argument to no avail and paid up with what grace we could muster. Duty also had to be paid on all shotguns, but a receipt was given and repayment allowed when leaving the country.

After endless haggling we finally shook ourselves clear of the dockside, got into our trains and rumbled off to our new station, which was Lucknow in the United Province.

The journey took a couple of days and our progress was leisurely. The tracks appeared to be well laid, but we seldom travelled more than 30 or 40 miles an hour. On Armistice Day 1931 the train was duly halted somewhere in the blue, the buglers got out and we had a three-minute parade on the side of the track. We also stopped at Jhansi for an hour or two in order to avail ourselves of the hospitality, which was generous, of the Seaforth Highlanders who were stationed there. We finally arrived in Lucknow on the afternoon of November 12th.

At this time of the year in India, the weather on the plains is delightful. This meant that whether it was training or sport of any sort, everything was compacted into the period from October to the following March. Our barracks occupied a considerable area and the military cantonment was spread out over some dozen or so square miles. Lucknow had a very good racecourse and the Army

38

Cup Meeting was due to be held only a week or so after our arrival. This meant that all senior officers in the chain of command descended on us for the purpose of 'Inspections'. Amongst these came the Army Commander, General Sir John Shea, who had greatly distinguished himself in the Palestine Campaign under Lord Allenby fourteen years previously. On first arrival we had no horses, the system being that mounted officers provided themselves with horses, the Indian Government providing stabling, the fodder and the pay of the syce (groom). The purchase of a horse was fraught with far more dangers in a place like Lucknow than in almost any other place, as there were serried ranks of prospective and frequently unscrupulous vendors. The horse, in any case, would be required to serve a dual purpose, as in addition to the normal military requirement for parades and exercises, it would need to be a polo pony as well.

The Army Commander was quite a character, sported white gloves and a monocle, and, for a General, was remarkably benevolent. After the parade we were drawn up and he addressed us. He said some nice things about our turnout and bearing, which of course we were very pleased to hear, and then went on to say how much we reminded him of the 1st Battalion when he last saw it at the Battle of Mons and Le Cateau and how magnificent we were. He retired the following year, and I next saw him striding down the passages of the War Office, after war had been declared, dressed as a Commissioner of the Boy Scouts, still wearing his white gloves and with his monocle still firmly screwed into his eye. He cut a magnificent figure whether in uniform or otherwise and lived until he was 96.

The atmosphere of the Indian Mutiny of eighty years before still hung about in the 1930s. There was no Indian Regiment of Artillery and very strict orders existed for the safeguarding of arms. In each barrack room there was a rifle rack holding all the rifles and pistols of the men living and sleeping there and it was double padlocked. When we went to church on Sunday we took our rifles with us. The barrack rooms, during the hot weather, were kept reasonably cool by means of 'punkahs'; these consisted of a succession of wooden flaps with matting nailed on to them, which moved backwards and forwards below the ceiling, either operated by hand or by a machine. Offices had 'kus-kus' tatties; these were curtains of thin bamboo covering the doorways, with a coolie throwing water over them at intervals. This water rapidly evaporated and caused quite an appreciable drop in temperature.

The cost of living was so low officers and men had considerable scope. All the officers were encouraged to buy horses, and either play polo or go pig-sticking. Most of the officers who could afford it played polo and a few of the others would borrow money for it, without interest, in order to get horses, making repayment over a period in monthly instalments through their mess bills. It took me three or four months to get a suitable horse and I repaid the loan from the Polo Fund over a period of about twelve months. It proved to be a very good pony indeed. It was not until we had been in India for three or four months that we got going, in a small way, with our polo team. In the spring of 1932 we started to take part in games organised on a District basis, in which we would be included in sides containing players of much more skill and ability than we ourselves possessed. We had some splendid games and the two cavalry regiments were most helpful. Our Commanding Officer made his charger available to me on these occasions, which enabled me to play four chukkers a day, as a pony was really only good for two, played alternatively. The original members of the Polo Team were: Number 1 Henry Alexander; Williams Anderson was No. 2; George Collingwood, the inspiration of the whole thing, was No. 3 and I was the Back, presumably because of my name and my record in football.

The officers lived in spacious bungalows and I lived in a wing of the Commanding Officer's house. These bungalows had all sorts of outhouses and it was staggering to discover how many people were tucked away in them. There was a bearer who was a sort of major-domo and personal servant and the house servants, known as khit-magars, were the next in importance in the hierarchy and there might be two or three. Then there were the 'syces' that looked after the horses, never more than one syce to a horse, and finally, the 'bhistis' who did the menial work. These official servants were not only accompanied by their families, but by a host of hangers-on, either relations or otherwise, because as the successful member of the family it was incumbent on them to look after the less fortunate members. Consequently most of the compounds of the officers' bungalows and officers' messes were veritable beehives, teaming with humanity of all ages and sex. The bearers were paid the princely sum of thirty rupees a month, the equivalent of about two pounds ten shillings, and the syce about a pound and that was all. Nevertheless, this was good money in India in those days and the jobs were eagerly sought after. The bearer would look after everything, keeping your quarters spotlessly clean, take care of all your equipment and clothes and handle the laundry. We would always have a hip-bath ready with boiling hot water at any time of the day at very short notice. If you wanted anything from the bazaar one of the camp followers would be sent flying down the road to get it. All this came as something of a surprise to those who had never been in India before and some of the younger officers revelled in it. Nevertheless it was delightful to see the troops availing themselves also of the cheap labour available. They even arranged to be shaved in bed before they got up. It must have been an odd sensation to have a hand groping for your chin in the darkness, followed by the liberal application of a quantity of warm soap and the arrival of the cool incisiveness of a 'cut-throat' razor. This particular practice made a bit of nonsense of our security arrangements, but we were not prepared to do anything about it. A strong loyalty sprang up between the employer and the employees, and I never heard of an Indian exploiting the special position which he would enjoy in these circumstances. If there were any thefts they were never traced to the household staffs.

We arrived too late in 1931 to take part in the usual winter competitions both in football and cricket. In Scottish regiments it was the New Year which took pride of place. The 1st of January was an important day in India because on that day all the garrisons paraded in strength to commemorate Queen Victoria's proclamation as Empress in 1877. The parade was almost a replica of the Royal Review of Aldershot days, being held on the 'Maidan' about 2 miles away from the barracks and off we marched at an early hour with the Jocks in remarkably good trim, all things considered. We arrived on the parade ground and were joined by all the other regiments in the garrison. There would be about 8,000 troops on parade and we were drawn up in line. We were surprised to find that the Indian populace considered this to be the big event of the year and behind the saluting base were thousands upon thousands of colourful and excited people waiting for the 'Tamasha' to start. It did not have the best of starts because, on arrival at the saluting base, the Brigadier noticed that the Union Jack was being flown upside down. He was in a somewhat choleric mood and we could all clearly hear his comments on this situation.

The Battalion was drawn up with the Commanding Officer in front, being flanked by the Second-in-Command and myself, all three of us mounted on horses borrowed from the Gunners. Mine was different and ambled along in a suspiciously quiet manner from the outset. The parade proceeded, the inspection took place and the Brigadier returned to the Saluting Base, and there the order came 'The Parade will remove Head-dress'. This was done and left me with my sword in my right hand together with the reins and my sun helmet (always worn on such occasions no matter what the weather) in my left. Then came the order 'Three cheers for His Majesty, the King Emperor – Hip-Hip-Hoorah'. This was all my horse needed to know and without any hesitation broke at once into a scrambling gallop, with the aim of placing the maximum distance between him and anything to do with the parade. I was taken off guard to start with as both my hands were fully occupied holding something, but with both hands working on the reins I sawed away left-handed and shot past the front ranks of the spectators, who scattered in the most flattering way and described a wide circle towards the left flank, the rear of the parade, and, I hoped, oblivion. The manoeuvre ultimately achieved its aim and I vanished in a cloud of dust from the view of the Saluting Base and a horrified-looking Brigadier. We nearly came to grief when we were in sight of victory when the second cheer rolled out, but the full force of it eluded us and I was ready for any other tantrums from my faithful charger. I spent the next five minutes restoring some sort of order and then crept back, somewhat ignominiously, into my position.

My brother officers thought I had stolen the show, which was only marred by the fact that I had not lost my seat altogether and been compelled to walk back to barracks. A sadistic lot, I thought.

In the spring of 1932 most of us managed to get our own horses. I collected a delightful pony, which served me well for the remainder of my stay in India. It was the only horse I ever owned and I left it behind in India with great regret.

There was another parade, which we held in the early spring of 1932, which took quite a different form from the ordinary. The 2nd Battalion of the Regiment had taken part in the relief of Lucknow in 1857 during the Indian Mutiny. We erected a memorial on the spot where this reunion took place and on the 26th of February it was unveiled by the Governor of the United Provinces, Sir Malcolm Hailey. It was draped with an old Residency flag, which was presented to us. The old Residency in 1932 was exactly as it had been left in 1857 at the end of the siege, complete with the holes torn in the walls by shellfire.

I had hoped to go down to Calcutta with the Regimental Football Team to play in the Calcutta Shield, but I had been given a vacancy on a course of instruction for prospective Staff College candidates, which was being held in Simla, and the Commanding Officer insisted that I should go. As usual, anyway in those days, I did what I was told, although I was very anxious to take part in the only football tournament we had entered for so far. There were about forty of us on the course and we came from British and Indian Regiments and Corps, with an Indian preponderance. We were housed in various hotels and it was strange, in India, sometimes to go into breakfast with a heavy mist outside. It reminded us, almost too much, of the autumn in London. Equally, when we first arrived, we had to be aware of the fact that we were over 6,000 feet above sea level and it was disconcerting to find the blood pounding in the throat when walking up an average slope. The course was one of four weeks and at an early stage it was clear that Staff College students run in all shapes and sizes, but it was equally clear that we had a great deal to offer to each other in our predicament. The lectures were given in a room which more resembled a classroom, but which was the debating chamber of the Indian Government when in the hills.

Towards the end of the course, all the students at what was referred to as 'the Backward Boys Course' were invited to dinner at the Vice-Regal Lodge, together with their wives. It was the first time in my life that I had moved in such circles and I found it most impressive. On arrival we were met by the household staff and presented with a brochure, which was beautifully prepared and which gave the names of all the guests and included the table plan.

We all then moved into a large anteroom and were marshalled in order of precedence. These were followed by two gorgeous-looking ADCs who paced slowly down the line of guests, preceding Their Excellencies.

These ADCs were what we would call 'clued up' because, without appearing to consult any notes, they presented each of the guests in turn as they drew level with them. When the presentations had been made, we moved through into the dining room, which was almost breathtaking. It was a high panelled room of gracious proportions with the coats of arms of successive Viceroys displayed in rows above head height. There were two large, highly polished oval dining tables, parallel to each other and laid with silver, glass, flowers and other decorations. The Viceroy sat at the centre of the table on the right and the Vice-Reine at the centre on the left, facing her husband. I found myself sitting at the latter table on the inside with my back to the Viceroy, but with a good view of the occupants of the Vice-Reine's table.

Dinner came to an end and there was a 'move'. The Viceroy had obviously caught the eye of the Vice-Reine and we all rose from the table. I watched all this with the greatest interest. The ladies were beautifully dressed and seemed to float along, providing me with a vision of loveliness. The Vice-Reine arrived at the entrance, turned and swept me the most marvellous curtsey, before turning away into the next room. As I was about to recover from this exquisite surprise I saw that the ladies were moving forward in pairs to the same spot, presumably in order to curtsey in their turn. It was only then that I looked over my shoulder; not only was I on the direct line between the door and the Viceroy, but also the remainder of the male company who had vanished from the centre and were ranged against the walls. I stood, therefore, in splendid isolation for one of the great moments of my life, but not for long. It was unreasonable to expect the floor to be sufficiently accommodating to open and swallow me up, therefore I went into rapid retrograde movement, propelling myself backwards until I reached the safety of the other spectators. The ladies finally departed and the men then returned to the table in typically British fashion for coffee, cigars and liqueurs and there we sat until the Viceroy finally rose to his feet and we rejoined the ladies. Having made myself sufficiently conspicuous already, I successfully effaced myself amongst the other officers I knew who were grouped together, I imagine, for mutual protection. Then, suddenly the Vice-Reine broke away from the group she was standing with, came across to us and holding out her arm to me said, 'I wonder if I could have your arm. We are now going to see a film and I would like you to escort me there.' It was one of the nicest things that ever happened to me and I have always been grateful to Lady Willingdon. The film was a very good one and featured Gloria Swanson; one saw so few films in those days that this part of the evening was an event in itself.

When the film was over Their Excellencies withdrew and we took our departure shortly afterwards.

The next time I met the Marchioness was in a London restaurant just after the War and we were in the same party. Rationing was still in force, but we had an excellent dinner just the same. To my intense delight, just before the main course was about to be cleared away, in one lightning movement Lady Willingdon swept the remains of her plate into a specially designed bag, which she had kept under the table. Turning to us with a smile she said, 'The dog's dinner is now ensured.'

I will always remember with gratitude how kind she was to me, an impecunious subaltern in the days when she was the First Lady in India. The course came to an end and a delightful stay in the hills soon joined the other memories.

I made my bow on New Year's Eve to Lucknow and the adjutancy, but took part in the New Year's Day parade as a staff officer. I took the Staff College Examination in 1933, and to enable me to do so and to put in more study I was left behind in Lucknow when the Battalion went off to the manoeuvres. When they returned, the examination was behind me.

In March 1933 I took over a company command and spent the summer in Ranikhat and Dehra Dun. It was then that I heard that I had failed Staff College. This came as a bitter disappointment and was made no more palatable when it emerged that I had failed in one obligatory paper by only 10 marks out of 1,000 and but for that I would certainly have qualified and might even have had a competitive vacancy. There it was, but the competition was far too keen for examiners to be soft-hearted as normally 600 sat for the examination with only 30 competitive vacancies for both Camberley and Quetta.

I left India from Bombay and on the ship I was given command of a draft of another regiment. We arrived at Southampton, but I had no further duties in respect of my draft and so our ways parted and I took a train to Winchester and the family. I had not expected to be back in the United Kingdom quite so soon, but it was very acceptable.

Chapter Eight

Hamilton and Staff College

After a couple of weeks in the south I went north to the Regimental Depot at Hamilton in Lanarkshire as a subaltern in the Training Company. The Depot was then commanded by S.A.H. Graham who later achieved great distinction when commanding the 56th (London) Division in Italy, and later the 50th (Northumbrian) Division in Normandy.

The barracks were ghastly and more resembled a prison than anything else, being a typical Victorian product. At the top of the barracks, which was shaped in a long rectangular form, was the Officers' Mess, a somewhat pretentious-looking building with an enormous Royal Coat of Arms planted above the entrance.

My tour at the Depot was made particularly interesting as a result of coming into contact with the Territorial Army both during the winter and, more especially, in the summer when they went to camp. The regimental area covered the whole of Lanarkshire up to the south bank of the Clyde, which was very thickly populated. In the First World War we had had twenty-eight battalions of various types, and even in 1934 we had three Territorial battalions. In Hamilton we had the Headquarters of the 6th Battalion, commanded by the Rt Hon J.D. Colville, with its companies scattered throughout the country; the other two battalions, the 5th/8th and 7th had their drill halls in Glasgow itself. During the winter months the Territorials did very little before the New Year but had a few 'drills'.

There was a Depot shoot, which was run by Pat Waller, an Irishman. We had rented a moor from Lord Lamington somewhere near Abington and thither we repaired one week. Volunteers were collected from amongst the recruits to act as beaters and there was sharp competition to be included. They would all go down to

Abington in a bus, suitably clad, and off they went. It was a modest moor and for the most part we walked up through the heather, interspersed with the soldiers, putting up the occasional grouse, but with quite an amount of other rough shooting, which made the expedition interesting and worthwhile. From the time we started there was always something happening, even if it only amounted to dogs being restive and ill-disciplined, to the sudden appearance of a hare. These shoots could not have been more different from those highly organised parties in India and were infinitely more enjoyable. We would walk most of the day in marvellous country without being too much bothered what the bag might be. In the late afternoon we would return to the area of the Home Farm and then we would have a couple of drives, at which I was seldom seen to advantage. I doubt if we collected more than fifteen brace of grouse on any one day but it was a form of shooting which I thoroughly enjoyed. We returned to Hamilton in very good order, the troops had a first-class dinner and we normally would have a little party in celebration.

The time came when I found myself a member of a shooting party on Lord Lamington's moor with the 'professionals'. Of course I had no right to be there but the invitation had come to the Depot Commander who was away and so were the 'guns' in the Mess who were well qualified to play this particular sort of hand. I went down by road and the party duly assembled. It was abundantly clear from the outset that I was about to be outclassed. The other 'guns' looked horribly professional, having two guns and bags of cartridges and their own loaders. We moved off up the hill through a welter of rhododendron bushes and away through the heather. I suppose the shoot was one of the more prolific in this part of Scotland, because we had a train of ponies on which the results of our work would be brought down the hill at the end of the day. This in itself was faintly intimidating. However, the column moved on remorselessly, and as the conversation was mainly to do with slaughter on the grand scale I was something of a listener. We solemnly went through the business of drawing for butts, and moved out along a slope to take up position. I was somewhere in the middle and on arrival at my particular butt deployed my ammunition and waterproof to the best advantage. It was a lovely autumn day with a hint of rain in the air and clouds massing to the south-west behind us. But the sky to the north was a brilliant blue, flecked with small flying clouds and the mistiness which seems to go with this time of the year in Scotland. The butts faced more or less to the north-east and the skyline was no more than 100 yards away. The beaters must have got under way as soon as we were in position, but it was a long beat and we heard nothing of them.

The weather, the view and a breeze ruffling the heather led to daydreaming and I was soon miles away. There was a faint rustling noise as of 'innumerable angels' and I suddenly found myself almost completely surrounded by grouse. They had planed almost noiselessly over the crest and seemed to think that the safest place for them would be somewhere near me because, at this stage, not a single bird went anywhere else, otherwise I would have been alerted by shots from the other butts, which had remained ominously silent. I felt rather like a policeman and by discharging my gun issued the order to them all 'To move along please'. They obliged me by doing so, with relative little loss to themselves after which the 'engagement' became general, the other guns concentrating on the killing process. I was sorry to see my birds go, as I am sure we would have got along well enough. This first flight was followed by a number of others and it may have been my imagination but there appeared to be a mastermind directing the birds, as they all, I think rightly, seemed to make a bee-line for my butt, feeling that there stood the best hope they had of survival.

I remember during the war reading a book called *The Glorious Twelfth** in which an expert shot went into a coma in his club in London and woke to find himself a grouse on the moor of his greatest rival. He and one or two other similarly placed thereupon organised the grouse with such skill that the shoot was a complete fiasco. This first experience of mine on a first-class moor bore a slight resemblance to this operation, except that birds were so plentiful that my inability to hit many of them did not seriously detract from the size of the bag, which nevertheless, was smaller than anticipated. I think the main trouble was that there were too many of them, and one was apt to 'brown off' into a covey instead of selecting a particular bird. On such a shoot nothing would be said about individual performances, as might happen on a syndicate

* A.G. MacDonald, *The Glorious Twelfth*.

shoot, but a glance into my butt showed a great number of expended cartridges and remarkably few birds.

When the beaters finally came over the crest and the drive was over, the dogs were let off the leash and a search was made for birds in a range of about 80 yards or more. This meant that birds falling some distance away could have been brought down by one of two or three guns and this provided a form of face-saving. We had two or more drives before lunch and then sat inside a mountain hut and had an excellent lunch, which had been brought out from the house. The party was quite convivial. There were two more drives after lunch and during the second the rain came and we were soon extremely wet. We squelched our way down the hill and back to the house for tea and on arrival I found to my horror that I had forgotten to put a change of stockings and shoes in the car. I therefore made my excuses to Lord Lamington, but he would not hear of me going back without tea and I enjoyed it, but the longer I sat the larger grew the pools of water on a lovely parquet floor under my feet. There was nothing I could do about it, but I was grateful when the time came to go and I could make my escape from the slightly scandalised household staff. It was certainly a day to remember, even if it fell a little short of being a red letter day.

In November I attended another backward boys' course for the Staff College which was held in Edinburgh and we took the examinations the following February when I was reasonably satisfied with my performance. I left for the south in June and stayed with my old Commanding Officer, Colonel Hyde-Smith, where we had one or two games of golf in Mildenhall and on one such idle afternoon came a telegram from the War Office that I had passed into the Staff College, and the relief this gave me was immense.

On my return to Winchester I found two letters addressed to me from the War Office, the first of which was official offering me accelerated promotion into the Cameron Highlanders and the second a follow-up letter from Captain B.G. Horrocks in the Military Secretary's Office asking me to go into the War Office as soon as I could in order to discuss the implications. This Captain Horrocks I came to know much better in later years, apart from the fact that he became a Corps Commander in the Eighth Army in the Desert and in Normandy, and also Black Rod and a television personality. All of this was to do with the future, but he could not have been more friendly and kind when we met in June 1935.

Even at that stage in our acquaintance it was clear that he could sell almost anything to anybody. He pointed out that I was 8th subaltern in my regiment, and the indications were that I should not be promoted to Captain in under three or four years. He realised that it would mean that I would take my place on the regimental list of the Cameron Highlanders junior to some who had less service. He said that he appreciated what a wrench it would be to leave the Regiment in which I had served for so many years, but on the other hand if I refused this offer it would almost certainly go to another regiment, with the result that promotion in the Cameronians would not have been eased at all. Lastly he pointed out that I had just passed into the Staff College and that my regimental days were numbered in any case. I must have showed that I remained unconvinced because he suddenly jumped up and said, 'Now, before you make up your mind on this I want to introduce you to two Cameron Highland officers working in the War Office and they may be able to help you.' So, without further ado we marched off down the corridors of the War Office, which appeared to be endless and he left me with Colonel James Drew, who later became the Divisional Commander of the 52nd Lowland Division, who then took me on to see Lieutenant Colonel Douglas Wimberley, who later became famous as the Commander of the 51st Highland Division in the Western Desert and Sicily. Both of these very distinguished officers could not have been more welcoming. They stressed the fact that it would be well understood that my first regiment would always have a special place in my affections, but their regiment had a saying which was 'Once a Cameron, always a Cameron', and they would be delighted if I decided to change regiment. This was all very disarming, and at the back of my mind was the point that, if I refused this promotion, the lot of those junior to me would continue to be bleak. If I refused, it would be almost as bad to have been the senior subaltern, having failed to pass my promotion examination and to have an officer from another regiment imported. It was also very flattering to be offered a promotion into a first-class regiment.

The result was, I accepted, and was thereupon ordered to report to the 2nd Battalion of the Cameron Highlanders in Aldershot in

August. It was sad to say goodbye to the Regiment, but, in fact, I remained in the closest of touch with it until we finally disbanded over thirty years later.

Looking back on this challenge in the middle 1930s it is interesting to record that the outcome was entirely unpredicted because the question of promotion did not prove to be the decisive factor. What proved to be the crux of the matter was when war broke out, I was in a Highland Regiment as opposed to being in a Lowland Regiment, and therefore found my way into the 51st (Highland) Division 1942, instead of the 52nd (Lowland) Division two years later. The latter Division was held back, being specially trained as a mountain division. There was no doubt that, provided you survived, it was important to get into the War sooner than later.

I turned up in Oudenarde Barracks, Aldershot in August 1935 as the Junior Captain of the Cameron Highlanders. It was an odd coincidence that these barracks were immediately adjacent to Ramillies Barracks, where I had joined the Cameronians twelve years before.

The Camerons were to go to Palestine that November as part of the garrison there and in the meantime were carrying out exercises within the 2nd Division, commanded by (then) Major General A.P. Wavell. Although the infantry was not fully mobilised at this time and still retained a full establishment of horses, motor transport was included for the first time. This consisted of only a few Austin Seven cars, but it was indicative of a change of wind.

I went south again soon after this and in the middle of December went to the wedding of Dick O'Connor to Jean Ross at Stoke Poges, an event which gave all Cameronians immense pleasure and, late in January, I went by train to Camberley yet again, to commence the two-year course at Staff College.

I had never been inside the Staff College before I reported in the third week of January 1936. My Division, as it was called, consisted of sixty students of whom about thirty got competitive vacancies, the other thirty being nominated. Our ages ranged from 30 to 35 and it was all rather like going back to school at a somewhat advanced age.

The Commandant when we joined was Major General Clement Armitage who was a Gunner. He was succeeded later in the year by Major General the Viscount Gort VC who only lasted a few months before going off to the War Office as Military Secretary at the behest of the new Secretary for War, Mr Hore Belisha. He was followed by Major General Sir Ronald Adam, another Gunner and he held the appointment until we left. The Colonel who was in charge of our Division was Colonel Curtis, late 60th Rifles, and he remained with us for the whole of our first year.

A feature of the Staff College was that each officer had his own horse and groom and we were encouraged to ride as much as we could. In the winter there were two drag lines a week, and also two 'hunts'. The drags were a miniature form of point-to-point. One moved from one line straight on to another and although it was excellent exercise it was extremely exhausting to anybody like myself who had not ridden a great deal in previous years. Often we hacked out a number of miles followed by a long hack back again, the result being that I often got rather more exercise than I bargained for. The Cavalry officers and the Gunners were very quick in ensuring that they got good mounts and the infantry officers more or less got what was left.

I gather that at some previous time an Air Force officer who was a student at the Staff College was horrified at this 'archaic' army practice, pointing out that the cost of it would be worth another bomber squadron for Bomber Command. Luckily nobody took any notice of him; otherwise we should have 'missed out' on about the best form of exercise one could have wished for. This remark was typical of many of a similar nature made in the days immediately preceding the War by those who were convinced that the War ahead would be won by air power alone. It would have been too galling if their mistaken conception of the War had been heeded to the extent of depriving us unnecessarily of this splendid sport, particularly as it was never to come my way again.

In our Division, during our first year, we had HRH the Duke of Gloucester as a fellow student. He took part in everything and although I doubt if he enjoyed writing some of the military papers, he was excellent in discussions on tactics. He only lasted one year, because in December Edward VIII abdicated and the Duke was forced to return to public life.

It was in the summer of 1936 that the King, Edward VIII, came down to the Staff College from Fort Belvedere, where he stayed from time to time, in order to dine with us. This came as a very pleasant event as a reigning monarch had never dined at the Staff College before. He was beautifully turned out in the mess kit of the Seaforth Highlanders of which regiment he was Colonel-in-Chief. We were all lined up in the anteroom and presented. He had a word with one or two whom he recognised and although quite charming seemed to be somewhat withdrawn. Few of us were aware of the personal problem, to do with Mrs Simpson, which must have been plaguing him at the time. The soup was served and cleared away and then, to our astonishment, the Commandant rose to his feet and said 'Gentlemen, it is the King's wish that should anybody want to smoke they have his permission to do so.' When he sat down the King immediately drew out a cigarette case and lit up. Lord Gort did not smoke, but this was the signal for quite a number of those present to follow suit. I hardly smoked at all in those days, but carried cigarettes with me. The chap sitting next to me said, 'Have you got a cigarette because I never smoke them, but I am not going to miss this one!' It was all quite funny to be sitting there smoking cigarettes while the fish was being served at the beginning of a mess night. It later became obvious that the King found the thought of sitting the whole of the way through dinner without a cigarette quite out of the question and we therefore were witnesses of something most unusual.

When dinner was finally over Lord Gort got up and made a charming welcoming speech to which the King replied. His speech was warm and friendly and when it was over we all moved out to the anteroom where he moved around having a word with as many as possible. He seemed to be enjoying the evening very much indeed, as I imagine the opportunities to relax that year must have been few. It was certainly an evening to remember. He went off on a cruise in the Mediterranean the following month, and one was aware of the fact that one of the passengers was a Mrs Simpson.

Our first year at Staff College came to an end shortly afterwards and each of us in turn was summoned to the presence of the Commandant and told how we had fared. My report was not too damning, in fact it was very constructive and helpful. We saw more of Lord Gort than either of the other two Commandants we had, although we had him barely for a year. He was a man of the highest integrity and worked immensely hard, being a dedicated soldier in the best sense of that overworked word. We heard that, as a result of Mr Hore Belisha seeing him on a bobsleigh run in Switzerland, he was taken away from the Staff College to be his Military Secretary. This was in 1937 and we were rather astonished when, the following year, or so it seemed, he was made Chief of the Imperial General Staff. He certainly filled the latter appointment in 1939 and went from it to be the Commander-in-Chief of the British Expeditionary Force in France when war broke out.

His handling of the BEF was first class and my generation felt that insufficient credit was given to him for bringing out the BEF through Dunkirk more or less completely intact. Only he was in direct contact with the Belgians, the French and 10 Downing Street and only he could take the decisions required for the conduct of the campaign as a whole. His Corps and Divisional Commanders gave him splendid support throughout, but none of them could claim with any justice that they had 'saved the BEF'. It seemed to me that this withdrawal was Gort's main claim to fame, although attempts by some writers to place the credit elsewhere is unworthy of them and did a great wrong to a highly meritorious officer. He was never given high command which seemed petty, but he showed his mettle when he took over in Malta during the height of the siege. We much admired him.

In May 1937, during our second year, I received a letter from Lieutenant Colonel Douglas Wimberley, who was still working in the Training Directorate in the War Office, in which he said that as I was a German interpreter and a Staff College graduate, I was eligible to do an attachment to the German Army for a period of about two months. It was understood that if I accepted I would get no summer leave and might even have to go before the end of the term. It emerged that, in his efforts to woo the British, Hitler had agreed to a few officers being exchanged between the German and British Armies for a period of up to three months. We sent every year a Cavalry officer, a Gunner, a Signaller and an Infantryman.

I crossed over from Dover to Calais and then set out through Belgium and Holland heading for Hamburg. It was one of the dullest drives I have ever made, but I finally arrived at my destination, which was Wandsbek on the outskirts of Hamburg. The following morning I set out for the barracks. I suppose I should have been more carefully briefed, or alternatively, have played for safety, but the fact was that I reported in plain clothes; it did not occur to me to turn up in anything else so much as it was the fashion in those days to wear plain clothes on practically all occasions. I presented myself at the barrack gates and addressed myself to the Guard Commander. It was eight years since I had spoken German and he was highly suspicious of the whole operation from the very beginning. He had got to the stage when he started to look over his shoulder to make sure that the guard were within supporting distance when I produced the letter, which was the authority for my presence. This was a letter prepared in the German Foreign Office and signed by Ribbentrop himself. The Guard Commander took it from me and tried to read it at the same time as keeping me under observation. Then he saw the Foreign Office stamp and finally the signature. He stood there practically paralysed for a few seconds clearly trying to think whether he had said anything which might not be to his advantage, shouted all sorts of orders, which included one which sent one of the guards flying across the square to the Orderly Room. In no time at all an officer came hurrying out, I was ushered into the presence of the Commanding Officer and all was well. I do not think I wore plain clothes again for the rest of the trip. The German officer loves wearing uniform at all times.

I had arrived a few days before the Regiment was due to move out to the Lüneburger Heide for collective training, so there was no Officers' Mess as we understand it, the equivalent being what they called the Casino where one occasionally dined, but in which there was no accommodation for officers. The officers made their own arrangements for living out in the town or elsewhere, whether they were single or married. One quarter was reserved in the barracks themselves for the equivalent of the Orderly Officer. The barracks appeared to be run by the Feldwebel and Unter-offizieren, the equivalent of our Warrant Officers and Sergeants. The barracks were absolutely new, and all ranks were extremely well turned out. The men were, almost without exception, conscripts doing a two-year term of service. I wandered around the barrack rooms from time to time in the company of other officers and there were two notices which appeared in all of them. The first read, 'Ein Reich, Ein Volk, Ein Führer', and these words appeared above three profiles, those of Frederick the Great, Bismarck and Hitler. The second notice read, 'Die Politiken des Soldaten ist Gehorsam', that is to say 'The politics of the soldier is obedience'. This was the year 1937 and Field Marshal von Blomberg was still Chief of Defence Staff, and General von Fritsch Chief of the Army Staff. The dismissal of the first and the attempted disgrace of the second within the year saw a drastic change in the attitude of the Army to the regime and to Hitler personally. But the Army I saw was very confident and independent and the only concession I saw to Hitler was that officers on meeting would exchange a very perfunctory 'Heil Hitler' salute. It was embarrassing to be greeted in this way by German officers as there could be no adequate response, except a bow. There were one or two parties before we left for camp and they were both held in restaurants. The evening seemed to be largely taken up with drinking German champagne in which it was usual to drop a peach into the glass having punctured it with a few holes and the fruit proceeded to rotate. Such occasions were invaluable in brushing up one's German and there is no doubt that the champagne had the effect of loosening up the tongue.

Within a few days we left the barracks and marched off to the training area. This was some distance away and as we marched the whole of the way it took us three days to reach camp. We bivouacked on both nights in open fields and on the first night, 'Tapfen Streich', the equivalent of our Tattoo, was played. Naturally it took a different form and one item was the singing of 'Stille Nacht' which was very moving. The men marched well and I thought I would stretch my legs a bit and march along with them. I was rather enjoying this, but at the next stop the Commanding Officer took me aside and said that he had no objection to me walking a little but he could not agree to me marching any distance. The purpose of the horse was to ensure that commanders arrived at the other end sufficiently fresh to be able to attend to the needs of the soldiers in all respects and he asked me therefore to conform with this custom, which of course was understandable.

The column was halted just short of the camp gates, steel helmets were put on, the band brought to the front and we were 'off'. The Colonel accompanied by myself cantered ahead and drew up at the side of the road where he was intending the march past to take place. Then we heard the order, 'Parade Marsch' and the Battalion as one broke into the goose-step. On parades such as these the leading files were composed of the best specimens of the German race available and they were tall, well built and in the peak of condition. As soon as this order was given out, out shot the left legs, absolutely straight and stiff, then to be brought down with a resounding crash on the road. The right leg followed suit and I noticed that, in order to get the required leverage these leading files raised up on the ball of the foot on the ground, the better to ensure the power and velocity of the descending leg.

Altogether it was an impressive entry, but as the battalion moved past it was obvious that a price had to be paid for having all the biggest and best in front, because the stature of the later files was considerably less impressive. Apart from that, the long strides of the leaders made impossible demands on this lesser degree sort when it came to keeping step and not losing ground. There was one casualty that I remember, a little chap who lost his balance, and in the process his steel helmet fell off his head. I nearly had hysterics watching this poor unfortunate darting about at ground level trying to recover his hat with feet flailing the ground remorselessly all around him. The Colonel was not amused.

The Lüneburger Heide was then one of the best-known training areas of the Army, and of course became better known in our own country, as it was the place where Field Marshal Montgomery took the surrender of the German Army in 1945, which was only eight years later. It became obvious that this training area was used to the full throughout the year and when I was there, at all hours of the day. We normally started the day with a Continental breakfast taken sufficiently early to enable us to be on our way to the training area by 5 o'clock in the morning. We were eaten by midges and our eyes and nose filled with the fine dust that our progress occasioned. I could think of better ways of starting the day.

As soon as we were clear of the area the gunners, or other infantry, would take our place. No time whatever was wasted on any of the days I was there. The camp was hutted but very comfortable, each of the officers' quarters having their own telephone. I was given a batman called Gefreiter Lankbehn, who came from the

Baltic coast and who followed our treks driving my Ford in case it might be needed. The lunch at midday was held in the Camp Casino, was à la carte and one paid for whatever one had on the spot. It was a moveable feast and a meal could really be had almost at any time of the day. There was formal dinner in the evening, and sometimes we were joined by other ranks who were probationary, or being considered for a commission, with the object of ascertaining more about them. These dinners also provided me with the best opportunities of talking with the other officers and discussing general military topics. These discussions frequently went on until past midnight, but we were away the following morning just the same at 5 o'clock.

While training was going on I moved about freely, except that an officer always accompanied me and directed my movements to a certain extent. On one occasion my companion (or Bear Leader) was in some difficulty with his horse and I lost him for a couple of hours. I stumbled upon some armoured troops with tracked artillery who were as surprised to see me as I was to see them and for some time there was an 'atmosphere'. I managed to explain my predicament and ultimately made my way back where I should have been. This made me a little more alert and I began to notice that there were quite a number of officers in the camp who were there for reasons other than training. Some were administrative officers and others observers and all seemed to be outside a framework of the known Field Army. Some of my observations helped to confirm the War Office in their belief that the German Army of thirty-six divisions was in the process of being triplicated.

One night in the Mess they asked me about my Regiment and I explained that it was the 79th Foot.

'Ah,' said one of them, 'then you are very junior.'

'Yes,' I replied, 'we were only raised in 1793.'

There was a sort of hush as if they could hardly believe their ears. Then one of them muttered, 'Du Lieber Gott'. They were quite dumbfounded to discover such a degree of antiquity. Hitler had created the 'New' German Army from scratch and ensured that there were virtually no links whatever with the old Imperial German Army. Nevertheless the Army felt the lack of tradition very keenly and so much was this the case that the 2nd Battalion of the Regiment (the 69th) to which I was attached adopted the tradition of the German East African Corps of the 1914–1918 War, because it happened that its commander, General von Lettow Vorbeck, was still alive and living near their barracks at Bremen. On this question of tradition, it was not surprising that the German Army, which was the senior of the three services in Germany and which had had a great record in Europe for upwards of 200 years, should have felt so strongly about the lack of it. At the same time they were deeply grateful to Hitler for putting the Army back onto a proper footing after the years of humiliation imposed by the Treaty of Versailles, and all he did in respect of the provision of new barracks, modern equipment and the overall expansion of the Field Army, including raising the Panzer Army and the Parachute Corps. The overall result was the creation of an Esprit d'Armee and it seemed to me during the 1939–1945 War the German Army fought every bit as well as did those famous old regiments in previous wars. The tempo of the training I saw was on a considerable scale, even for the Germans, and could not continue indefinitely without some purpose behind it. The officers were apt to say that a second world war was out of the question because it would mean the end of European civilisation. They rather hinted that perhaps the time had come for Germany to take up the torch of Western civilisation from, what appeared to them to be, the failing hand of England.

My attachment to the German Army was not only a considerable physical strain, but also the mental effort required to discipline oneself into speaking and thinking in German for weeks on end took a lot out of me. My German improved by leaps and bounds, but it took time to engage the soldiers in prolonged discussions. One day, when riding back from an exercise with the Commanding Officer and one or two others, we ran into a General (von Lettow Vorbeck). The latter was standing, impassively, under a tree watching us. The Colonel barked an order, upon which all immediately dismounted, came to the salute and moved forward, still at the salute. The Colonel reported who he was and who we were, with a special explanation to include me. The General at first said nothing, his eyes slowly sweeping through the group and then wanted to know a bit more about me. I could not help comparing this encounter with many I witnessed in the British Army; a German General was someone who really did matter. Towards the end of my attachment I actually met General von Brauchitsch, who later became Commander-in-Chief of the German Army. He came to dinner one evening and was extraordinarily pleasant. His son was the famous racing motorist. It emerged that the 69th Regiment was to be converted into a motorised regiment prior to joining the Panzer Corps, which the General then commanded, and he had come to inspect this new addition to his command. I used to have conversations from time to time with civilians, who were always intrigued by my uniform. One or two thought I might be an Italian, and were frequently delighted to hear that I belonged to a Scottish regiment. They clearly hoped that if there was to be another war we would be on the same side and at the same time showed great contempt for their Italian allies.

The training finally came to an end and the Regiment left the camp, moved down to the railway siding and entrained for the Baltic coast where the manoeuvres were to be held. I was very sorry to say goodbye to this excellent Battalion and its Commander, who had been most kind and considerate towards me. There was no patronage or condescension and everything remained on a very friendly and professional footing. The next time I met or talked with German soldiers was with prisoners at El Alamein five years later.

On leaving Lüneburg I went by road to Berlin to meet our Military Attaché there, Brigadier Hotblack, late of the Royal Tank Corps. He was most interesting about affairs in Germany and it would probably have been better had I met him before instead of after my attachment. He agreed that the pace of preparation for war in Germany was too hot to be maintained indefinitely, but such observations as I had been able to make seemed to help to confirm some general conclusions regarding German rearmament and were therefore helpful. I have always considered it delightful that, although I served for twenty-four years after this attachment to the German Army, I was never given an appointment where my knowledge of Germany and the German language was made use of in any way. Such are the inscrutable ways of the War Office.

I got back to England about ten days before the autumn term started at the Staff College and later on met my 'Waterloo' out with the Drag. The magnificent horse which I had in my second year and I sallied forth on the November drag hunt in the vicinity of

Winkfield. The autumn had been dry and it was a warm and sunny day, but there was no scent. There must have been about fifty of us out on this day and we filed in succession into a field from which the line would start. The hounds raced off but soon lost momentum in the absence of anything to work on. The Master and others moved slowly up the field, which was wide and about half a mile long. We all, in turn, got into the field and followed decorously behind. The hounds by this time were getting a little worried at their lack of success but redoubled their efforts at the exhortation of the Huntsman. In the meantime the field moved inexorably forward. To start with we would be moving forward in groups of three or four, then those in the rear moved up on the flanks of those in front, then we had three lines, then two and finally the whole field was in line riding abreast. It was a point-to-point on the grand scale and it did not suit me a bit. My tactics were to start as far back as I could, knowing that only by so doing would we avoid roaring through the hounds well before the end of the run. It was at this point that the hounds picked up the scent and the whole field was 'literally off'. There was only one way to avoid catastrophe it seemed to me because, in any event, the fence at the far end of the field would not have accommodated more than a dozen at a time at the outside. I wanted none of that and I swung the horse around in a wide semi-circle before bringing her back onto the line. This was successful and the way was reasonably clear when we started on our run. Actually it was not so much a run as a furious gallop. My splendid steed was absolutely enraged at being deprived in this manner of the opportunity of really getting amongst the thrusters up in front at the earliest possible opportunity. We came at the first fence like a tornado, cleared it by feet, shattered the second fence, but it was too good to last and at the third fence we hit a pole which had the effect of bringing us down with a resounding crash some distance on the other side. We shook ourselves clear but apart from the fact that my bowler was crushed beyond repair, I found that I had also broken my right arm. There was a volunteer to take my beloved horse down the next line, but with this performance I made my bow to the Drag and to serious riding. I had gone out with a bang.

In the middle of December the course finished and we went our various ways, scattering to the four points of the compass. It was remarkable how few of my fellow students I met in later years. It is true that, unknown to us, the War was only two years away and also, many were posted abroad for staff appointments or returned to Australia, Canada, India or South Africa. I saw quite a lot of Guy Simmonds, an outstanding Canadian officer, first of all in 1940 and later in Sicily and Normandy, by which time he was a Lieutenant General. There was Roy Urquhart of Arnhem fame, with whom I served in the 51st Division. The only other student was James Martin, against whom I had played football when playing for the Royal Military College sixteen years before, and whom I met in the Middle East during the War, and also when he became General Officer Commanding Salisbury Plain District after the War. It was altogether surprising that I should have seen so little of the remaining fifty-odd officers and went to show how wide the responsibilities of the Empire at that time were.

I took the normal month's leave and towards the end of January 1938 I reported to the 1st Battalion of the Queen's Own Cameron Highlanders at Catterick. The Battalion was now commanded by Lieutenant Colonel D.H. Wimberley, fresh from the Military Training Directorate in the War Office and one of the best trainers for war I have ever met. We embarked at once on a number of indoor exercises and field exercises without troops, usually one a week. It was quite a salutary experience to come down to the earthiness of a Battalion after two years in a sort of stratosphere.

The indoor study periods were usually held each Wednesday morning in the dining hall, and on Monday we would receive a note from the Adjutant informing us what the subjects to be discussed would be. I was commanding a Rifle company and I would assemble the subalterns. We would discuss these and agree upon the form a solution would take and who would be our spokesman. On one occasion the problem was what action would you take if you found yourself moving down a road with your platoon and you were attacked by low-flying aircraft. We came, unanimously, to the conclusion that with as little delay as possible, we would dive into the nearest ditch. Our spokesman, in the clearest possible manner, made it clear that survival was the first consideration and a ditch was the best method of achieving it. There was a slight pause and then Douglas Wimberley exploded. He was appalled that an officer in the Regiment should have the effrontery to suggest such negative action. He would have none of it and shouted to the assembled company that the policy of the 1st Battalion the Queen's Own Cameron Highlanders would be to 'fill the air with lead' and he wanted that to be clearly understood by everybody, no matter what other 'clever' alternatives might be suggested.

Unlike most stories of this nature, there was a sequel. The scene changed from a cold and drafty dining room in Catterick in the spring of 1938 to a very hot and dusty road in July 1943 on the Plain of Catania in Sicily. The actors were the same except that Douglas Wimberley was commanding the 51st (Highland) Division and I was commanding 153 Infantry Brigade under his command. We had just sighted Mount Etna to the north and things were going very well. General Wimberley was sitting in his Jeep with an enormous contoured map on his knees, his headphones on, and covered with dust. I had been summoned to meet him when he explained the situation and gave me orders for the next move in the Jeep. We were completely immersed in studying the various issues involved when I became aware of a disturbing, almost menacing noise. Looking up I saw a flight of Messerschmitts, line ahead, in the middle distance strafing the road with machine-gun fire and heading for us at about 400 miles an hour. That was really all I wanted to know and the ditches in Sicily are very big and handy. I took a dive into the nearest one in a way reminiscent of my best days as a goalkeeper. It was a very impressive performance and I was in the process of congratulating myself on a fine piece of avoidance, when a heavy body descended from the sky above, landed in the middle of my back, driving most of the air out of my body and ensuring that I could hardly breathe. The planes passed over and when we unravelled ourselves to my great surprise and delight the heavy body was possessed by Douglas Wimberley. Of course it was a great privilege to have accommodated him in this way, but I was staggered that he could have disengaged himself from his map, his headphones and the Jeep in about the same time that I merely 'took a dive'. We unravelled ourselves without comment, dusted ourselves down, climbed out of the ditch, looked around to see whether there was the likelihood of a repeat performance and then resumed our debate.

It was not time to recall that debate in the dining hall of five years before, but many years after the War I did have the temerity to draw his attention to this problem and what the two of us did on that hot and dusty day in Sicily. He was quite unrepentant and roared, 'I was a General and you a Brigadier then, our action was nothing to do with the Queen's Own Cameron Highlanders who will always fill the air with lead!' This incident in no way lessened my respect and admiration for a very great Commander.

Part 2

The War Years 1939–1945

Chapter Nine

The War Office and 3rd Division

[**Editor's Note:** Nap Murray spent from the middle of 1938 to the summer of 1940 at the War Office. He served on the staff as General Staff Officer (GSO) grade three in the Staff Duties Directorate until August 1940, when he became GSO2 until he left the War Office to become a Staff Officer with the 3rd Division in Frome, Somerset. His post of GSO2 was taken over by Dick Hull, later Field Marshal.

Unfortunately nothing of this chapter remains in the memoirs describing that period, but to have been promoted within the General Staff just prior to the outbreak of war in September 1939 would have been a sign of things to come.

All that remains is his own description as a brief comment in 'Envoi', chapter 23, and an appearance he made on a later BBC television programme *The Day War Broke Out*, in which he describes the effect the warning sirens made on the Staff in the War Office on 3 September 1939.

The Editor recalls that during this time he lived with his brother-in-law Terence Donovan, quite close to the War Office in the Middle Temple.]

I left London by train for Frome in Somerset where the Headquarters of the 3rd Division was located. The summer of 1940 was perfectly lovely and the fact that the German armour made such deep penetrations in France was in some measure due to a very favourable period of excellent weather, which made their going good. The English countryside was looking its best and although the train was packed almost to suffocation one could not help thinking of the predicament of France and that portion of the British Forces which were still operating in south-west France, retreating back towards the Brittany peninsula. People were very matter of fact and it was not easy to realise that there was a war on. I imagine that the contrast provided to the returning troops from Dunkirk beaches to the English scene must have been startling. I arrived at Frome and was driven to 'A' Mess where the senior officers of the Divisional Headquarters were living. They had taken over a complete hotel and the service was excellent. The following morning I made a bow to the Divisional Commander who is now better known as Field Marshal the Viscount Montgomery of Alamein. A short, lean and hungry-looking General with cold blue-grey eyes and a clipped manner of speech. He asked some pointed questions regarding my military background, not being at all sure that a Whitehall Warrior was best suited for a Regular Division of the Field Army. He was faintly reassured when he discovered that I had been employed on the General Staff and that I knew Brigadier Archie Nye who was in his own regiment. He stressed the fact that I was joining a highly trained and battle-experienced Division and it was up to me to establish myself in it. He wished me luck and I got the impression that I might need it.

Within a couple of days I was sent for and given two specific problems to work out and one was to do with the timing of an exercise in relation to the position and size of the moon to fit in with a night operation he was planning, requiring me to make recommendations. It was an amusing study and I duly reported my conclusions. He studied them carefully, asked one or two questions, after which I rather thought that perhaps I had passed muster, but I never took it for granted.

He had a splendid chap as his ADC in Charles Swiney of the Royal Ulster Rifles, a reserved and level-headed officer, who had no difficulty in speaking his mind. (I gathered that they had first met in Palestine during the Arab revolt, two years before, when Swiney was serving with his regiment there.) Monty went to lunch one day and embarked upon a dissertation upon the Cavalry (then horsed) for whom he appeared to have little use. He moved on to those who rode horses and in particular those who hunted. He was in fine fettle and was in the process of developing the theme when a quiet voice, that of Charles Swiney, floated up from the bottom of the table, 'Sir, it is obvious that you have never hunted.' Monty was delighted with this retort and in due course he became his ADC.

I was present at dinner in the hotel one evening when Monty embarked upon another theme. Charles Swiney was at the same table, with his head in a bandage, having been wounded on his way out to Dunkirk. The subject on this occasion was the need for careful reconnaissance and good map-reading and he then graphically described an incident when the Tactical Headquarters of the Division was withdrawing towards Dunkirk, when in close contact the column, led by the ADC, entered a village, but turned to the left prematurely and finished up in a cul-de-sac. The move was carried out at night and with very strict orders regarding lights and therefore it was easy to grasp that the business of unravelling the column was extremely difficult and lengthy. The whole thing had to start at the back with those in front gradually easing themselves clear. The situation was further complicated by the fact that the Germans selected this particular moment in time to shell the village. Monty was revelling in his story, sparing no details at all and when he finished he turned, smiling brightly to Charles Swiney, and said, 'Do you remember, Charles?' There was a noticeable pause and then Charles said, 'Sir, I have had very little opportunity to forget.' There could be no answer to that; little was gained by trying to tease Charles Swiney. He went back to regimental duty later on, but returned to Monty's staff in 21st Army Group in Normandy in 1944. He was killed in the last few days of the War and Monty wrote a beautiful obituary notice, which was much appreciated by those who knew Charles and his very great qualities.

I gradually picked up the threads of the work of a Regular Division with an exceptional commander, experienced in battle, and I found it amusing to be confronted with relatively junior staff officers, who, as a result of their experiences in France, regarded me as a complete novice. It was not the first time that this was to happen to me, but one always learned something from it. There was little doubt that here was a Division of high morale and very professional. The General went one day to the Senior Officers' School at Erlestoke Park, which curiously enough was commanded by my old Commanding Officer, now Brigadier R.C. Money. He spoke for about an hour giving his experience of commanding a Division in France during May. The two points, which struck me most, was the rapidity with which he sized up the Germans, and the other was his insistence on concentrated artillery fire whenever it could possibly be brought to bear.

There were other lessons that I learned from this famous commander, which could be titled 'Know thyself'. After a big exercise, when Montgomery was commanding V Corps, he said, 'I have discovered that there is one major difference between Napoleon and myself.' We fairly sat up when this announcement was made. He said 'The great difference between Napoleon and myself is that, whereas he needed no more than five hours' sleep, I need eight hours nightly in order to make decisions. A tired commander cannot hope to make the right decisions and control slips from his hands.' To illustrate this, I heard of an occasion with the 3rd Division in France in 1940 when one of the brigades fell back from a village and the Brigadier rang up Divisional Headquarters and asked that the reserve brigade should counter-attack and restore the situation, or that the other leading brigade should fall back to conform. It was a very difficult situation to be resolved by a staff officer and it led to a somewhat lengthy conversation. While it was in progress Monty came in from a visit and asked what it was all about and was told. With little hesitation he took up the telephone and said 'Jack, what is this that I hear that you have been driven out of . . . village?' A stuttery voice came back over the line, which was quickly cut short with, 'But Jack, you must drive them out, you must drive them out.' This, the Brigadier proceeded to do. A tired commander could not have made such an impact.

He had a great understanding of human nature and the potentialities of officers of whatever seniority and standing. Soon after I arrived a conference was called to be attended by the Brigadiers, including the CRA (chief Gunner). He said to me, 'Now, I want Brigadier "X" to be invited to come half an hour early and Brigadier "Z" to stay behind afterwards for a bit. The others can turn up at the proper time', and this was arranged. It emerged that Brigadier 'X' was a bit slow to grasp a point and needed a form of prior briefing, whereas Brigadier 'Z' was highly imaginative and was apt to ask a great number of questions which bored the General stiff. I saw a further evolution of this technique when he was an Army Group Commander, because he always saw to it that his subordinate commanders were given tasks which accorded with their natural abilities. I was particularly interested in this technique because I saw it being applied to Brigadiers and it helped me to realise that, no matter what the rank, officers run in all shapes and sizes, and each differs completely from his fellows and must be given separate and individual treatment. General Montgomery's knowledge of the officers in the Division was incredible. This was helped by the fact he seemed to have an almost photographic memory.

I had been in the Division for only a few days when a group of officers descended upon us from the Mobilisation Branch of the War Office, because it had been decided that the 3rd Division would be remobilised with all speed in order to return to France and come under command of General Sir Alan Brooke who was gathering a force together in Brittany which included the 51st (Highland) Division and the remnants of units and formations which had been driven south by the German armour. It seemed something of a forlorn hope, but it was clearly of vital importance to try and sustain France as long as we could. I suppose it was a measure of the high regard in which the 3rd Division and its commander were held that it should have been singled out for this special duty and was somewhat flattering. The reaction in some of the regiments, however, was quite otherwise. Although the cry did not go up, as it was to do later in the War, 'Who else is fighting?' the fact was that there were a considerable number of men in the ranks who felt that they had an entitlement to leave, and that the War could wait for a little to enable them to get it. Within a week, however, the French had collapsed and General Alan Brooke and his force returned to the United Kingdom.

[**Editor's Note:** It must have been at St Valéry, close to Dieppe, the 51st Highland Division was surrounded and captured by Rommel in June 1940.]

During this time we completed our mobilisation and were probably the only formation apart from the Canadians in that happy position. The possibility of invasion now arose and at very short notice the Division was ordered to move to the South Coast and take up defensive positions between Chichester and Brighton. The move was carried out with all the slickness for which it was famous and the operation was completed in less than twenty-four hours.

We spent the first night in a private house, but this was far too modest by divisional standards and the following day we moved into Wiston House near Steyning. The Divisional Commander spent most of the day travelling throughout the divisional area, visiting headquarters, meeting commanders at all levels, and also meeting a number of civilians. The latter frequently asked his opinion about the chances of invasion and were assured that it was more than probable and that the front held by the Division was the most likely place for it to take place. In fact he strongly advised them to leave the area altogether if they could manage to do so. Many took his advice and this, together with the building of strongpoints at suitable places, including evacuated houses, raised quite a storm when the threat of invasion disappeared and we went on to other pastures. He became very unpopular in the Division with the married officers and men when he ordered all wives out of the divisional area. His reason for doing so was that, in his opinion, if a battle developed how could the husbands do their duty effectively if their wives and children were sharing the same perils as they were? He could properly point out that this was the first time that the country had been threatened with invasion since the days of Napoleon and exceptional circumstances called for exceptional measures. It all seemed very logical but the reaction of the husbands was one of great indignation.

The Local Defence Volunteers, the forerunners of the Home Guard, were springing into existence and the zeal in Sussex was almost frightening. I accompanied Monty when he addressed two or three meetings of the officers of this force, many of whom wore the ribbons of the South African War and all of the 1914–1918 War. They turned up in faded regimental uniform, completely ready for the fray. The more outspoken Monty was regarding the policy to be followed, which basically was the extermination of all invaders, the louder became the grunts of approval from the front rows. It was clear that many of these officers had had high rank when they were serving and were quite happy to take command of battalions or companies for that matter in the general interest. It made one very proud to be alive in such circumstances. Travel at night was full of hazards as all crossroads were manned with men waving a remarkable assortment of arms in a highly dangerous, even aggressive manner. All road signs had been ripped out, which put a high premium on map-reading. The Gunners had the remarkable experience of deploying on the South Downs behind Brighton, and trying out their new guns by firing over the houses into the sea.

We had no armour, and the brigades were widely deployed, but our deployment took us right forward to the beaches which I believe is the best policy in defence against invasion by sea, because in later operations the vulnerability of troops in the process of landing was painfully apparent.

While we were still on the South Coast the Prime Minister, Mr Winston Churchill, visited us. He drove up to Wiston House and he and Monty left on a tour of the front, finishing up by having dinner together in a hotel in Brighton. When he returned Monty was in high good humour. He was amused that the Prime Minister selected the table at which they would sit and even went as far as arranging the flowers. It is said that this was the occasion when Monty enunciated his doctrine on fitness exclaiming that 'I never smoke nor drink and I am 100 per cent fit.' 'General,' came the rumbling reply, 'I both smoke and drink and I am 150 per cent fit.' This may well have been their first meeting, although there were to be a great number more in the years to come. Monty decided that perhaps the Prime Minister was possibly an exception to his dictum and he said, 'He smokes enormous cigars and he drinks, but he is a very great man.'

It was early in July that Divisional Headquarters was required to plan two separate operations; one was for the occupation of the Azores and the other the Cape Verde Islands. We worked out the full implications of these, the maps provided being quite excellent and it gave us opportunities of discussing these islands with a number of interesting people who had lived there. One Brigade was to go to each, but the plans were no sooner complete than the whole thing was cancelled. It would have been odd to spend the rest of the War in such delectable surroundings, but it was not to be. We were so busy with plans and training while we were in Sussex that little opportunity arose for other forms of exercise, but when we moved elsewhere those weekly cross-country runs, which were a feature of every command Montgomery held, came into force. The Commander never came down to breakfast, and had a light one in his room; he might be in for lunch, but that depended on his programme, but he was always in for dinner. He would stay in the Mess until we had heard the nine o'clock news, then he would retire for the night. On the door of the anteroom would be a notice reading 'No Smoking'. This meant that throughout the day no smoking in the anteroom was possible and only permissible when Monty had gone off to bed. We frequently had to move in quickly when a guest failed to grasp the full implications of this order. During dinner he was always lively and amusing, although it is true that he expected to dominate the conversation. It came as little surprise that after about a month in Sussex we were moving inland as a form of strategic reserve and our place was taken by another division less well equipped. Within thirty-six hours of getting the orders we were deployed in the vicinity of Andoversford near Cheltenham. We were not here very long before we moved down to Cirencester, and it was here that we received the code word 'Cromwell' and deployed ready for the invasion, although the scare was soon over.

Higher Command insisted on carrying out large-scale exercises from time to time. The result was that there was never a dull moment. When we arrived at Blandford the full force of the Monty regime hit us with the weekly runs and the rest of it. His chief doctor formed up one day and protested that some of the more elderly officers should be excused this exercise as they might suffer from it. It is alleged that Monty merely said that it was preferable to die now rather than in the middle of a battle.

We carried out another large-scale exercise over Salisbury Plain, which was deemed to be a desert for the purposes of the exercise. It was carried out during a very cold spell of weather and I have never been more uncomfortable. The usual 'critique' followed, conducted by Monty, which was very illuminating, if somewhat devastating. The usual rules regarding coughing and smoking were applied. We moved on to Christmas (which was spent at Blandford) and the New Year, and after only seven months with the Division, I was appointed AQMG Northern Ireland, in the rank of Lieutenant Colonel.

Chapter Ten

Northern Ireland

An Assistant Quartermaster General was a grade 1 'Q' Staff Officer and I had been appointed to Headquarters British Troops in Ireland (BTNI). It was commanded when I arrived by Lieutenant General Sir Henry Pownall, but he left almost as soon as I arrived in order to go to the War Office as Vice Chief of the Imperial General Staff and was succeeded in Ireland by General Sir Harold Franklyn.

In 1941, in the early months of that year, there was the possibility that Germany might invade Southern Ireland and one of the first aims would be to capture two airfields to the west of Dublin. In such an eventuality the Corps would be required to invade Southern Ireland in order to anticipate such a move, or to recapture them if the Germans were ahead of us. My job was to organise the administrative backing such an operation would require.

The Brigadier in charge of administration was Brigadier Brian Cuff, who knew much more about this game than I did, so it was unlikely that I would go off the rails. He had a lovely red setter, which went about with him everywhere. He came out of his office one day and found a junior staff officer patting his dog.

He said, 'Do you like dogs?'

'Yes Sir, I do.'

'Then why don't you buy a dog of your own instead of wearing mine out?' was the reply. He had a slow drawling voice, which made such remarks all the more telling.

From time to time groups of gentlemen in plain clothes would arrive from Dublin, escorted by our Military Attaché there, and went into secret discussions with the General Staff. The purpose of these discussions was to acquaint the Staff of the Irish Army with our plans to ensure the necessary coordination. Whereas I do not doubt that Eire would have cooperated to the full if the contingency arose, they nevertheless allowed themselves the luxury of a re-insurance policy by mining all the bridges down which the Corps would move.

The situation started to change during the spring consequent on Hitler's invasion of Yugoslavia and Greece, culminating in the massive use of airborne troops against Crete with appalling losses. We heard that the losses were on such a scale that German diplomats in Istanbul refused to talk about it. The chances therefore of an invasion of Eire by the Germans became less. We kept the plans up to date but the Irish adventure became increasingly academic as the year went on, because on the anniversary of Napoleon's invasion of Russia, Hitler followed suit. It was just over a year since Dunkirk but it seemed much longer. When news of this invasion reached us I had a visit from the Colonel commanding the Pioneer Corps units in Northern Ireland. He said, 'What do you think of the news on the Eastern Front?' I could only say what a relief it was to have somebody in, on our side, at last and as most of us had been very unimpressed by the Russian Campaign in Finland the year before I said that all we could hope for was a long, sustained campaign well on into the winter. The Colonel then said, 'The Germans have made a colossal miscalculation. You mark my word: the Russians will ultimately defeat the German Army in the field.' He was the only person I met in early 1941 who came out in such a categorical way in support of the chances of Russia winning.

We went down into Eire once or twice in plain clothes, on affairs disconnected with the planned operation, but on short leave. The War had now been in progress for nearly two years and complete blackout on all occasions was now a way of life. Consequently to travel down into Southern Ireland was to us like a trip into Fairyland with light blazing out of all the houses and the streets fully lit. It was the best tonic in the world and it was a pity that we were not in a position to enjoy it more often. On one occasion, when an air raid on Northern Ireland was under way, we 'bent the beam' of their direction-finding system and the aircraft flew to Southern Ireland instead, by mistake. How they could have mistaken this brightly-lit country for Northern Ireland I cannot imagine, but they dropped their bombs just the same.

That summer GHQ Home Forces laid on what was probably

the biggest exercise ever staged in Great Britain, and a considerable number of divisions took part, including at least four
armoured Divisions. The Commander of Eastland Forces was
General Sir Lawrence Carr, and Westland, General Sir Harold
Alexander. I was allowed to go over as a spectator and was
provided with a car for the purpose. The two sides advanced
towards each other and it appeared to me that at the end of
twenty-four hours of manoeuvring, the advantage rested with
Eastland. The exercise lasted nearly a week and as it progressed it
became increasingly obvious that Eastland had lost the initiative
and in the end, victory lay with Westland. It is too long ago for
me to be able to recall the details of the exercise, but I was
impressed at the manner in which Alexander gradually wore down
his opponent and emerged the victor.

In the autumn of 1941 another plain-clothes invasion took place,
and this time it was across the Atlantic from the United States, and
was part of the plan authorised by the President, Franklin
Roosevelt. It was a highly secret affair because the United States at
this time were not in the War at all. In their number they included
Dwight Eisenhower. I was just about to get involved when I was
ordered back to London to take up the appointment of GSO1
Home Forces. It was a bare nine months since I had arrived and in
that time the danger to Eire had virtually disappeared.

Chapter Eleven

GHQ Home Forces

I reported to GHQ Home Forces in October 1941 and it was fun to be back in the centre of things although it was barely eighteen months since I had left London for the 3rd Division. Home Forces contained the whole of the Field Army in Great Britain and as the Prime Minister wanted the Commander-in-Chief to be immediately to hand, a special set of offices were made available to him in Storey's Gate.

The new Commander-in-Chief was General Sir Bernard Paget, an outstanding infantry soldier who had commanded the Andelsnes column going into Norway the previous year and was an indication that the younger generation of Generals were coming into their own. His previous command, South Eastern Command, was taken over by General Sir Bernard Montgomery. This Headquarters was the predecessor of 21st Army Group, which was created for the invasion of France in 1944. The main Headquarters was in St Paul's School and the Army had taken over the greater part of Latymer Court on the other side of the road in which the staff officers lived and had their messes. As I was in the inner circle I worked at Storey's Gate. The Chief of Staff was Lieutenant General Sir Henry Lloyd, whose deputy was Brigadier Philip Gregson Ellis, under whom I came. We were responsible for all operational matters affecting Home Forces as a whole, including the Home Guard, which was commanded by Major General Lord Bridgeman.

The day's work was of average length. We normally went by car up to Storey's Gate in the morning, and worked there throughout the day, getting our lunch there in a canteen or going out to the club. At this time the United States were not in the war and we were concerned primarily in building up the Home Guard and, in conjunction with the Air Ministry, the creation of the Royal Air Force Regiment. They normally only trained at the weekends but many of the officers and men went off on courses of varying lengths. The aim was to bring the Home Guard to such a pitch that, with the passage of time, they could largely replace the Field Army when the latter finally went overseas. We used to go to the various centres, give lectures and attempt to answer questions. These latter could not be undertaken lightly as the students were very wide awake and asked the most pertinent questions. Such lectures were usually given at the end of the day, but this meant a lot of travelling.

I made a point of getting out once a week to visit units and establishments. It was particularly interesting to visit the chain of radar stations along the South Coast dealing with high and low intruders or air attacks, but I got best value from travelling along with the Commander-in-Chief in his special train to carry out inspections. Every second or third week this train would take him off to some command and he would spend a complete day touring and inspecting. My brother staff officers were a bit slow in discovering the excellence of these trips and for a time I had the field much to myself so far as the General Staff was concerned, provided you went properly briefed. General Paget was a very high-class trainer and was deeply imbued with the traditions of the Light Division, trained by Sir John Moore at the beginning of the nineteenth century. He and his generation of infantrymen, including Monty, were determined that in no circumstances would the infantry ever again docilely wander forward behind a barrage carrying heavy equipment on their backs as they had done in the First World War with such disastrous results. The new approach was to train the infantry to fight their own way forward with their own weapons, and making the best use of ground they could. In order to concentrate attention on this all-important matter he created a battle school at Barnard Castle and gradually every Division had its own. The whole approach to the employment of infantry in battle was drastically changed and it led to the troops in the United Kingdom in 1944 being undoubtedly the most highly trained that ever left these shores. So, when the Commander-in-Chief went off in his special train, known as 'Rapier', I did my best to go along.

This train consisted of two first-class sleeping coaches, a coach which served as an anteroom and the working office of the Commander-in-Chief, a dining room and a kitchen. There was an additional coach at the back into which two cars could be end loaded. We usually left late in the evening having already had dinner, but if we started early we would have dinner on the train. Either way we travelled through the night, had breakfast on the train and by 9 a.m. would find ourselves at our destination, the cars unloaded and all ready for a full day.

On the first occasion I went on 'Rapier' we got out at Berwick-upon-Tweed and carried out a whole day of inspections, which took us down the coast as far as North Shields, whence we went on to Newcastle. This inspection included a few coast defences, but was mainly concentrated on indoor and outdoor training. Having then returned to the train, we had dinner, went to bed, arrived in London in time for breakfast and by nine in the morning were back at our desks in Storey's Gate. Other trips that I can remember were to Yorkshire, to visit the Battle School at Barnard Castle and two formations nearby, and the other to East Anglia to inspect the armour deployed near Newmarket.

No matter what unit it might be, the inspection was very thorough, Paget missed nothing, and could be most unpleasant where things were not as he wished. On one occasion, in East Anglia, we stood on a forward slope watching a small exercise, which consisted of the approach to and crossing of a river of no great size. It had not been laid on particularly well as we could see far too much of the forward movement, the troops were not under control and the actual crossing was clumsy.

When the exercise was over the troops formed up on the near side of the river, obviously well pleased with their performance, but the officer in charge was called forward to the Commander-in-Chief who took him aside. Paget was possessed of a pair of piercing brown eyes, which could be either warm or icy. At the Staff College, when he was Commandant, he was known as 'Beady Eyes'. On this occasion his eyes were icy. He said, 'Captain . . . the exercise I have just seen was thoroughly bad, it is not training for war at all, and it is my business to eradicate this sort of thing whenever I meet it. Now, I will tell you what was wrong.' Then followed a detailed and scathing indictment of the exercise from the time it started onwards. It was a shattering experience for anybody even if it was beneficial. I do not think General Paget took any particular pleasure in 'dishing it out' and was certainly generous with his praise when the circumstances warranted it. On the other hand, when he got really angry it was noticeable that the back of his neck reddened, which was a great help to those who worked with him, as it provided a sort of danger signal.

He suffered severely from arthritis and the winter of 1941/1942 was sharp. We were watching some trials of an anti-tank gun, standing out in a strong north-easterly wind. He was wearing a thick British warm [officer's overcoat] and scarf, but he was shaking quite violently. His strength of mind was such that he never allowed this disability to interfere in any way with the work that was before him. It must have been a grievous disappointment to him that, in 1944, command of the 21st Army Group passed to another, but there can be little doubt that the man who forged the weapon for the invasion of Normandy so splendidly was Bernard Paget.

From time to time General Paget had discussions with Army Commanders, which I attended as Secretary. The morning's work consisted of examining the training state of the Army Group, and amongst the issues discussed were amphibious training and the vessels available to carry it out. By this time a training centre had been formed at Inverary, where specialised training was now in progress. Nevertheless the amount of equipment available at this time for amphibious operations was very small indeed and when one heard the cry that was going up for a second front it was laughable. It was an interesting experience to sit in on these discussions and to study the respective Army Commanders and their performance. The two outstanding personalities were General Sir Harold Alexander, before he went out to the Far East, and General Sir Bernard Montgomery.

After lunch at Storey's Gate the CIGS, General Sir Alan Brooke, would come in and give a survey of the world situation. The one I particularly remember was given late in February 1942 when the position in the Far East was in the process of collapsing. He stood on an improvised stage in front of a map of the world, with a staff officer behind him carrying a pointer with which he followed the talk across the map. Without once turning around to consult the map, and without any notes, he spoke at top speed for about an hour commencing in the Far East, moving on through Burma, India, Persia, Iraq, Russia, to the Middle East and the Mediterranean. He gave the overall situation in all of these areas in succession, sketches of the leaders and commanders in each and the likely developments in the months ahead. It was a brilliant performance.

I remember his reference to Singapore after it had fallen; a brigade of the 18th (Australian) Division had got into Singapore, but the situation deteriorated so rapidly owing to lack of sea power and air cover, that it was clear Singapore was doomed. From a purely military point of view the despatch of the remainder of the Division into Singapore was throwing good money after bad and it would have been preferable to divert it to Rangoon. Such a course was, however, politically out of the question because, although the Australians had done nothing pre-war to build up Singapore as a naval base, there would have been an outcry from that country that we were pulling our punches and that the arrival of this Division could well save the situation. So the remainder of the Division went in and more or less straight into the bag.

In the spring of 1942 I had been on the staff for four years and although I was fortunate enough to see a great deal of the Field Army, the time had come for me to get back to regimental duty. It was in fact nine years since I had said goodbye to 1st Battalion the Cameronians and I was now 39. So I 'formed up' to the Deputy Chief of Staff and he promised not to get in my way, although I had been in Home Forces for only just over six months.

In April 1942 the reborn 51st (Highland) Division was selected for service overseas and moved south into the area of Aldershot ready for despatch. This Division had been in France in 1940 and the greater part of it had been captured at St Valéry. It had been reformed mainly by calling on the Second Line Division, the 9th, and during the past two years had trained hard in Scotland under its famous commander, Major General Douglas Wimberley. It happened that the command of the 1st Battalion the Gordon Highlanders fell vacant at this time, as its commander, Lieutenant Colonel Joe Malcolm, was considered to be too old to take the Battalion overseas. Furthermore, this Regiment had lost both of its Regular battalions, one being captured at St Valéry and the other in Singapore, consequently there was a dearth of senior regimental officers. It was into this void that I stepped, being appointed Commanding Officer of the 1st Battalion the Gordon Highlanders in May 1942, never having served in the same station as this Regiment in my life and knowing nothing about them. It was a piece of great fortune for me and it was thus that I finally got into the Army in the Field, where I stayed until the end of the War. The height of my ambition had always been to command an Infantry Battalion, but I was especially fortunate to have got command of a Battalion about to go overseas on active service.

I made my bow to my palatial office in Storey's Gate and having fitted myself out in the uniform of the Gordon Highlanders, went by train to Camberley and took over command. I spent a little time getting the feel of the Battalion, spending a day with each company in succession. I think that there was an air of doubt amongst the officers to start with because it was well known that I had already served in two other Scottish regiments, and might conceivably be something of a careerist, but as I did my best to identify myself with everything to do with the Battalion the atmosphere improved. Within a few days of my arrival all the Battalion transport disappeared on its way by road to the port of embarkation, which was Liverpool.

I collected as my Second-in-Command, Major 'Hammie' Fausset Farquhar, who was also a Cameron Highlander, and was initially no more acceptable than I was, but it all worked out extremely well. The days were too few in number to get to know the officers, but it was soon apparent that the Regular officers tended to keep together and there were one or two other clearly defined groups. I remembered my experience with the Cameronians twenty years before, and made a mental note of the need to watch developments. Our preparations proceeded apace, we were issued with tropical clothing and the time for departure was now on top of us.

It was the custom, during the War, for His Majesty King George VI to visit all formations immediately prior to their embarkation for service overseas and just before we left, the King, accompanied by Her Majesty Queen Elizabeth, came down to see the Division. My Battalion was formed along a road in Camberley two deep on either side – I escorted the King up the right side and 'Hammie' and the Queen moved up the other side. The King was in rather a difficult mood and although I drew his attention to one or two of the men in the ranks for some particular reason he evinced no real interest, with the result that we reached the top of the road in very little time. We looked back and discovered that the Queen had hardly started and was talking animatedly with one of the Jocks. The King and I stood about at the end of the Battalion inspection and I was in a bit of a quandary because I had always understood with Royalty that it was for them to start a conversation if one was called for. I was about to break the silence in the absence of any opening gambit on his part, when he uttered an expression of impatience and stalked back down the line. The Queen was still talking when we joined her and she turned to the King and said, 'George, here is —. Don't you remember him at Balmoral?' How the Queen came to spot him I never knew, but it was a great moment for the man and made all the difference to the King. He thawed out at once, his ill humour left him and all four of us moved slowly up the road with the Queen continually stopping to have a word with one or other of the men. It was altogether a most impressive performance and made one realise what a tower of strength she was to the King at all times. When we reached the top and as they were about to get back into their car the Queen turned to me and said, 'Colonel Murray, I think your battalion looks perfectly splendid.' It was a gracious tribute to the Battalion and my predecessor and gave me the greatest pleasure to pass it on to the Battalion.

A few days later we entrained for Liverpool where the Movement Control Staff, as usual, took complete command of all matters to do with embarkation. The same evening we sailed north and by the following morning we anchored in the Clyde and waited for the convoy to assemble. It contained the whole of the personnel of the 51st (Highland) Division and others who were slipped into Gibraltar on the way. When we finally sailed we knew that we were calling in at Freetown and later to Cape Town, but our destination could be Suez or India.

At this time Rommel was in the process of driving the Eighth Army back and the situation there was such that Egypt could easily fall, in which case we might be forced to go initially to India. Our ship was the *Empress of Australia* with a displacement of about 23,000 tons and easily the largest ship I had ever been in. In addition to the 1st Gordons, we had the 5th Black Watch, commanded by Tom Rennie, Brigade Headquarters commanded by Brigadier Douglas Graham, the full complement of sisters for a General Hospital and Field Battery Royal Artillery. I suppose there must have been 2,000 of us in the ship all told. We finally moved down the Clyde towards the open sea. It was a most glorious summer's day, brilliant sunshine and small white fleecy clouds chasing each other across the sky. It was quite impossible to link this scene with war, but it was a glorious vision and stayed with me for the rest of this venture.

We gradually got into some sort of order and then cruisers and destroyers put in an appearance from nowhere and we were off. The strictest blackout orders were in force and they included no smoking on deck. We moved out past the coast of Northern Ireland, which I had left only nine months before and which now seemed part of another world. We must have gone some hundreds of miles out before turning south. One morning we woke up and found a battleship wallowing along in the middle of the convoy. It was so much lower than we were in the water that the thought came that it might not be more than a large cruiser but the matter was settled when we became aware of its enormous guns, it was the *Malaya*.

We travelled south and opposite Gibraltar part of the convoy turned away and disappeared towards the Mediterranean. This voyage was quite invaluable to a commanding officer trying to get to know both the officers and the men. One was in daily contact with the officers in a relatively confined space, with few distractions to worry one. I made a point of meeting half a dozen NCOs every day in the afternoon, and before the voyage was half over had met them all, without knowing them as well as I would have liked to do. The situation, which I sensed in Camberley in the Officers' Mess, was brought under control. The division of the officers into groups was not as obvious as it had been when I joined the Cameronians, but it was there just the same, but during the two months that the voyage lasted it was possible to eradicate this. Nevertheless, on arrival at Suez I was obliged to order a senior regimental officer to stay on board rather than join us as I had discovered that he had been intriguing against my command with connections in England, which I had discovered thanks to my friends in Storey's Gate. He returned to England on the same ship.

We arrived at Cape Town on the 21st of July and we came in sight of Cape Town as night fell, providing us with another glimpse of Fairyland, with the cluster of lights at the foot of Table Mountain and others stretching all the way up to the top. We just stood there drinking it all in and saying very little. Then, to our delight, we were told that we should be staying in Cape Town for three days and that all ranks would be allowed ashore. We were docked alongside a wharf so that disembarkation was a simple affair. Each morning all troops disembarked and we went off on a route march lasting two or three hours. It was astonishing how necessary this was because, although we took as much exercise in the ship as we could, space was so limited that none of us got more than twenty minutes at a time. These route marches did not exhaust us, but demonstrated that we were by no means fit. We went back to the ship for lunch and the rest of the day was free. Three of us, Tom Rennie, Chick Thomson and myself went off on successive afternoons to play golf, where we were given a very warm welcome. On each of the evenings several parties were organised for our benefit, the Cape Town Highlanders, being affiliated with the Gordon Highlanders, excelling themselves. This break did us all a world of good, but it was at this time that we heard that we were bound for Egypt, and that the Divisional Commander and GSO1 (Roy Urquhart) were flying on ahead.

When the ship first docked there was normally a row of private cars lined up on the quayside whose owners were prepared to drive officers or soldiers anywhere they pleased and also to entertain them. One Cape Town family collected one of the men in the Battalion and drove him away, finally returning to their own house for supper. When supper was over he got up to take his departure, but his hosts said, 'Why don't you stay the night? We always know when convoys are due to sail and we can ensure that you do not get left behind. Stay as long as you like.' The temptation was too great and the soldier not only stayed the night, but for the rest of the time we were in port. The following morning he was posted as an absentee and remained so until about an hour before we sailed when a car swept up to the side of the ship, a Jock jumped out, farewells were taken, and he bounded up the gangway in fine fettle. His Company Commander was not amused, but when he came in front of me all I could see was a completely transformed soldier, and was very grateful to that Cape Town family for effecting this.

We stopped for half a day in Aden in order to disembark some personnel, and then turned west and made for Suez, where we dropped anchor on August the 12th, of all the days in the year.

Chapter Twelve

The Middle East

I had not been down to Suez by train from Cairo in the old days, but since 1931 a whole network of railways and roads had sprung into existence, mostly built in the previous four years. On both sides were a great number of camps of various sorts, intermingled with a large stretch of desert. The Jocks gazed out onto the scene with complete detachment, only making from time to time some dry comment; they might have been looking at such a scene all their lives.

Our destination was Quassassine, a place that had not existed eleven years before so far as the Army was concerned, although it was only about 12 miles inland from Ismailia. When we arrived it was already dusk, but we picked our way into the area allotted to us as our camp and which, apart from a couple of huts and some cooking stoves, was merely a piece of sand. A nearby regiment had cooked a meal and the men set about it as if they had never eaten in their lives. It is true that sand seemed to be in everything and one company sergeant major brought along a dixie of tea for my inspection, which undoubtedly had a layer of sand on the surface. It was something we had to live with and it had disastrous effects on some stomachs. Initially blankets had been dumped and the men were issued with a couple each. There was little moon at this time but the sky was completely clear, the stars shone in a way they only shine in the desert and the night was delightfully cool after a hot and humid day. Not only that but the thousands of flies, which had been in attendance since we landed, disappeared as if by magic. I often wondered where they spent the night.

One of the officers came up and asked where they were to sleep. I, by way of a reply, could only make a wide sweep of the arm and indicate that there surely was all the room in the world from which to select a suitable encouchment. They looked at me with some disbelief until my batman, Frazer, arrived with my valise and laid it out within a few feet from where I was standing. The day had been long, there appeared to be no point in debating the matter and all dispersed into the company areas to make the best of it. We posted some sentries to deal with marauders, unrolled our blankets and 'under the wide and starry sky' slept like logs right through the night. I could not help laughing to myself when comparing the luxury of the *Empress of Australia* of the morning in the open once again, away from the noise and fug of the ship.

We roused ourselves in the morning by degrees and then the main consideration was to keep the men active and get some sort of a camp organised. Camp equipment, digging tools and tentage arrived throughout the day and in no time at all we had a proper camp. We slept on the second night in what were called 60-pounder tents shaped like a 'V' inverted, and all of them were dug down 2 or 3 feet to deal with bomb blasts.

Unknown to us at the time there had been changes in command. Commander-in-Chief, General Sir Claude Auchinleck, was to return to India as Commander-in-Chief there and was being replaced by General Sir Harold Alexander. Command of the Eighth Army was to have gone to General 'Strafer' Gott, but an enemy fighter aircraft had shot him down and his place was to be taken by Lieutenant General Sir Bernard Montgomery. It happened that these changes were announced at about the time we arrived at Quassassine and one of my officers asked me one day what I thought of these new commanders, of whom they knew very little. In reply I said, 'If these two fail we have had it, because I can think of no others who could do the job half so well.' I said this from my experience of both of them at Home Forces and as it turned out they proved themselves more than adequate for the purpose. This remark seemed to cheer one or two of them up a bit.

We were at Quassassine for about two weeks, the remainder of August, and we proceeded to embark at once upon an intensive training programme. Douglas Wimberley did a marvellous job in Cairo and at GHQ Middle East after he flew up from South Africa. He had served in the 51st (Highland) Division in the First War and he was in the process of achieving a long-held ambition of

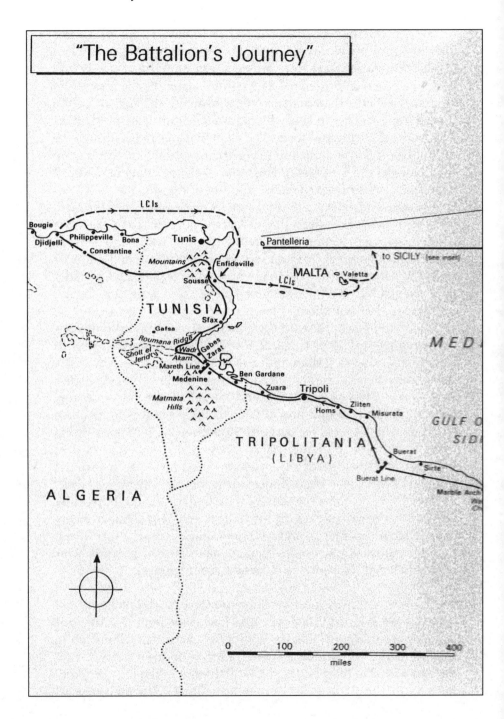

commanding it himself, consequently he arranged that we should be amply provided with training teams, and also extracted a promise, which was kept, that the Division would go into its first battle as a Division and not be split up. The last provision was vitally important to a division which had never been in action before as it would be very difficult to achieve any degree of cohesion at a later stage. In a very short time a training team turned up composed of officers who had considerable experience of desert warfare and we were in a very receptive frame of mind because we knew that the whole subject was a closed book to us. At a later stage in the War, before the landing in Normandy, it was otherwise for several reasons, but the penalty exacted was very heavy. This team was composed very largely of young but enthusiastic officers and they set about their task of making us 'desert worthy' in a highly professional manner. The first lesson was that the desert had to be 'woo-ed' in the same way as a sailor woos the sea.

We first of all had to accustom ourselves to moving about in trackless country without losing our way by day or night, and for that matter not losing our nerves. Secondly, we had to get used to living in the open for days, if not weeks on end, and becoming part of the desert scene. Of course we also needed to develop techniques to deal with both ground and air attacks when on the move. In addition the Intelligence Section were taught the use of the sun-compass which enabled us to maintain direction during the hours of daylight. 'Hammie' and I used to spend some evenings working out suitable desert formations. This was done in a small marquee with the aid of flash lamps suspended from the tent pole. We came to much the same solution as most others, arranging a screen of carriers and anti-tank guns, with the 'soft-skinned' vehicles behind it widely dispersed.

The desert was featureless, and even the famous 'Kidney Ridge' at Alamein was not more than 30 feet high. The main obstacles to movement were patches of soft sand, whose location was unpredictable and which varied in size from a few square yards to square miles. The important thing in such circumstances was to maintain the momentum of the vehicle, but this was easier said than done. Often it was quite a problem to decide whether a halt was justified to extract lame ducks and it was usually resolved to press on without them. It always seemed to me that it verged on the miraculous how they all toddled home by the end of the day. The drivers accepted it as a challenge to their skill and ingenuity, a challenge they seldom failed to meet. The training team never hesitated to put us right, even if it was sometimes crudely done, and we were quite happy to take the medicine, as we were fairly certain that time would soon start to run out; their criticisms covered all and sundry, including the Commanding Officer. On one exercise, travelling in an acquired Jeep, I was followed by an imposing escort of despatch riders and it smacked somewhat of Napoleon or Marlborough galloping forward with their staffs to points of vantage in some great battle. The senior officer with the training team assured us that such a technique was almost certain to lead to the total liquidation of the whole of Battalion Headquarters – it might have been justified a century or so ago, but had nothing to do with movement in the desert in the face of hostile aircraft.

Movement in the desert by day was, in fact, a hazardous procedure, whether you had air superiority or not, because the vehicles and the dust they raised could be seen miles away. On one occasion Brigadier Douglas Graham* was travelling across the desert by himself when an enemy aircraft caught sight of him and came in for a 'kill'. The Brigadier kept firmly on his course until the Messerschmitt flattened out for his run-in and when this happened he gave the wheel a sharp turn and shot off at right angles, a simple manoeuvre where the ground is suitable, but requiring a cool brain. The aeroplane banked over but missed by miles. The plane repeated the performance on two further occasions, but finally gave it up as the Jeep was much too expertly handled.

We extended the scope of our training to include movement by night. We would start off sometime in the middle of the day and then created one or two situations, which called for deployment in a hurry, during which we remained widely deployed. As the light began to fade it was noticeable that the companies steadily closed

---

* Douglas Graham, Major General, a highly decorated officer earning two DSOs, a CB, a CBE and an MC. Commanded 153 Brigade in North Africa and the 56th Division in Italy, being badly wounded at the landings in Salerno. Later commanded the 50th Division in Normandy and North West Europe where he was awarded Legion of Honour and the Croix de Guerre (twice). Colonel of the Cameronians and a big supporter of 'Nap'.

in on each other until the Battalion resembled a Grecian phalanx more than anything else. Darkness fell suddenly, but we had a scheme of coloured lamps, which enabled us to distinguish individual companies, and this enabled us to form a laager without too much difficulty. The food on this occasion came out separately under the Quartermaster and it became distinctly possible that we might lose him. In such circumstances it is quite fatal to send out scouts in all directions, mainly because you are most unlikely to see them again. There is usually some spot, which has some slight elevation, even of a few feet, and on this we would install a shaded lamp with an all-round traverse. It was astonishing how far the light from such a lamp extended and on this occasion it worked well and the dinners were served on time.

Soon after our arrival we had a visit from the Prime Minister and the CIGS, General Sir Alan Brooke, on their way back from Russia and the first meeting with Stalin. Winston was in his blue boiler suit and also wore a 'Bombay bowler', a sort of light sun helmet. We lined up two deep, about 50 yards apart and he went up one side and Alan Brooke went up the other. It was rather a rushed job as they wanted to visit as many units in the Division as they could. It was a very hot day indeed, but Winston was full of vitality in spite of the fact that he was then in his 67th year. When he got to the top of the line we went into the officers' marquee and gave him a drink. He decided upon a glass of tepid lemonade, which took us by surprise, but the visit was much appreciated.

We were in the middle of the night operation towards the end of August, when I received an order to hand over the Battalion to 'Hammie' and join Brigade Headquarters that was about to leave, by road, for Cairo. I got back to the camp at daylight and by the middle of the morning the Brigade Orders Group was travelling down the road to Cairo. The reason for this sudden move was the news that Rommel was about to make one last effort to defeat the Eighth Army and occupy the Nile Delta and the 51st Division was to deploy west of Cairo as soon as it could get there, as a sort of longstop to the Eighth Army. On arrival at Cairo we were briefed regarding the deployment of the Division and made plans for the necessary reconnaissance the following morning. I always thought that the Eighth Army was very fortunate to have Cairo within striking distance, a privilege which the forces in Burma did not have. The following morning we went out to look at the ground and found that we were to take up defensive position to the west of the paddy fields in the general area of the Pyramids, the Sphinx and not least the Mena Hotel. The following day the troops arrived and we deployed. The battle of Alam Halfa followed and it was a most successful defensive battle in which we took no part. As usual Rommel attacked the open or southern flank, in the vicinity of the Qattara Depression, but Montgomery had given this flank so much depth that it could not be turned. It led to a stalemate, with Rommel holding on to the ground he had won, but unable to do more than that. It meant that a considerable part of his force was exposed for some time to heavy air attacks, which must have been wearing to them.

After about a couple of weeks near Cairo we were ordered to proceed up the road in the direction of Alexandria, to join the Eighth Army and this brought to an end our sojourn in the Delta. We had arrived at last, at the 'sharp end'. We could not continue the sort of training we had been carrying out hitherto, and spent most of the time studying the methods of the 9th Australian Division on our right and the 2nd New Zealand Division on our left, and discovered what worked and what did not. At an early stage we started to do our share of patrolling and to begin with they were not very impressive; on one occasion we lost a complete patrol.

When we were in Cairo we saw something of the Australians and the New Zealanders and they admitted that, up to August, they had not had a great opinion of higher command, but the battle of Alam Halfa had changed this. In the first place Montgomery foresaw the form Rommel's attack would take and had a signals exercise before it started in order to practise the lower headquarters in the part they would be required to play. Secondly he stopped all 'penny packet' attacks and ordered that no attacks would be made in less than the strength of a division. Thirdly, artillery would be used in mass and in one of the attacks at the time 150 guns were employed. The last order he gave was that all troop-carrying transport would be sent out of the Eighth Army areas, as there was no question of withdrawal so long as he was in command. The collective effect of these actions on these veterans was that from then onwards their confidence in the Eighth Army Commander was unqualified.

In the early half of October we carried out two full dress rehearsals of the Battle of Alamein. These were staged behind the front line in a southerly direction towards the Qattara Depression. These lasted for twenty-four hours commencing in the late evening, going on through the night and continuing on through the next day. They included the firing of an artillery programme and what the Germans thought of it all I do not know, except that they brought down a considerable amount of defensive fire on the main front. Our final objective was the north edge of the Qattara Depression, and the leading Company Commander reported back that the depression was not there. He could only be ordered to go on until he found it. This made him somewhat indignant, but he put spurs to his horse and charged off into the blue. Shortly afterwards we heard a shout, loud clangings, a crash and then complete silence. The Company Commander had clearly found his objective rather earlier than he had expected. What was fortunate was that there was some nice soft sand at the bottom.

There were two features of the Alamein position which we exploited, the first being the sea that was no more than 20 miles from our position, and the second was the proximity of Alexandria. As regards the sea it is difficult to express in words what a boon it was to leave the desert with its heat during the day, the occasional high wind which blew sand into everything including eyes, ears and nose, the drabness of life during the day and the endless nights, and to plunge into cool sea water and wallow. We behaved rather like children on these occasions and stayed as long as possible, coming back to the 'box' in quite a different frame of mind.

I was more concerned about the officers because once they started to get stale everything would have tended to fall away, rather like a tyre going flat. They did not get away for more than twenty-four hours but it was worth it. The plans for the big battle were known in outline, but it was well into October before we were told the date, although had we studied the course of the moon and its various phases we could have got very near to the mark. The planning was meticulous. As soon as we got up into the Western Desert, Douglas Wimberley had a large sand model made which showed the deployment of the Division, the start line, boundaries and objectives. It was only after prolonged discussions of this sort that the two full dress rehearsals were carried out. Officers down to the rank of Lieutenant Colonel were there and we had our own exercises and discussions within our own units. In broad terms the Division was to attack on a two-brigade front, with our Brigade, 153, on the right.

The 'break-in' battle was to be fought by the infantry with the object of overrunning successive enemy minefields, thus creating the opportunity for the armour to 'break out' into the big wide-open spaces available beyond. It was to be a night attack commencing at about 9.40 p.m. In our brigade the leading Battalion was to be the 5th Black Watch, with orders to capture two successive objectives, which would take them 3,000 yards into the enemy positions. We were to follow up in the rear and when the time came, to pass through and extend the penetration achieved by a further 3,000 yards.

The code words for the objectives were named after Scottish towns in regimental areas, so our final objective was 'Aberdeen'. The hope was that having penetrated 6,000 yards we should be right through, but in the event the enemy minefields were even deeper, which prevented a clean break until much later in the battle.

About a week before the battle, somewhere around about 16 October, all officers down to the rank of Lieutenant Colonel in XXX Corps (commanded by Lieutenant General Sir Oliver Leese) were ordered to a conference to be addressed by the Army Commander, General Montgomery. This was my first experience with the technique he developed more and more as the War progressed, to ensure that all ranks were aware of the plan as a whole and the particular part each would be required to play in it. We duly assembled in a marquee which was stiflingly hot, it being in the late morning, lowered ourselves gingerly into those collapsible wooden chairs which were in rickety condition and, settling our feet into a bed of soft sand, awaited events. It was accepted that the possibility of being attacked from the air existed, but it was important not to cower away in holes in the ground all the time. Nevertheless the bag on this occasion would have been impressive. We were sitting fairly close together and one could single out General Morsehead who commanded the 9th Australian Division which would be on our right, with his officers grouped near him; on the other side there was the redoubtable Bernard Freyburg, the Commander of the New Zealand Division, which would be on our left; there was Douglas Wimberley with the rest of us; and finally the 2nd South African Division, of which we had hitherto seen very little, but who appeared tough and hardy. It was a great privilege for us to find ourselves in such select Commonwealth company for our first battle in the desert. General Leese made a few remarks and then quite unostentatiously Monty came in, looked around the company, moved up to a lectern and leaning against it started to talk.

He had not changed a bit, except that he might have been even leaner than when I last saw him. The steely blue-grey eyes, the clipped phrases, the rolling of 'Rs' and the occasional repetition of a phrase which pleased him or which he wanted particularly to stress. The first part of the address was to do with the thinking which led to the plan, and why he had decided to eat into the enemy's position with the infantry, before putting the armour in. He gave a detailed appreciation of the enemy position and resources, which led to the conclusion that the enemy was not in a position to fight a long battle and that his limit was ten days. He stressed the fact that the enemy could only be worn down by hard fighting and that once we got to grips there was to be no let-up at all; by unrelenting pressure we should bring about the destruction of Rommel's army, after which it would be our aim and purpose to knock him for six out of North Africa. This was pretty heady stuff. We had only been in the desert for two months, whereas the other divisions there had been active for two years or more, and when occupying defensive positions it is difficult not to be unaware of the superhuman effort required to get up and go forward, after a long period of inaction. And here was Monty talking about advances of hundreds of miles; suddenly it all appeared to be eminently feasible. The speech consisted of a sober examination of the possibilities of the situation without any heroics, which made the conclusions convincing. I sat there drinking it all in and so far as I was concerned he could have gone on talking forever, but it terminated almost as abruptly as it had started and suddenly we were rising to our feet and drifting out again into the glaring sun.

Looking around it was difficult to assess the other people's thoughts, but my heart was lighter and I returned to the Battalion with real and genuine hope welling up within me that we were going to win this battle and that we would thereafter set in motion a campaign which would carry us far to the west.

My task was to hand on to all ranks what they needed to know to enable them to play a full part in the impending battle. Where we were, marquees were out of the question and no overhead cover was available apart from the trenches themselves. Therefore we arranged for a few camouflage nets to be suspended on some low poles and, assembling under its cover each company in succession, I proceeded to explain the whole battle in so far as it affected us. The men would arrive in groups of two or three and gradually fill up the greater part of the covered space, sitting on their haunches. I suppose there would be 100 men in each session of which there were five or six. I crept in from the other end, proposed a diagrammatic plan up against one of the poles and started in. The talks were given in the middle of the day when the heat haze reduced visibility considerably. I first of all dealt with the overall plan showing the Australians on our right and the 2nd New Zealand Division on our left, and this piece of information undoubtedly was very acceptable to the audience, judging from the buzz which followed.

From there we went on to the Divisional plan with ourselves leap-frogging through the 5th Black Watch with the 5th/7th Gordons on our left. They were told when the operation would start, an outline of the artillery plan and some details regarding the employment of armour in the opening stages. There would be a full moon and I suppose history will compare Napoleon's 'Sun' at Austerlitz with Monty's 'Moon' at Alamein. The light anti-aircraft regiment was to fire tracer down the inter-divisional boundaries to help us keep direction. We were going to attack with 'A' (Hugh McNeill) and 'C' (Hubert Skivinton) Companies forward, with 'B' (Mike Duboulay) and 'D' ('Scrappy' Hay) following through to the final objective. There was nothing much more to be said about the actual mechanics of the battle, but I added the Army Commander's forecast that he did not expect the battle to last more than ten days and that we would win that battle and 'knock the Afrika Corps for six out of North Africa'.

Even the most phlegmatic Jocks thawed out on this and it was one of the few occasions before a battle that I looked into shining faces. A lot had been said about 'the light of battle in the eyes of the soldier', but in my experience it did not happen very frequently and hardly ever after the first encounters, because they knew too much. The untried and inexperienced 51st (Highland) Division, however, had it in large measure on that October day in 1942 and their confidence in the Army Commander and themselves rose to greater heights when, eleven days after the battle was joined, the Eighth Army did break out and the pursuit commenced.

My talk came to an end, but I could hardly leave things there. In October 1942 I had had exactly nineteen years' service, but had never been in action before. This applied equally to the Battalion as a whole, except for a handful of men who had been in France two years before with the BEF. There we were, with no battle experience at all, and most of us wondering to what extent we would measure up to the ordeal ahead. After a pause I said, 'I believe that this battle has been laid on, at all levels, with great professional skill and I am personally convinced that we are going to win. Whether it will prove to be the turning point remains to be seen, but it is a very important battle indeed and we must not fail. It must be the determination of each one to do his very best and as the present generation of Gordon Highlanders I am absolutely certain that we shall live up to the high standards our predecessors have set. I feel they will be with us in this battle, as will be the thoughts of all our people at home. We cannot fail them. Good luck to you all.' What effect this had on the Jocks was impossible to tell, as their faces remained impassive and immobile. In the event their performance excelled our highest hopes.

A few days before the battle part of the Battalion, under the command of Major Jimmie Hay, went right up into the forward defended localities opposite that part of the line through which we were to attack, and on three successive nights dug shelters for the rest of the Battalion. These trenches were extremely well dug, but it meant that we spent the night of the 22nd/23rd and the daylight hours of the 23rd on the edge of 'no man's land'.

It gives some idea of the wide deployments forced on both sides by the nature of the desert that it took us four hours marching to get to this somewhat exposed position. We started to move up as soon as darkness fell on the 22nd, moving in open file down a track marked by white tape. On both flanks we could hear and partly see similar columns making their way forward to their battle positions. The night was warm, our feet stirred up the fine dust and we were soon engulfed in a wall of sand, which gradually settled on any exposed parts of the body and became a sticky amalgam. The other columns gradually faded into the darkness and we ultimately reached our lying-up area. There we had a first-class meal, and then vanished into the ground just like a lot of troglodytes. We emerged just before first light, had breakfast, and disappeared whence we had come, because to be in the open at first light with the sun rising behind us would have been fatal.

There was a light meal but when it got dark things started to happen. We got out of our holes and had an excellent dinner. The companies then grouped themselves in accordance with their respective tasks. Water bottles were filled and a check made that each man had his iron ration. We wore khaki drill shirts and shorts, with boots and puttees. Our equipment consisted of belt, shoulder straps, small pack and ammunition holders. All carried rifles, the revolver not being very effective at any distance and making the officers conspicuous. These were the days before the arrival of the Tommy gun. Of course the Bren gun and machine-gun teams had to manhandle their guns and weapons forward because we would have to move through the minefields on a broad front and before the mine-sweeping parties could clear the mines away. When passages through the minefields had been cleared our transport would join us, but not before.

At this stage of my career I could afford the luxury of a cigar, and I always carried a dozen in my small pack. It was the custom in those days to have a 'left out of battle' element, as there had been many occasions in the past when battalions were decimated and no nucleus existed upon which they could be reformed. Our 'LOB' amounted to about eighty officers and men, including the Second-in-Command, 'Hammie'. As things turned out this precaution was justified in our case as two of our rifle companies had to be amal-gamated on the second day of the battle owing to the high rate of casualties sustained on the opening day.

The Battalion deployed with 'A' and 'C' Companies forward and we commenced the forward move. At this stage Battalion

Headquarters moved with the leading companies so as to be immediately available when the time came to pass through the 5th Black Watch. With this group was also the 'Taping Party', under Captain James Keogh, which had the task of taping out the Battalion axis on a compass bearing, thus ensuring direction. It only came into operation when we got through the Black Watch. The night was clear, and as we were already deployed there was relatively little dust. The visibility, under a full moon, was considerable and must have been about 400 or 500 yards, but beyond that it was difficult to see anything. It meant that the Germans might be able to see targets, but they would be difficult to hit at any range. I walked along with Hubert Skivington for a mile or so, and we talked about his house at New Malden and his plans for the future. It was an odd experience to be walking across this open space between the two sides in almost complete silence, but as the Black Watch were already ahead of us they provided us with the necessary protection. 'H' Hour was 9.40 p.m. and about half an hour previous to that we halted and lay down waiting for the start. Exactly as planned the artillery opened up and it was as well that we were by this time well forward as the noise was quite deafening. I think there were 800 guns in this opening salvo and as we lay on the ground we could see the gun flashes rippling up and down the skyline behind us and it continued, with occasional pauses, all through that very long night until dawn.

It was difficult to know how the Black Watch were faring, although we collected odd scraps of information from casualties on their way back and also from Brigade Headquarters. We advanced for another half mile and then lay down again. The rests were very welcome to the machine-gunners of the 2/7th Middlesex Regiment and also the bearers of the '22' wireless set back to Brigade, who carried it on an improvised stretcher. Communications within the Battalion were by means of an '18' wireless set, an unpredictable instrument which gave uniformly poor service even in the desert where conditions for wireless could hardly have been improved upon. Communications became a nightmare to most Regimental Signals Officers, who were roundly berated by all and sundry almost incessantly. From the front, piercing through the intense artillery bombardment, came the skirl of the pipes. Douglas Wimberley had been determined that they would be played, and played they were. As the campaign progressed the casualties in pipers tended to mount and they gradually played an increasingly small part. Whether the sound of the pipes affected the morale of the Germans, history does not relate but it was an unexpected and eerie experience for any who had not heard them before. We gradually moved forward, until some figures loomed up and we found ourselves on the near edge of the first minefield. The figures were those of the Royal Engineers who were employed in clearing a passage for the 'soft-skinned' vehicles and the armour. They could proceed in the darkness, unimpeded as the Black Watch were, by now, well forward. The width of the gap was intended to allow two-way traffic for all types of vehicle, and the depth was about 200 yards. With only a momentary pause we stepped over the wire running along the near side of the minefield and started to advance through it. We admired the calm and purposeful way in which the Sappers inched their way forward with the detectors and the professional group of attendants who marked the mines, defused them and finally lifted them.

We knew that they were working against the clock, because with the arrival of daylight their work would become apparent and would receive a great deal of attention both from the air and from artillery fire, which was, in fact, the case. Taking a deep breath we picked our way slowly through the minefield. We had the incredible luck to discover that in this particular minefield there were no anti-personnel mines, only anti-tank. The anti-tank mines were large and cumbersome and had been laid in the ground, which had a hard top surface, but with very soft sand underneath. The result was that the soft sand was gradually blown away by the action of the wind leaving the mines exposed to the naked eye. We placed our feet with the utmost care, every one of us being entirely absorbed in avoiding any spot which looked in the least bit uneven and it was a delicious thought that we were moving into this most important battle with our eyes literally glued to the ground to the exclusion of everything else. We suffered very few casualties and emerged more or less intact on the other side.

We had not advanced more than a mile beyond this minefield when we ran into the rear of the Black Watch. It was now about 11.00 p.m., and the Black Watch had captured their first objective and were moving on to the second against stiffening resistance. At midnight the Black Watch were on their final objective and the time came for us to go through. The Battalion moved forward and 'A' and 'C' companies at once seemed to become engulfed when they moved on by dust and shellfire. It was my impression that the shellfire, which caused this heightening of the artillery battle, was the defensive fire of the other side, but there were those who thought we might have advanced through our own barrage. The din was so deafening that it could have been a combination of the two. It was always one of the most difficult problems to resolve where a great amount of artillery was employed, but whereas we went on, and suffered heavy casualties, some did otherwise.

The Direction Finding Team went forward, but were quickly forced to ground and never made much progress for the rest of the night, so it seemed to indicate that our trouble came from the enemy and not from ourselves. The two leading companies soon went out of contact. We had only the '18' set and the two sets moving forward must have been knocked out. Any attempt on the part of 'B' Company or the Direction Finding Team to make progress ran into increased fire. At 3.00 a.m. I decided that until we knew more about the success or otherwise of those two leading companies we would have to dig in. Time was running out, and to be certain of being below ground at first light at least two hours was needed, so we could wait no longer. To launch the two reserve companies into a fluid and uncertain battle might have been disastrous, and certainly very costly.

When the order to dig was given, I was treated to a sight that is never seen on peacetime training: that of the soldier digging with the greatest possible enthusiasm. We soon got down a couple of feet and then struck solid rock, through which even the most industrious could not penetrate. And so it was that, when dawn came, we were nominally dug in with no news of 'A' and 'C' Companies. The 'douvres', as they were called, were sufficiently deep to give protection if a crouching or prone position could be adopted, but the parapet consisted only of loose sand and could afford very little protection. The dawn came, and with it some armour from the rear. Of course it is always a pleasurable feeling to have armour about, provided it is not too close, as it is apt to attract artillery fire. From then onwards the position we held was subjected to harassing fire throughout the day. Most of it came from medium guns some distance off, but what we feared most was the airburst against which we had no protection at all.

At about 8.00 a.m. one of the Company Sergeant Majors of the leading companies arrived at Battalion Headquarters, having come by a circuitous route, and reported on the situation. The companies had successfully captured their objective, 'Braemar', but had suffered very heavily casualties in doing so. Hubert Skivington, the commander of 'C' Company, had been killed and the other Company Commander (Hugh McNeill) seriously wounded. The other casualties were on such a scale that, after the battle, I think the Battalion suffered about 150 casualties all told. I returned with the Sergeant Major and joined the leading companies to find them in great heart, in spite of the heaviness of their casualties in their first battle, with flying colours and there was little fear that they would lose what they had gained. Most of the position was in the middle of a minefield, but no-one seemed to mind too much about that. I returned to Battalion Headquarters telling the two new company commanders, relatively junior subalterns, that I would return later in the day to plot the next move.

When I got back I found that the armour was now engaged in a long-range duel with enemy armour, more or less over our heads. I then went back to Brigade Headquarters, but found that the Brigadier had gone back to Division for a conference; nevertheless it was fairly clear that that night the operation would be resumed with the object of taking out our final objectives. It was not obvious when the Brigadier would return so I went back to Battalion Headquarters. There we sat for two or three hours being steadily shelled throughout; it provided me with the opportunity of smoking one of my cigars, which may well have had a reassuring effect on those nearby. There was one battery of medium guns, which was particularly tiresome, as they seemed to have got our range almost too accurately.

The slowness of flight of the shells was such that you heard the discharge well in advance, counted about eight, and then they arrived. When they started off one was relaxed, but as the time ran out tension became high. Having established the sequence and knowing that there were only four shells to bother about we could relax for a second time when they delivered their burden. Ultimately one shell came so close that my batman and I thought it must be making for us and we cowered even further down the trench. There was a shattering explosion some yards away; it had missed us after all. I looked over the top and saw that it had hit the parapet of the next trench, which contained the Adjutant and the Signals Officer. I was just in time to see the small pack of the Adjutant flying through the air, and then the emergence of two faces, covered with sand and displaying a certain measure of concern. I was so relieved that they had not actually been hit that it was difficult not to laugh as they looked for the entire world like black minstrels. They were, nevertheless, badly shaken for a time.

At about 4.00 p.m. there was no news from Brigade and as it was now five or six hours since I had visited the two forward companies, I decided that I should go up and see how they were, and give them some indication of the probable course operations would take that evening. So I went over the top telling Jimmie Hay, who was acting Second-in-Command, I would be away for about an hour and set off. I went by myself and it was a relief to stretch one's legs after a fairly long period of inactivity, but I had not been on the move for more than about ten minutes when things started to happen and, looking over my shoulder, I saw to my horror that our armour was moving out in order to 'engage the enemy more closely'. Of course we had no notification of this move, so I was fairly caught between two angry nests of wasps, and could have wished myself many miles away. I decided that my presence was superfluous and decided to make myself scarce. Looking around for some sort of protection I saw, some yards away, a slight fold in the ground which was all one expected and all one needed, and hastened thither with what speed I could muster; even then I was too late and I collected a shell splinter through my right wrist. It was just like being hit with a solid leather hammer, and there was none of the 'searing pain' one had read about in so many boys' magazines in days gone by. I looked down and saw a ragged gash on the back of my hand, and a bump on the inside of the wrist where the metal had stopped on its way through. I felt slightly sick but completed my journey into the fold in the ground and was forced to stay there for about half an hour until the armour had moved away. I then returned, somewhat ignominiously, to Battalion Headquarters. I thought I could make light of it, get it tied up and start again, but the Brigadier turned up and ordered me out of the battle.

For a moment my indignation very nearly got the better of me, but I realised that I was not, in fact, feeling all that hot and did as I was told. It was all quite maddening: here was the great battle for which we had trained so assiduously for weeks, and here was I out of it all in less than twenty-four hours. I was evacuated that night, just when the reserve companies were about to go forward and finish the job, under the command of Jimmie Hay. It was nice to hear, some time later, when I was right back in Alexandria, that they were successful, but Jimmie Hay also became a casualty that night when his carrier ran into an uncharted minefield and went up. Jimmie was very badly wounded in the legs, and was never fit thereafter to take the field again. 'Hammie' Fausset Farquhar turned up to take over command of the Battalion, which had lost at least ten officers including a Major and three Captains, and one third of the rank and file. He bore a charmed life and continued to command the Battalion throughout the remainder of the Desert Campaign right into Tunisia, with great distinction.

I was picked up in an improvised ambulance and sent back to the Advance Dressing Station where the surgeon operated at once, removed the shell splinter and tucked it into the breast pocket of my shirt as a keepsake. As I had suspected, it had just failed to force its way out through the wrist, but had broken most of the bones in its path. I was put into an ambulance convoy the following afternoon and that night arrived in Alexandria. We were carried into a vast hall with beds stretching out as far as one could see in the half-light. I was put on a sort of pallet, still wearing the same clothes as I had worn in the field. I think they must have given me a 'shot' here, because I later woke up to find myself in pyjamas and in a proper bed, in a hospital ward. I was in this hospital for about a week and it became obvious that the wound had turned septic, as I was beginning to run a temperature. I remember waking up one morning having had the most lurid dreams, with the other members of the ward looking at me with a mixture of alarm and sympathy, which meant that at the worst I had been raving, or at best talking loudly in my sleep.

I think I was kept in Alexandria for a whole week because I was too ill to move, as the casualties of the first two days of Alamein were on a considerable scale. In any case I recovered sufficiently by the end of October to make me eligible for a passage in a very small hospital ship, the *Abber*, to Haifa. We sailed on October the 31st when the Battle of Alamein was still undecided and reached Haifa the following day. It turned out that my destination was a General Hospital in Nazareth and it was located in a convent, which had been evacuated for the purpose.

The hospital in Nazareth had a highly professional staff but it had little modern equipment. Here they carried out three operations over a period of time. The first two operations consisted of cutting slits in the back of my hand to help to get the pus out, but I made such little progress that I began to wonder whether, after all, I would not lose my right hand. Then, quite unexpectedly, at the beginning of December, my temperature went back to normal and stayed there, and at long last I had turned the corner. This led to a third operation to set the wrist, the after-effects of which were unpleasant.

A few days later the surgeon in charge of my case came in and informed me that he had graded me 'Six Months D' and that I would be evacuated to Egypt. Six months 'D' meant that I was considered unfit for all duties during that time and it sounded at the time almost like a death sentence. I said so. He replied, 'You must go to another hospital which is better equipped than we are, and that without delay. It is only now that you are fit to travel; otherwise we would have got you away before this.' He was quite immovable and before the week was out I found myself in an ambulance convoy heading south.

The first night we stopped at Sarafand and the following morning continued the journey down to the Suez Canal, finally coming to rest at 13 General Hospital at Suez. It soon became apparent that this hospital was there to send casualties by sea to South Africa, so I at once set to work to avoid going there, as it would be the end of the War so far as I was concerned at a time when my actual battle experience amounted to exactly twenty-four hours.

I was in the charge of a Maltese medical officer who clearly thought I was slightly deranged in not wanting to slip away to South Africa and all that that great country would have to offer. The more I pressed my case the more difficult he became, until he reached the stage that he was quite convinced that he must ensure my departure by boat at the earliest opportunity. Just before Christmas the *Queen Wilhelmina*, an enormous hospital ship lent by the Dutch Government, arrived and we were all booked to go, as there was masses of room. There was a chap in the ward who had very nearly recovered from his disability. He came in one evening not looking particularly well. The following morning he was discovered to be suffering from diphtheria, and the whole ward was put into quarantine. This lucky break meant that the hospital ship sailed without us.

Towards the New Year of 1943 I was allowed to move about, and even to go down into Suez on occasional expeditions, which was a marvellous experience. Then, to my horror, up turned the good old *Abber*, the ship that had taken me across to Haifa two months before, ready to take a further shipload down to Durban. I knew that its capacity was limited, so I popped into the Orderly Room, saw the Orderly Room Sergeant and arranged for my name to be put at the bottom of the list, which he was kind enough to do and, sure enough, the *Abber* sailed without me. It became clear that I could not expect my luck to last much longer, so I asked for, and obtained, leave to go up to Cairo for two or three days. My hand was giving me very little trouble at this stage. The following morning I set out for GHQ Middle East, which was installed in the Semiramus Hotel. I looked down the staff list and found that the Deputy Adjutant General was Major General Moorehead, who had been in a branch of the Adjutant General's Department when I was in SD2 at the outbreak of war in the War Office, and with whom I had had quite a lot to do.

I marched in, got a temporary pass from the NCO at the entrance and called in on the General's private secretary. I was lucky in that the General was in and half an hour later I was ushered into his presence. After the usual pleasantries I got down to the purpose of my mission, which, quite crudely, was his help to keep me in the Middle East, as the only hope I had of remaining in the War was to be in the same theatre as the 51st Highland Division. He was rather amused at the request, because I think he had something of the reverse attitude. When he saw that I was quite sincere in my wish, he picked up the telephone, rang up the Medical Directorate and a lengthy conversation ensued. He admitted that, since the actual Battle of Alamein, the casualties had been relatively light, and the fear of the hospitals in the Delta being flooded out had disappeared. He thought my chances of having my way were relatively good and he wished me luck.

The following day I betook myself by train back to the wastes of Suez and from the station took a taxi back to the hospital. I had just paid off the taxi cab driver and was turning away when I found myself confronted by the Maltese doctor, who was obviously extremely angry.

'What have you been up to in Cairo?' said he.

'Nothing much,' I replied, 'just met a few friends up there who were very kind.'

'Then why do I get this peremptory telegram ordering me to send you to the 15th Scottish Hospital in Cairo?'

He was beside himself with indignation, accused me of working behind his back, which was true, and consigned me to the devil.

Thither I went the next morning and by the afternoon had been admitted to the 15th Scottish General Hospital.

I realised that, provided I hung on, the way for a cure was at last open. This hospital had been raised at Cruden Bay, in Gordon Highlander country, and to have the former commander of the 1st Battalion with them ensured almost preferential treatment. It was installed on the south bank of the Nile, having been built just before the War for the benefit of rich Egyptians, and was modern. I was looked at that afternoon, but no decision was taken as the hospital had been notified by GHQ that the surgical specialist would come in the following morning in order to satisfy himself that my injury justified being dealt with in Cairo. He unwrapped the bandages in the presence of the hospital surgeon and there was a long pause, at least it seemed very long to me. The hand looked pretty miserable and hung awkwardly and lifelessly on the end of a bent wrist. The specialist turned it over to see the exit wound and then looked at the wasted forearm. He gave a grunt and then asked when it was last operated on; I told him that this had been a month previously. He seemed surprised to hear this, but then tied the hand up, looked at me and said, 'Well, we will do what we can, it is in poor shape but they should be able to deal with it here, given time.' I thanked him, much relieved and then became an accepted patient in one of the best hospitals one could wish to be in.

The months of January and February were taken up with a series of operations, of which the first two were the most gruelling. The trouble was that the wrist had been set at the wrong angle and the wrist had to be broken and re-set properly. I think that, before I was finally released from the operating table, I had had thirteen operations. There is no doubt in my mind that in World War One I would have lost my hand and possibly the whole of the arm. To have finished up in what was probably the best hospital in the Middle East was almost too good to be true.

It was in early March that the forefinger was finally induced to touch the base of the thumb, and a very painful experience it was to start with. Then the second finger followed suit, which was a great triumph, but there success stopped because the third finger and little finger were never again to close properly and have remained aloof ever since, with the little finger stuck out in a most uncompromising manner. It was also possible at this time to go into Cairo on shopping expeditions. On one of these I ran into an officer in the Scots Guards who, eleven years before, had travelled in the same Bibby Liner which took me back to Egypt after my leave in 1931. He was employed in GHQ and was responsible for officers' postings in the Adjutant General's Department. I told him that when I had had my medical board I wanted to be posted back to the 51st (Highland) Division. He said he would do what he could when the time came, but naturally could give no undertaking until the medical papers were received in his office.

Throughout my stay in the 15th Scottish Hospital I had kept in touch with the Brigadier and one or two of the regimental officers, and it was particularly pleasing to hear that the 1st Battalion the Gordon Highlanders was the first infantry battalion to enter Tripoli in the third week of January 1943. Their advance continued on towards Tunisia until they took up a defensive position at Medenine early in March, to fend off the expected attack by Rommel after he had delivered a heavy blow against the First Army at Kasserine.

Monty issued one of his famous orders of the day, one of the paragraphs reading much as follows: 'We will stand and fight the enemy in our present positions. There must be no withdrawal anywhere, and of course, no surrender.'

An officer from Brigade went forward after the battle, met one of the leading Company Commanders and in congratulating him added, 'I suppose you read out the Army Commander's Order of the Day to all ranks?'

'Not bloody likely,' came the answer, 'I didn't want to be left here all by myself.' The possibility of his company de-camping was slight but it is not uninteresting to record the reaction of a down-to-earth Company Commander, on the eve of an important engagement, to exhortations from the highest.

In the second week of April I was transferred to Lady Lampson's Convalescent Home for Officers. Soon after this I was summoned back to the hospital to appear before a medical board, which examined my case with great care. They finally decided that I should be graded 'B'. This was the last thing I wanted, because it meant light duties, which was certain to lead to a further appointment on the Staff. So I said to the President, 'Why not "A"? After all, as a lieutenant colonel, the fact that my hand is not completely 100 per cent does not matter in the slightest, because all I have to do is to sign my name. I do not have to fire even a pistol.' They were rather amused at this, but, bless their hearts, they graded me 'A', fit for all duties.

I dashed off to GHQ and told my Scots Guards friend that I was in the 'clear' and would be grateful to him if he could get me posted back to the 51st at the earliest opportunity. On the 17th April I had lunch in the convalescent home and then drifted across to Gezira to watch some cricket. The spring had come and it was a delightful day, but in the early evening I returned to the home to see if anything had turned up and sure enough there was a message from GHQ to the effect that I had been posted to the Eighth Army and that I would be picked up at Shepheard's Hotel at 5 a.m. the next morning in order to be flown up. I was so anxious not to 'miss the bus' that I slept, or tried to sleep, on a settee in the lounge leading off from the front hall. I had a word with the doorkeeper to ensure that I was not 'overlooked' when the bus came. It was not a comfortable night as the settee was alive with bugs, against which I fought a losing battle for most of the night. They finally won and

I went out onto the balcony and sat on one of the seats there watching the dawn gradually making itself felt.

There I sat while the nearby buildings took on a more positive outline and then suddenly realised that I was 40 years old that day, which was quite a thought as I was now really middle-aged and getting on a bit. My reverie was cut short by the arrival of a very ropey-looking bus and in I got to find half a dozen others, of all shapes and sizes and differing ranks from mine to private soldier. Off we went, rattling through the streets at a round pace and took the road towards Alexandria. There were several airfields in this direction and we pulled off the road. The thought of being left behind was unthinkable. We were eventually called forward and went outside to get into our aeroplane. I do not remember what type it was, but it looked astonishingly small. We got inside and found that it had been completely gutted, with no seats, no belts, just the bare walls.

The engines started up and they raced them for quite a time before trundling off to the end of the runway. On arrival there they put the brakes on, raced the engines madly and suddenly we shot off. Only when the aircraft was on an even keel travelling to the west were we permitted to unravel ourselves. We could see nothing, and even if we had been able to look out we would probably only have seen the inevitable sand. The first stop was El Adem, where one or two got off. We did not stay long but flew on to Benghazi, where we landed for a meal before going on, this time to Castel Benito, outside Tripoli. It was now early afternoon and it seemed faintly crazy that the Eighth Army had taken three months to cover this distance, which we had done in a few hours. We had a cup of tea here and flew on to Sfax which we reached at about 5.00 p.m.

The airfield was no more than a landing strip as Sfax had been occupied only ten days before. It was thrilling to hear later that the first infantry into Sfax had been the 1st Gordon Highlanders. The first person I saw was a Major General wearing the Divisional sign of the 56th (London) Division, Major General E.G. Miles, but he also seemed to be waiting for something and in any case it was impolite to approach Generals on minor issues. It then occurred to me that I had seen the transport of the London Division passing through Cairo during March, on its way westwards from Asia Minor, so the Division was now about to join the Eighth Army after an approach march of 2,000 or 3,000 miles. What did not occur to me was that my career was about to be affected by this move and the fate of its commander, but that was to come later and to my great relief it emerged that the 51st (Highland) Division was resting within a few miles of Sfax. I borrowed a truck from them and that evening reported to Douglas Wimberley in 'A' Mess. Altogether quite a full day, with Cairo 2,000 miles away.

I stayed at Divisional Headquarters for a day or two, while my fate was decided. So far as Douglas Wimberley was concerned the aim of every officer or man in any way connected with the Highland Division was to return to it by hook or by crook. This I had done, but it was not quite so easy to decide what to do with a Battalion Commander. Douglas Graham came over and it was decided that I should return to the command of my beloved 1st Battalion; I returned with him to the Brigade area to do so. 'Hammie' Fausset Farquhar could not have been more under-standing, in spite of his brilliant performances through the long haul since Alamein, and made my return a happy one with no reservations.

I went around having a word with the officers and men and, not unnaturally, there were a great number of new faces. Tunisia was a great change for these old warriors and they were revelling in it. The Division was not expected to take any further part in the North African Campaign and the forward divisions were now the 2nd New Zealand Division and the 4th Indian. The overall campaign in the Mediterranean was to be further prosecuted, no-one knew where, and the 51st was to be kept ready to prepare for the next venture. So, on this 19th day of April 1943, it looked as if I would have time to get to know the new Battalion as well as I had known the old. Early on the 20th of April off we went with the Battalion Orders Group streaking on ahead, heading for Enfidaville. We bumbled along down the coast road, making good time, when to our astonishment a complete Roman amphitheatre loomed up to all intents and purposes just as it was nearly 2,000 years ago. This was too much for our curiosity and we simply had to go in and have a look, no matter what the state of the battle ahead might be. It was El Djem and we spent an hour there, having something to eat as we did so. Thence on to the north, through Enfidaville and towards the Garci Mountains.

Just before first light we ran forward in our Jeeps across an open plain for 2 or 3 miles, through a dry wadi and thence under the lee of the Garci Mountains. These were formidable and it took the skill of Indian soldiers to penetrate in as far as they did. We spent quite a long time forward, as we picked our way from one company position to another, all of which were separated from their neighbours by deep gullies.

The plan was for the Battalion to take over that evening. We had a good midday meal and spent the afternoon ensuring that we were ready in all respects for the takeover. In the middle of this Brigadier Graham turned up and told me that General Wimberley and Roy Urquhart, the GSO1, had been ordered back to Cairo for planning, that he was to take over command of the Division temporarily and that I was to go back with him to take Roy Urquhart's place. Hey-ho, so after all, command of the Battalion had lasted only thirty-six hours after all, but I could only bow myself out, hand over to 'Hammie' again and push off. It was to be my last appearance as a battalion commander. On the evening of this day, April 21st, I reported back to Divisional Headquarters and by the following afternoon Roy Urquhart was on his way to the fleshpots of Cairo.

At Divisional HQ one became aware of a bigger picture. The 56th (London) Division had moved up and were taking over on the right from part of the 2nd (New Zealand) Division. Neither of these divisions were to take part in the next Mediterranean Campaign initially. It was decided that the 51st Highland Division should send advisers over to the 56th Division to help them with battle procedures and generally be of assistance in much the same way as it had been provided for the 51st six months or more previously in the Western Desert. The Corps Commander on the front at this stage was Lieutenant General Sir Brian Horrocks, who commanded X Corps Headquarters, XXX Corps having also gone into reserve ready for the next venture. An occasional Orders Group would assemble at X Corps Headquarters which I attended and there I discovered that although the 51st Division was not to be required to carry out any offensive operations, this did not apply to the newly-arrived 56th Division.

The following week the 56th put in an attack, which was only partially successful, in spite of being put in with great spirit. It seemed to demonstrate that a thrust up the coastal plain was not really on. Soon after this the 4th Indian and the 7th Armoured were ordered across to join the First Army, and the Eighth Army front thereafter became secondary. Lieutenant General Brian Horrocks went across with these two Divisions, taking his headquarters with him and command on the front passed to Lieutenant General Bernard Freyburg. The same day I decided I would go forward and pay a call on the 1st Gordons with Jock Sorel Cameron (CO 5th Camerons). We took one of the Headquarters' Jeeps, which belonged to one of the liaison officers, and set out. We got up forward, dropped onto the plain which had to be crossed in order to get to the Garci Mountains and ultimately got under the lee of the hills, until we reached a point below the location of Battalion Headquarters. We then got out, climbed up the hill for about 100 feet and reached our destination. It was a nice warm sunny afternoon, and as it faced south the Headquarters was undoubtedly snug.

After about ten minutes there was an ominous whistle followed by a partial explosion in our midst, which sent stones flying in all directions. That was all we wanted to know, and the move towards some sort of cover was impressive, but not before we were deafened by a shattering explosion further down the hill. We had had an astonishing bit of luck as there was only one shell and it happened to go off at the second bounce. Many of us had scratches from the flying stones caused by the first bounce, but little would have remained of most of us had it gone off first time. It may have been a complete fluke, but we counted ourselves extremely lucky to get away with it. I think it was a remarkable piece of opportunism on the part of the Germans and I am quite certain that the shell was fired as a result of our visit. It went to show that the Germans never missed a trick and you had to be constantly on guard.

On our way back Jock Sorel Cameron turned to me and said, 'You know, we really had no business to come up here in daylight and had we been wounded we would have had precious little sympathy.' Within a matter of days a similar incident took place on the front of the 56th Division with very different results. The Divisional Commander (General Miles) decided one afternoon to go up and visit the Regiment. He had been equipped with an armoured command vehicle and travelled in it on this occasion, and also took his GSO1, Lieutenant Colonel Ely, with him, which was an unusual thing to do as normally one or other needed to be available at Headquarters. The route forward was quite safe, but it was completely overlooked from the high ground to the west. His arrival at Battalion Headquarters, where the Commanding Officer and Second-in-Command were standing to receive him, coincided with the arrival of a 'stonk' of German artillery fire. It was an incredible piece of timing and in this case it killed the Second-in-Command, severely wounded Colonel Ely, who subsequently died of his wounds, while the General had a shell splinter through his head. It was a disaster, and had a very depressing effect on the whole Division. The first we heard of this was the receipt of an order from Army Headquarters ordering Brigadier Graham to go over to the 56th Division to take over command and he disappeared that day, with Brigadier George Murray coming into 51st Divisional Headquarters to take his place. It was now that at last the time came for the Highland Division to be pulled out of the line, being relieved by a Free French Division. This Division had a number of British liaison officers with it and the reconnaissance parties went forward in the time-honoured manner to start to take over. Early in May the Free French were concentrated behind us and one night the relief commenced. In the middle of this relief we received an order requiring me to go over to the 56th Division to assume the duties of GSO1 in the place of Ely. Of course it was out of the question to go before the relief was complete and it was not until first light that I went to take up this appointment. The 51st (Highland) Division was going across country to Algeria at a place called Djidjelli.

Once there I found myself gazing once more at the problem of the thrust north towards Bou Ficha up the narrow coastal plain, and the more one looked at it the less likely it appeared. The acting Corps Commander, the redoubtable Bernard Freyburg, was not the sort of man, however, to wait upon events, and plans were already in training for a joint attack by the 56th Division and the Free French. I turned up at about 10 a.m. on May 7th and spent the rest of the morning taking stock of the new headquarters and those composing it. I went forward with the Divisional Tac Headquarters when it got dusk and ran past some of these troops resting in the ditches on both sides of the road. An hour later they were filing past us to take up their positions forward. The attack went in at 10.00 p.m. with a considerable weight of artillery support. The first objective was captured with relative ease, and the reserve companies moved through at about midnight against the main ridge, but at once ran into heavy opposition and were held. Three separate assaults were put in, but all were repulsed. The Division was very anxious to succeed but time was running out, as the objective dominated the whole of the battle area and if caught in the open after first light they would be decimated.

They had one last crack, but by 3.00 a.m. it was clear that they were still short of the crest, and the Divisional Commander ordered the action to be broken off and the troops recalled. He just had time to clear the battlefield before the day broke. The Division had suffered heavy casualties and was extremely disappointed that they had been unsuccessful, but they had fought with great skill and determination.

The following morning Bernard Freyburg came up and I was an interested spectator as he cross-examined in great detail all those concerned in the previous night's battle. He clearly could not understand why it had failed and he remained unconvinced to the end. I think the trouble was that, by this time, his New Zealand Division was probably one of the most formidable formations in the Eighth Army with a wealth of battle experience and he was apt to judge others by the very high standards they achieved. I was, personally, impressed by the élan of this inexperienced Division, which put up such a splendid show in their first engagement after an approach march of some thousands of miles.

Tentative plans were at once drawn up to stage a resumption of the attack, but the rapid advance of the First Army caused the plans to become increasingly academic. Grombalia had been captured and Hammamet was about to fall as well. During the 10th of May we commenced picking up signals from the 6th Armoured Division and by the 11th we had netted our own artillery with theirs. The great day came on the 12th when the forward troops reported the appearance of tanks on the front and these proved to be those of the 23rd Armoured Brigade commanded by Brigadier 'Pip' Roberts. The encirclement was complete.

As the day wore on white flags commenced to flutter from the hills to the west of the road, which had hitherto looked so formidable, indeed unassailable. The hills which had for so many days gazed down upon us, stark, silent and full of menace, assumed quite a different aspect, when trickles of men started to appear and move down the slopes towards us. These trickles gradually merged to form a long straggling column making towards the bridge over the road, which had been blown by the Germans when retreating. In the meantime the tanks of the 6th Armoured Division moved forward into hull-down positions supervising and dominating the whole area.

We finally grouped ourselves near the bridge on our side and watched the early stages of a mass surrender unfold. The column came across country towards us at an angle and seemed to be almost exclusively composed of Italians. The Germans were to be pulled in later. These Italians looked rather woebegone and scruffy, but glad to be out of it all. At long last the head of the column arrived on the far side of the wadi, wavered and came to a halt. They were ordered to cross over where they were, but seemed disinclined to do so until the orders became peremptory and, somewhat uncertainly, they moved down the far bank and descended into the bed of the wadi. In a matter of seconds there was a series of shattering explosions and cries of anguish.

When these explosions took place we instinctively thought that the bridge was being shelled and the speed with which very senior officers made themselves scarce was impressive. The bridge was virtually untenanted in no time at all. Then we heard the cries coming up from the wadi and saw the head of the column of Italians recoiling up the far bank, which showed that the explosions had been anti-personnel mines, which had been sown in the bed of the wadi. They were not as lucky as we had been at Alamein. No further attempt to cross was possible and we called up a team of the Royal Engineers to clear a passage through. The mines were cleared away and a passage made, not only allowing the column of prisoners to be on the move again, but enabling us to meet the commanders on the other side. The photograph of the Corps Commanders, Horrocks and Freyburg, and the Divisional Commanders, Keightley and Graham, is historic, because this was the fateful scene which saw the end of the campaign in North

Africa. While this was going on I suddenly realised that the 56th Division would have the task of collecting, housing and guarding thousands upon thousands of prisoners.

The first night saw the arrival of huge numbers of Italians and it was not until the following day that our old opponents the German 90th Light Division marched in, looking just as formidable as they had been in battle. It was nice to think that the long duel between these desert veterans and the Eighth Army was now satisfactory resolved in our favour. The other late arrivals were the Generals for whom we created a special camp and whom we entertained to an English breakfast, which I think they ate merely out of politeness.

Within a few days it was confirmed that General Miles was too badly wounded to resume command of the 56th Division and that command was to pass to Douglas Graham. The following day I was sent for by Graham and told that I would have to rejoin the 51st (Highland) Division, which I had hoped for and expected but he went on to say that Douglas Wimberley had decided to give me command of his old Brigade, 153. This was a bit breathtaking, but before I left, Douglas Graham and I wrote out an order of the day. We had both been very impressed by the performance of the 56th Division and felt that in spite of the exceptional demands that had been made upon them, by being involved in operations in very difficult country, against some of the veteran German divisions, they had shown quality of the highest order. They had not had the satisfaction of distinguishing themselves in a spectacular battle of their own, but they had nevertheless played a part in a campaign, which culminated in the surrender of over a quarter of a million Germans and Italians. It was a German military disaster, which compared with the recent German surrender at Stalingrad.

So the campaign in North Africa ended. It was a far cry back to the days of the Western Desert Force, to the days of General Sir Archibald Wavell and General R.N. O'Connor. The 51st (Highland) Division arrived at a time when the tide was turning, with tanks which could compare with the German Mark IV and with the best tactical commander on either side, but we never doubted that the glory rested with those veteran Divisions which had borne the heat and burden of the day in those earlier years: the 9th Australian, the 2nd New Zealand, the 4th Indian and the 7th

Armoured. I think that the flamboyance of the 51st was irksome to many. The less charitable resented the way in which the divisional sign was plastered on every building of note all the way up through the desert and on a sufficient scale to earn them the title of the Highway Decorators. It had started with the simple desire not to lose the way and we did not mind if some thought it smacked of self-advertisement.

We had organised a park for captured enemy matériel, equipment and transport and I went down there without too much waste of time, but was far too late to get transport of any quality, so swift on the draw had others been. The best I could do was to collect a couple of anaemic-looking and very small Fiats. I drew a quantity of hard liquor to be on the safe side and one fine morning we took the road for Djidjelli. We still had no idea what the next venture was likely to be, except that it would probably not be too long delayed.

Chapter Thirteen

Sicily

The weather was quite magnificent and we set off one morning in the middle of May 1943 in high spirits. Our two little Fiats constituted a 'flying column' and our only shortcoming was that we had no real mechanic amongst us. We sailed gaily along until we were approaching Medjez-el-Bab, a scene of much fighting on the front of the First Army during the previous six months.

Evening came and we found ourselves way out in the blue near a high wooded hill, and there we rested for the night. It was all a little fabulous because we had everything to ourselves with the First Army milling about in the Cape Bon peninsula miles away.

We reached an RAMC Mess, in a marvellous villa, very near to the edge of the Mediterranean at Bougie and sat down to an excellent dinner. One thing seemed to lead to another and at one stage of the evening I found myself standing on the shoulders of one of the others signing my name on the ceiling. It was a poor effort, but was greeted with shouts of applause. In no time at all we were in the sea splashing about like a lot of boys and coming out ready for almost anything. It was a reminder, if one was needed, that the RAMC know how to make the best of their leisure and I could not have been more grateful for having this opportunity of sharing this sort of evening.

I went straight on to the Headquarters of the 153 Infantry Brigade, which had been set up near the sea on the far side of the town, a splendid site. My Brigade Major was Major James Scott Noble of the King's Own Scottish Borderers, a Lowland Scot who was later to be a big figure in the wool trade. He was highly efficient and imperturbable and altogether a great blessing.

The following morning I reported to Divisional Headquarters and then discovered for the first time that the next venture was to be the invasion of Sicily. This operation was to be launched early in July and left less than six weeks for training. The plan required the 51st Division to attack astride Cape Passaro, in the South East corner of the island. We were part of XXX Corps again under Lieutenant General Sir Oliver Leese and would assault with XIII Corps (General Sir Miles Dempsey) on our right and the 1st Canadian Division, under Major General Guy Simonds (who was at the Staff College with me only six years previously), on our left. The actual assault was to be made by 154 Brigade under Tom Rennie, who would be reinforced for the operation by the 1st Gordons from my Brigade. My Brigade was to be the first follow-up Brigade and 152nd Infantry Brigade, under Brigadier Gordon Macmillan, was to be the floating reserve.

I saw the Corps Commander and he stressed that the first need was to get possession of airfields and ports and it was noticeable that XIII Corps, in going for Syracuse and Augusta with the Americans landing near the airfield at Gela, ran into much heavier opposition than came our way. Training teams turned up, this time from the United Kingdom and tried to teach us everything under the sun, including rock-climbing. As usual, they were very enthusiastic and considered the latter to be essential to all. But I showed little response personally to the latter accomplishment although I gave them every encouragement in other directions. These training teams were quite invaluable and helped us to shake ourselves clear, to a certain extent, from the technique of fighting in the desert, because Sicily was rugged, hilly, and almost mountainous, with indifferent roads and tracks and nothing like the same facilities for tactical manoeuvre that made the desert a tactician's paradise. We did what we could, but we had to combine this training with amphibious exercises, and when it is remembered that we had less than six weeks to cover the lot it is not surprising that we were weak when it came to minor tactics.

The troops revelled in the amphibious exercises but of course this was only the prelude to operations inland. In early June we sailed down the coast and carried out a couple of amphibious exercises, which were, for the most part a complete shambles. We were forced to use whatever beaches were available and these often had shoals off-shore which prevented even small craft from closing to the beaches; the ground, when we got ashore was totally different from

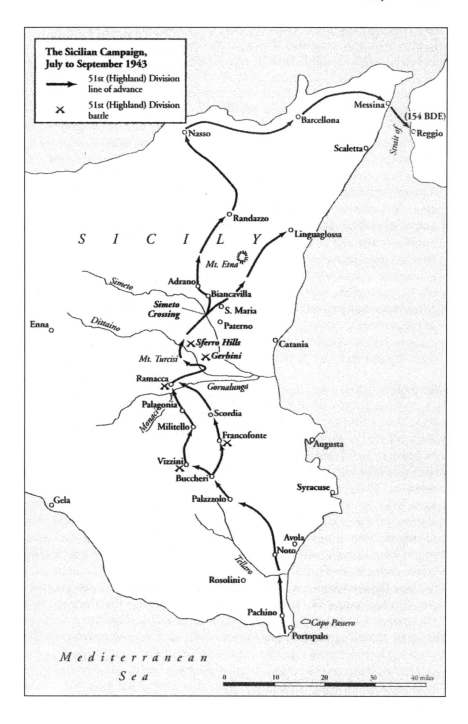

**The Sicilian Campaign,
July to September 1943**

→ 51st (Highland) Division
line of advance

✕ 51st (Highland) Division
battle

the ground we would attack over in Sicily. We attended two naval demonstrations, one of which was to travel in a rocket-ship and witness its capability. These contained 1,200 large rockets, which were fired off in salvoes of about sixty rockets at a time, electronically. The accuracy was not great, but it must have been most unpleasant to be at the receiving end and very demoralising.

We had a visit in June from Generals Alan Brooke and Alexander, travelling together and being very entertaining in the process. The idyll on the shores of the Mediterranean at Djidjelli came to an end and we started the long trek back to Sousse. I never travelled in convoys as it was boring and no-one wanted you to be there anyway. This time I had the highly professional support of the Brigade Headquarters team and we were never in any trouble. We went back through Constantine, which was very French, and where we had one of the best dinners I have ever eaten. So to Sousse and a very hot camp in the middle of an olive grove. I remember it well that while we were there, waiting, Will Fyffe, the famous Scottish comedian came to entertain the troops. It was one of the hottest days I can remember, the sun beat down through tents and trees and there was no escape from it. He gave a concert in the middle of the afternoon when the heat was almost unbearable, wearing his kilt, thick doublet and bonnet and gave a magnificent performance with the sweat pouring out of him in rivers. No wonder he got the rousing ovation he deserved.

As usual before amphibious operations, the troops taking part were completely immobilised at an early stage to enable their transport to be waterproofed and loaded well in advance. Consequently life was a little dull during the last few days before embarkation, but it was noticeable that all the troops had vanished back to the east and their place was taken largely by the airborne troops who were to precede the assault from the sea. We had a rehearsal of embarkation and disembarkation in the harbour which was witnessed by the naval commander, Rear Admiral McGrigor and at the subsequent discussion he could hardly have been less complimentary. It is not easy to get the soldiers interested in an exercise of this sort, which was bound to be artificial, and we treated it somewhat lightheartedly. It was a pleasant way of spending the afternoon, but it occurred to few of us that it was necessarily an operation of war.

*   *   *

It was on the early afternoon of the 5th of July 1943 that we finally embarked. We all travelled in LCIs (Landing Craft Infantry), which held approximately 150 men. As we were the follow-up Brigade we needed no assault craft. Each ship in turn pulled clear of the quayside and moved out into the Mediterranean, took up formation and then steamed away north with destroyers ploughing along on both flanks and with fighter aircraft overhead. We had nothing much to do except look at the sea, the ships and speculate. We were bound for Malta, where we were to stay for two or three days prior to the invasion.

Night came and we went below for a meal and bed. We carried everything we needed on us. We wore trousers instead of shorts, mainly because it was known that Sicily, in the summer, was malarious. After lunch, Malta which had been steadily looking up ahead was reached and we drove to opposite the entrance to Valletta harbour. The events of the next two hours were, to me, funny mainly because for once in a while, the Royal Navy put on what can only be described as an amateur performance. We bobbed about opposite the entrance for an appreciable time before we saw a few launches dart out of the harbour and make for the ships comprising the convoy. It transpired that the Captains of the ships in the convoy had no berthing instructions and these were about to be provided. This took quite a time, as there were a considerable number of ships to be berthed, and while this was going on (it lasted well over an hour), we provided one of the best floating targets any airman could have wished for. In turn we received the attention of a launch and a roneo-ed sheet was thrust up the side on the end of a pole. The Captain of our ship grasped the sheet as if his life depended on it, and from a distance it was fairly obvious that he was not really any wiser than he had been before. I went across to find out what he was supposed to do. The paper had on it the outline of the harbour. After a long and deep study of this sketch we finally agreed which berth we should make for and in the process I discovered that the Captain had never been in Malta in his life. This was staggering, as it never occurred to me that a naval officer existed who had never, at some time in his career, been stationed in Malta. Somewhat apprehensively we nosed our way into the Grand Harbour and it was my feeling that we should turn left as soon as we were clear of the entrance and thereafter proceed with 'the left hand down'. This did not appear to the Captain to be very helpful but in the meantime I was trying to recapture the picture of this harbour as I last remembered it in 1927. As a result of the uncertainty, we cruised gently around the harbour, peeping in first here and then there, for about half an hour. The Jocks thought that this was part of the show and were very appreciative, but not so the Naval Staff and words were exchanged between them and the Captain of a highly uncomplimentary nature. After this 'Royal Tour' we finally tied up at the correct berth, and disembarked with all speed. The contents of my LSI was composed almost exclusively of Brigade Headquarters and we finished up in an open field just off a very narrow and stony track.

So we relaxed in our stony fastness and wondered how we were going to fill in our time during the next forty-eight hours. As it happened this was a problem which resolved itself almost immediately with the arrival of Major Kent, who was on the staff of General Oliver Leese, and was acting as Liaison Officer to General Montgomery who was already on the island. It emerged that the latter wished, the following morning, to go around and talk to all the troops staging through Malta and that, as I was the senior officer of the Highland Division on the island, I would be required to produce a plan, and report to Monty by 10 o'clock the following morning with it and accompany him on the tour. This, of course, was very flattering, but when I asked Major Kent where the others were I discovered that he knew no more than I did. The only people who had the slightest idea where troops were located was Movement Control and thither we went, to discover them hundreds of feet below sea level in an underground headquarters which had been created as a result of the German aerial assault in 1941–2. Here we found a map of the island with individual locations of headquarters and units clearly set out. We spent some time studying the map and then worked out a plan in which we could arrange a circular tour through the island starting from the Pavilion, in which Monty was staying. We made a list of the units and headquarters, measured the distances between them, gave Monty fifteen minutes at each and arranged the whole thing so that we could be back at his house by 12.30 p.m. As we had no transport we borrowed a couple of Jeeps from the Headquarters and with an escort of

Military Police, who knew the island well, we set forth on our mission. It would be about 11.00 p.m. when we left on our journey and for four hours we travelled through the moonlit streets and lanes of Malta visiting each unit in succession, agreeing upon a place of parade, who would command it and the time we would arrive. Most of the local commanders resented being roused somewhat summarily, but were well pleased with the prospect of a meeting with Monty the following morning and while on the run it was also possible to discover what their problems were and get a general impression of their immediate needs. It was altogether a night to remember.

We finally got back to our remote field and I said goodnight to Kent and the Military Policemen and went to bed. At about 9.30 a.m. Johnnie Poston, Monty's ADC appeared in Monty's open car to take me down to the Pavilion. There was the Army Commander, just as chirpy as ever and I presented the plan. He examined it and then cross-examined me most carefully about the various commanders he would be meeting.

As I knew most of them fairly well I could play this with a certain amount of confidence and it appeared to satisfy him, although this was a subject to which he always paid the greatest importance. While we were in the middle of this in walked Freddie de Guingand, his Chief of Staff. Monty turned to me and said, 'Is there anything you want?' There were a number of requests, but there were two of particular importance. The first was whether it would be possible for the troops to be allowed out of their camps to which they were at present confined. The second was that there was no beer. Monty turned to Freddie and said, 'Of course they must be let out, otherwise they will blow up and how much beer should we let them have, two, three or four bottles each?' It was all fixed as easily as that.

Soon after 10 a.m. we left the Pavilion in the open car driven by Johnnie Poston. We had not gone very far when Monty waved to somebody standing on the pavement, who gazed back somewhat uncomprehendingly, but further on he repeated the performance to another, who was equally unresponsive until, suddenly, the first surfaced and let out a shout which was immediately taken up and echoed down the street and before we knew where we were we were running the gauntlet through crowds of excited Maltese. The technique was impressive and extremely effective. The tour worked out well enough but was a little uneven because Monty stayed longer at some places than others.

There were no inspections, but he met most of the officers and addressed all the troops who would be summoned forward to the car to enable him to speak to them from close quarters. He remained as fresh as paint throughout, although he must have visited at least eight gatherings during the morning. In his talk he made play about the creation of a 'Second Front' which had been bothering the politicians at home ever since Russia came into the War, and he said he was not certain whether we were creating a Second, Third or Fourth Front. Without specifically mentioning the fact that we were about to invade Sicily, he made it abundantly clear that the immediate enemy was the Italian. He went on to say that we should rid ourselves of the idea that the Italian was a good chap. He was not a good chap, said Monty; otherwise he would not be talking to them at that place, four years after the War had broken out as a result of Mussolini and all his works. 'So,' said he, 'your job is to kill one Italian every day and two on Sundays.' To the Jocks they knew perfectly well that a lot of it might be blarney, but it was the sort of talk they loved to hear.

When the last camp had been visited we returned to the Pavilion and lunch, to which I had been invited. On the way around Monty engaged me in conversation, more particularly to do with the officers and asked how old the Brigadiers were. The senior Brigadier was Gordon MacMillan aged 46, Tom Rennie was 42, and I was 40.

'And what about the Commanding Officers?' he asked.

I considered for a moment and, off-hand, gave an average between 35 and 38.

'Too old,' he replied. 'Brigadiers should not be over 40, nor Commanding Officers over 35.'

I protested by saying that these officers seemed to me to be in their prime and that although an age level served its purpose, it was inequitable to make it apply universally.

He remained quite unmoved, upon which, with some daring I said, 'After all, these age limits did not apply to you, because you got your Battalion at the age of 44 and you were 48 before you got a Brigade.'

'That,' replied Monty, 'has got nothing to do with it, because that was peace and not war. Anyway, what is the next unit we are due to visit?'

On balance I suppose he was right in drawing this distinction between peace and war, but many of us were conscious of the hardship inflicted upon highly meritorious officers when this rule was summarily applied, which deprived them of the privilege of command in the field which must always be the ambition of any soldier. They 'soldiered on' in command of training units, forging the weapon which others were to wield and it was very appropriate that their work was properly acknowledged when the War was over.

I stayed to lunch at the Pavilion, had a bath which was very welcome, and then stayed on for dinner. At dinner there were one or two American Generals as well as Lieutenant General Sir Charles Alfrey who had been one of the instructors at the Staff College when I was there, and who was now a Corps Commander earmarked for the attack on Taranto when the time came for the invasion of Italy. I was sitting well down the table and had a listening role. It was all very good value, but I remember in particular a part of the conversation initiated by Charles Alfrey. He was a Gunner and said to Montgomery, 'Sir, I think it is a great misfortune that gunners and sappers are not given the opportunity to command infantry, because when they reach high rank the greater proportion of their command is composed of infantry, of which they have previously had insufficient experience.'

'Charles,' came the swift reply, 'a gunner or a sapper will command an infantry brigade in the Eighth Army over my dead body.' This caused quite a laugh without convincing Charles Alfrey in the slightest. In fact, during the Italian Campaign, admittedly after Monty had gone back to command in Normandy, gunners and sappers did command infantry brigades and with quite a measure of success. Nevertheless, nobody was in any doubt what Monty's position in the matter was.

And so to July the 9th and in the afternoon we embussed, went down to our berth and then moved from the Grand Harbour to the open sea. A very different scene presented itself from that which we had experienced three days before, because there was low cloud and a high wind, which was to prejudice the invasion considerably. The wind whipped up the sea which hit us hard as soon as we were clear of the harbour. It was the sort of storm in which the Mediterranean specialises, coming from nowhere and spending itself relatively quickly, but it lasted long enough to put us to a great deal of discomfort and seriously prejudiced the airborne attack. These LCIs had a displacement of only 1,500 tons, so we were pushed about more than somewhat. The troops may have gained an inkling of what was ahead and any doubts may have been dispelled during their stay in Malta, but they had not, in fact, been briefed and this was reserved for this stormy afternoon.

When we were well clear of Malta the Brigade Major started to carry out his part by setting up a map against a hatch cover, where it was held by a couple of clerks, and the officers and men squatted down on the deck to listen. They followed the unfolding of the plan with what appeared to be rapt attention. We were landing at one or other of the beaches to the west of Cape Passaro in the wake of 154 Brigade. We would travel north and west as hard as we could go from there. They were told who were on our flanks and the supporting fire we could expect to get. The Brigade Major got through the opening part of his discourse, speaking slowly and distinctly, and then excused himself for a moment, went to the side of the ship and relieved himself of most of his lunch, returning to the next phase of the attack quite unperturbed, until another convulsion led to a further temporary withdrawal. It was one of the finest examples of the conquest of mind over matter I have witnessed and he continued on through with his disclosure until he reached its end. The whole affair lasted about an hour and it was not altogether surprising that when the Brigade Major got to the end of his discourse and asked if there were any questions there was no response, merely a firm move to get into the prone position as quickly as possible.

In the early hours of the 10th of July 154 Brigade touched down on the beaches near Cape Passaro, meeting little opposition and the rest of the Brigade was ashore by first light. Somehow or other, in our passage from Malta, the convoy was in a state of disarray and instead of my Brigade Headquarters bringing up the rear it was all too obviously well out in front.

There was little to be done about this as it would have been unseemly to back-pedal in order to give the others the opportunity of showing their mettle. We steadily got nearer and from half a mile out the prospect was not very inviting with the waves breaking high over the rocks and no obvious landing place. Our Captain handled the ship superbly and gradually closed to the shore until we were no more than 100 yards out, possibly less. He could go in no further without hazarding the ship, and down went the gangway. We were, of course, 'longing to be at 'em', but there seemed to be a disinclination to start the movement. Those about me seemed to be looking in my direction with the unspoken suggestion that this was when the leader actually led. There was nothing for it but to plunge down the ramp and jump into the sea, which I preceded to do. The water was delightfully warm, and only came up to my middle. I waded on for some yards, turned back towards the ship where many were contemplating their next move, gave the victory signal, put my foot into a pothole and vanished from sight. I think this unrehearsed ducking did more for the morale of my Head-quarters than anything else that happened in the rest of the campaign. I suppose it is not often that the troops had the pleasure of seeing a Brigadier emerging, like Venus from the foam, but looking more like a drowned rat with a steel helmet. When I got my breath back the troops were ploughing their way through the water in high spirits, laughing and joking to each other. I picked my way ashore, directed the area into which Brigade Headquarters would establish itself, looked back to sea, saw that the two battalions would be a little time in landing and then moved off to contact Tom Rennie to find out what the form was. Everything with 154 Brigade had gone pretty well according to plan and they had had few casualties.

In all such operations alternative plans are thought out in advance and we had three to meet varying conditions. In this case the plans had met with far greater success than we had anticipated and therefore Plan Four was adopted which gave wider scope. I think it was the Elder Moltke who once said that, in his experience, three plans were always prepared to deal with all contingencies and it was always the fourth that was adopted; he was 'too right' as regards our experience in Sicily. Having got the plan from Tom Rennie I returned to the area of Brigade Headquarters, took off my equipment and most of my clothes, hung them on a nearby wall, and then took out my mess tin in order to smoke a cigar. I should have known better, but when I finally got the tin open I was confronted with the sight of my beloved cigars floating and disintegrating in sea water. It was a moment which I can recall now with detachment, but it was quite infuriating at the time. However, the sun was now well up in the sky, my clothes were drying out and the battalions at long last were in the process of arriving. In my partially clad state I set the 5th Black Watch to drive to the east to clear the bay known as the Rada Di Portopalo, through which, during the opening stages of the campaign all reserves, stores, guns and equipment of XXX Corps would pour.

The 5th/7th Gordons, commanded by 'Scrappy' Hay was ordered to follow up behind the 154 Brigade to give further depth to the bridgehead. 'Scrappy' Hay had been the commander of the Divisional Battle School before the Division went overseas and if there was one thing he knew it was to do with battle drills. I gave him the orders sitting on the wall on which my equipment was hanging out to dry and he moved off at once, shouting 'O Group over here'. A collection of Company Commanders and others who were standing in the middle distance sprang into action and followed 'Scrappy' into a nearby orchard. The soil was loose and they flogged along as best they could until they reached the spot where he had come to rest. One or two of them were much the worse for wear and had a definite 'hangover' from the buffeting they had received on the way in. Eventually all were assembled and this had no sooner been achieved than a shot rang out, followed by a cry from 'Scrappy' that he had been shot.

Pandemonium reigned for a time, weapons were being levelled in all directions in the most frightening manner, directed at any would-be sniper. After a time it was noticed that the Intelligence Officer had remained completely immobile. He looked very ill and indeed he was a poor sailor. He had had a dreadful crossing and to make matters worse he had been thrown against a bulkhead and smashed his glasses, so that he could hardly see. He was in no shape at all as he flogged through the deep and when he joined the others he merely flung the 'Beretta' tommy gun, which he had 'acquired' from the Italians, to the ground, the cocking handle flew back and fired one round which proceeded to embed itself in the fleshy part of the Colonel's thigh.

There are many contingencies that we considered in our planning, but one of them was not the possibility of the Intelligence

Officer shooting the Commanding Officer: the latter, to his fury, found himself being evacuated in the same ship that had brought him ashore with his command passing to a relatively junior officer, Major Napier, who commanded with great distinction for the next ten days.

The first day's operation went like clockwork, against slight opposition, and we created a deep bridgehead. That night Douglas Wimberley sent on an armoured column which penetrated still further. As soon as darkness fell we were treated to a magnificent firework display as the anti-aircraft defences on the beaches went into action against enemy aircraft. We were up betimes the following morning, plunged on forward and immediately ran into Roy Urquhart's Brigade of the 50th Division, on our right. Roy and I were about to agree upon lines of advance when we got cornered as a result of some pocket of resistance coming to life unexpectedly, and took refuge in a ditch until it was cleared up. I went back down the road and almost at once ran into Monty, standing up in a DUKW (amphibious lorry) together with Rear Admiral Mountbatten, who was then the Director of Combined Operations. Montgomery asked for a map and quickly sketched in the locations of the leading infantry brigades of the 50th Division and our own, and then ringed around the areas into which he wanted the brigades of the 51st to move. We were required to travel more and more to the north-west, not only to give XXX Corps more room in which to manoeuvre, but also to protect their left flank whilst they drove north to Catania.

I got on the air to Douglas Wimberley and he later came forward and issued the necessary orders. We captured quite a large number of prisoners but they were all Italian. It was quite otherwise at Syracuse and to the west of Gela, where the assaulting troops ran into some of the best troops Germany could put into the field. It was only the dominating leadership of General Patton at Gela which stopped the Americans there being driven into the sea. The roads were in quite good order, but the tracks were indifferent and we started to think out a plan for ferrying troops forward instead of just marching.

It was too early to do much about this on the 11th of July, so we continued to march on the 12th, when we travelled 15 miles and climbed nearly 1,000 feet. That evening, however, we had a plan ready for the 13th whereby the whole Brigade was taken forward in lifts. This enabled us to be in a position to fight a battle for Vizzini five days after landing, 60 miles forward of the bridgehead.

Vizzini, like many Sicilian towns, is set upon a hill 2,000 feet up and we came upon it from the south. The previous evening an attempt had been made by another brigade to capture it from the east, which was unsuccessful. In the early morning we deployed on a ridge about 5,000 yards short of the town with the 1st Gordons on the right and the 5th Black Watch on the left. The 5th/7th Gordons at this stage had been temporarily detached and only caught up with us later in the day, then going into reserve. The ground was rugged and uneven, and when the troops disappeared over the crest they vanished from view, and must have made very good use of the cover because they managed to get right in under the lee of the town before the firefight broke out in earnest during the afternoon.

The town was approached by a series of steep ridges, the troops moving from one to another under cover of smoke they themselves provided. There was no artillery. By the late afternoon they had closed right on to the edge of the town and were beginning to penetrate it. The road leading to the town was covered by enemy fire, so in the afternoon, with communications very poor, I went forward and joined the Battalion Headquarters of the 1st Gordons which was installed about 500 yards from the town. I stayed there while the leading companies penetrated into the town. The troops were quite exhausted as it had been a very long and hot day. The ground had helped us to such an extent that our casualties were slight and we soon had complete possession of the town.

The following morning operations became mobile again and the 5th/7th Gordons were put onto tanks making for Scordia. This was the day when, having escaped the attention of the air since we landed, General Wimberley and I were taken by surprise by two flights of Messerschmitts. The Brigade, together with the Field Regiment, was moving down a road across the side of a hill when it happened. I was ahead on the road below and it was there that Douglas Wimberley and I made such a lightning descent into a ditch, which I have described elsewhere.

We moved on to Ramacca the following day and found ourselves looking down onto the plain of Catania. We had a marvellous view not only to the north but also away to the east. 154 Brigade had already entered the plain to the right and had run into opposition. It was therefore decided that we would cross the plain as a night operation, with the two Brigades advancing parallel to each other. We were directed to Sferro and 154 Brigade to Gerbini. In order that the two advances were properly coordinated, it appeared necessary for my Brigade to commence the advance two hours before it became dark. The leading battalion was the 1st Gordons and they redeployed on a wide front and moved out in broad daylight. Within half an hour when they were clear of the forward slope of Ramacca they came under long-range artillery fire, but suffered relatively few casualties and thereafter the light started to fade and progress was maintained. The advance was a silent one with the guns leapfrogging forwards by batteries so as to be available at first light if required. The armour was held back and would join us as soon as possible the following morning. We felt our way forward in the darkness, moving on compass bearings and astride a fairly well-marked track. We ran occasionally under mortar fire and tracked vehicles from time to time could be heard moving off in the darkness. The battalions had their anti-tank guns with them, but otherwise only their mortars, light automatics and rifles. About midnight the stubble in the fields caught fire as a result of the artillery and mortar fire and soon whole areas were affected. The flames were not high and there was quite a lot of black smoke. It tended to silhouette troops on their feet, but they would soon disappear in the smoke. I think the defence found it more of a handicap than we did, mainly because the two Brigades were on such a wide front and they were frightened of being outflanked.

So, by 2.00 a.m. the 5th Black Watch had reached their objective and the 5th/7th Gordons were lorried forward and passed through in their turn. The gamble appeared to be succeeding: we had already penetrated about 12,000 yards across the plain and moved out of close supporting distance from the remainder of the Division, so the Artillery Regiment was now moved up complete behind the 5th Black Watch, ready to provide defensive fire on a Regimental scale as soon as they could be employed. In the meantime the 5th/7th Gordons made good progress in the darkness and at first light were only just short of the crest of the ridge overlooking Sferro and the River Dittaino.

There they were halted. The total advance had been about 10 miles, our casualties had been light and the next night would be the time to complete the operation. I went forward to see the 5th/7th and had a look over the ground. The sun was up and already very hot. The scene was bizarre with clouds of black smoke sweeping across the front and welling out of the burning patches of stubble. The enemy was on the alert and planted some very well-directed shells nearby. At this stage, as was his custom, Douglas Wimberley arrived, gave information regarding 154 Brigade, confirmed the orders for the night and vanished in a cloud of dust. It was now the 19th of July, nine days after the landing.

We decided that we would have a repeat performance of the previous night, but with less ambitious objectives. This time the 5th Black Watch was to be the leading Battalion and their orders were to seize the bridge over the River Dittaino and capture the village of Sferro which lay about a mile beyond. The general feeling we had was that we were likely to run into organised resistance and that the previous night's 'swan' across the plain was unlikely to be repeated. The River Dittaino ran east towards Catania where XIII Corps had already been held up and the river line was an obvious continuation of a defensive position. The 5th Black Watch moved out over the ridge at about 9.00 p.m. and on down the forward slope towards the river. When the forward companies were approaching the river line they ran into heavy mortar and automatic fire and it was clear that a battle was on. When the Black Watch departed I wrapped myself in a blanket, lay down on the ground and went to sleep for about two hours. It is impossible for a Brigadier to fight the battles of leading infantry companies and his problems only arise when the situation calls for action by other troops.

It was just as well that I did because at about 11.00 p.m. things started to happen, so I got into my Jeep and went forward over the slope to meet Chick Thomson, the Colonel, who was in the process of launching his reserve companies in an outflanking movement in order to capture the line of the river, with the possibility of exploiting beyond to the village. It all looked suspiciously like a stalemate and I went back to my Headquarters, stood down the 1st Gordons who were waiting behind the crest and brought forward the Field Regiment to enable them to deploy forward.

The stubble was now blazing furiously and the scene down to the river and beyond looked like a modern equivalent of the inferno. The opposition seemed to be a combination of Spandaus, tanks and armoured cars. The battle went on into the early hours of the morning. By midnight the Field Regiment of artillery was deployed and started to register, but in the darkness it was difficult to discover where the ranging shots were falling. The guns probably were dropping the shells too far forward, but there was so much else exploding that it was impossible to judge. The only thing to do was gradually to reduce the range, and risk the odd shot falling short amongst our own people. The range finally dropped to 4,000 yards and then the FOO (Forward Observation Officer) picked it up. We at once put down five rounds of gunfire and the effect was almost instantaneous. The firing on the other side died away, the Black Watch availed themselves of this respite to get organised on the river line, we sent forward reserves of ammunition and when dawn came the situation was stabilised. It seemed to be a very long night.

The enemy harassed the Black Watch throughout the following day, but with our observation we were able to locate the areas from which it came and, as the whole of the Divisional Artillery was now linked up with our Field Regiment, we were able to give far more than we got. The Black Watch position had little depth, in fact it was almost linear along the river line. The river itself had practically no water in it owing to the heat of the summer and the lack of rain; it was therefore possible to establish platoons astride the two banks and provide flank protection as well.

The 1st Gordons were ordered to attack on the night of the 20th of July and to capture Sferro, which was about a mile further on. This was a night attack, but this time it was accompanied by a full-scale artillery plan. As soon as it got dark I went forward, joined Colonel Thomson in the river bed and established a Tactical Headquarters there. Then our artillery opened up and very impressive it was, but the enemy at once put down his own defensive fire, most of which fell in the Black Watch area and down the line of the river, but as most of them were well dug in the casualties were light. Then the leading companies of the 1st Gordons loomed up, went rapidly through the wadi and disappeared in the direction of the village. I scraped out a hole on the top of the bank and got a reasonably good view forward over ground which was quite flat. At that stage a conflagration developed forward and it emerged that the shellfire had set light to rows of wagons containing tar in the railway siding. In no time at all the whole countryside was lit up and although the attacking troops were silhouetted against it from our side, the enemy was forced to get out.

[**Editor's Note:** It was at this time that 'Nap' was recommended for an immediate DSO because 'the success of the operation had largely been due to his good planning, clear orders and the courage which he displayed day after day in visiting and encouraging the forward troops at times in positions where they were pinned to the ground; and on the night of 19/20 July 1943 when the Black Watch was being heavily attacked in the dry river bed at Dittaino he deliberately placed his headquarters there for several days to encourage his now very tired Troops, who had attacked, without respite, night after night, and thereby held the Sferro road bridge intact'. This description is taken from his DSO award which characteristically he does not mention.]

In the early hours of the morning the Battalion reported itself to be on its objective and was digging in. The anti-tank guns were already moving forward to join the infantry and so, by 3.00 a.m., we had to be satisfied with the night's work and consider what was to follow. At about 4.00 a.m. Douglas Wimberley jumped down into the river bed to find out for himself what the position was. I pretty well told him that he had no business to be there, but he was not to be put off in this way. He stayed for nearly an hour during which time he had a long talk not only with Chick Thomson, but many others. He was well pleased that we had gained the additional depth on this flank of the Division, particularly as by so doing we cut the lateral road turning east to Catania. He said he would let me know what the next move would be later in the morning, and then took his long lean figure back the way he came.

It was a typical Douglas Wimberley performance and explained why his reputation stood so high. He was known by the Jocks as 'Tartan Tam' and it was his determination to share the dangers to which the troops were exposed which ensured that he had a very special place in their affections. I suppose he was one of the best-known and loved of all the wartime divisional commanders. After he left, and as the Gordons were now well established, I went back up the hill to my Headquarters to be available for any further orders.

Later on in the day I went back to division and discovered that the night 20/21 July would see an attack by 154 Infantry Brigade on our right to capture Gerbini, and that my Brigade was merely to reorganise on the ground won, which we did, with the 5th/7th Gordons. The following day we heard that 154 Infantry Brigade had been only partially successful and had suffered very heavy casualties in the process.

It was at this juncture that the Army Commander decided to go over to the defensive and to press on with his left; consequently our task for the next ten days was to hold what we had. Well, the first twelve days in Sicily had been colourful and exciting, and now we had to experience the other side of the life of a soldier in the field, a patch of dull almost routine work combined with occasional alarms and excursions. This meant nightly reliefs of battalions in succession, which involved a great deal of movement and attendant risks. These risks had to be accepted as the days were incredibly hot with little overhead protection. If I wanted to get out of the sun I had to lie under a Jeep. Apart from that we were plagued with malarial mosquitoes.

Out on the left the Americans had made great progress and had already captured Palermo, while the Canadians were moving up through the centre of the island. It became obvious that the Germans were wheeling back, pivoting on Catania, with the object of easing their way back to the mainland through Messina. Catania was forward of Etna and the coastal strip was too narrow for it to provide a reasonable area for offensive operations in the absence of seaborne troops; so the closing days of July saw the steady shift of weight from east to west, with Sferro as the pivot. We followed the progress of the others and the advances were steadily maintained with 78th Division capturing Centuripe, and the Canadians Regalbuto. The Americans had now started their drive down the north coast towards Messina and the end of the campaign could not now be far off.

After the pause of ten days we went over to the attack again, having been relieved at Sferro by the 13th Infantry Brigade of the 5th Division which included the 2nd Battalion of the Cameronians.

From 31 July we carried out a series of attacks in a northerly direction, gradually eating our way to the foot of Mount Etna, finishing up in Linguaglossa, where the campaign finished so far as we were concerned. The Americans entered Messina on August 17th and it was all over. The campaign had lasted only thirty-nine days, but the end came unexpectedly quickly after the sticky fighting of the last few days of July.

The conquest of Sicily had just been achieved when it was announced that Douglas Wimberley would be leaving us to go to the Staff College as Commandant. He had been in command for three years, having reconstructed the 51st Division after St Valéry, trained it and then commanded it throughout the campaigns in North Africa and Sicily. He was just the sort of Commandant the Staff College needed at this time, having had a wealth of experience in and out of battle. He was such a character that he was likely to be a very difficult man to follow. His successor was Major General Charles Bullen-Smith.

The Sicilian Campaign was more a matter of manoeuvre than anything else. Nevertheless it had its hazards. The landing was the first assault landing since Gallipoli in 1915 and the element of chance was just as strong as ever. In the event we met little opposition on the beaches and thanks to using our assault scales of transport we managed to ferry forwards into the hinterland at a remarkable speed. It was not until we approached Mount Etna, on the line of the River Dittaino, that we met real opposition. We were held there for some days until the Americans and Canadians on the open western flank started to move eastwards and roll up the German right flank.

There were a couple of points of interest during the campaign. It was the first opposed landing of the War and provided a vast amount of material for the planning of the invasion of Normandy the following year. The other point was that, as a result of operating in the desert, it was normal for the Highland Division to attack at night and the two successful operations we had in Sicily were night operations. Nevertheless, there were several engagements which, necessarily, had to be conducted in daylight, and it was apparent that the Highlanders had lost the cunning that they had developed in the United Kingdom between 1940 and 1942. As our casualties were light, and as we avoided the worst effects of malaria thanks to Mepicrine, this shortcoming was not given the thought that it needed.

The campaign in Sicily was really rather disappointing. It is true that the run-in and the first ten days were very exciting, but thereafter the operations developed in such a way that we were merely driving the Germans back on their communications, which suited them very well, as the further they withdrew the shorter the line became. They pivoted on Mount Etna and finally withdrew, almost intact, through Messina. It may be that, as this was the first amphibious operation to be carried out against organised resistance, it was regarded as too ambitious to attack on two fronts, which could have led to something much more decisive. By attacking as we did, the enemy was able to 'run away' and fight another day. Another thing which many of us found difficult to understand was how it was possible for the Germans to travel by sea across the Straits of Messina with relatively little loss, despite our overwhelming air and sea power.

[**Editor's Note:** On August 8th 1943, when all Axis resistance in Sicily ceased, Montgomery told Douglas Wimberley that now the Sicilian Campaign was over he was needed in England as Commander of the Staff College at Camberley because 'battle experience' was required there and subsequently he was succeeded by Bullen-Smith as GOC. Soon afterwards Montgomery personally awarded medals earned by officers and other ranks in the 51st Highland Division and arrangements were made to erect a memorial at Gerbini to those who were killed. In November of that year the whole of 51st Highland Division, plus other regiments, left for England on the USS *Argentina*. They arrived at the end of November at Liverpool.

In February 1944, 'Nap' published his history of 153 Brigade in the Sicilian Campaign and was asked to give lectures based on that history to Troops in the Home Counties which included senior US Army officers. The presentation was based on the views of a Brigadier, a Battalion Commander and a Company Commander with the battle for Vizzini being the subject matter: *The Spirit of Angus*, p.110.]

Chapter Fourteen

Interlude in the United Kingdom

As much of the leave granted had to be staggered, we were into January before we could really get down to any training when we started to have sand model exercises for the invasion. No plans were divulged, but it was clear at an early stage that the centre of road and rail communications in the lodgement area must be Caen and, although the other areas were distorted for security reasons, we were not deceived, although we naturally said little about it. It was, however, possible even at this stage to give the overall plan of I Corps, in which we were under the command of Lieutenant General Sir John Crocker. The 6th Airborne Division under Major General Richard Gale was to drop to the east of the River Orne to form a bridgehead over that river, and in succession to the right came the 3rd British Division, the 3rd Canadian Division under Rod Keller, and finally the 50th Division under command of Douglas Graham. The 51st was to be a follow-up Division, and would not take part in the initial assault. In all this planning we would be given no concrete tasks, but would be employed as the situation demanded. I had had the same experience in Sicily. We were to land behind the 3rd British Division, but might also be used in support of the 3rd Canadian or the 6th Airborne.

My own Brigade was to be the first to land and it was therefore vitally important to be aware of the plans of the others. I think that our new Divisional Commander was unfortunate in our role, because it is the ambition of all commanders to fight their first battle as a complete team, as we did at Alamein. Major General Bullen-Smith not only did not have this satisfaction when we landed, but it was denied to him until the time came for breaking out of the bridgehead many weeks later. All this pre-planning was therefore unsatisfactory and to some extent too nebulous.

144

There were a great number of changes amongst the commanders. I was the sole surviving Brigadier, the other two, Gordon Macmillan and Tom Rennie both having been given Divisions, and 'Hammie' Fausset Farquhar, after a charmed life as Commanding Officer of the 1st Gordons and in battle for over twelve months, departed to another appointment. The same changes were also taking place in the other brigades. In addition we had the 2nd Derbyshire Yeomanry posted to us as the Divisional Reconnaissance Regiment and our beloved 2/7th Middlesex was completely reorganised so as to include a company of 4.2-inch mortars and a company of Oerlikon guns. I do not think the Oerlikons had much of a war, but the 4.2-inch mortars were worth their weight in gold as they provided us at long last with a mortar which could outrange and out-weigh the German 81mm. We were also very sorry to say goodbye to many of our Middlesex comrades.

Our new Divisional Commander was well qualified to prepare us for the campaign in France and we did a lot of special training in infantry/tank cooperation with the 6th Guards Tank Brigade at the Dukeries, river-crossing exercises, night operations in enclosed country, movement exercises and operations in semi-open country, all of which helped to re-orientate us. There were aspects of our training which gave me some concern. In the first place there was a tendency for units and formations of the Home Army (by that I mean the Divisions which had remained in the United Kingdom since Dunkirk four years before) to assume that the Divisions returning home for the invasion, such as ourselves, the 7th Armoured and the 50th Division, knew all the answers. Of course this was very flattering, but without any foundation, because whilst there was little about the conduct of night attacks we did not know (and we were battle-experienced), that the Home Army trained by General Sir Bernard Paget knew far more about the problems of fighting on the continent of Europe and their tactics were on a different level that we in the Highland Division never reached. This shortcoming was serious and, although time was short, there was a disinclination to remedy the situation. What was needed were training teams such as we had on the two previous campaigns; because we were supposed to be the experts, this was not done. The result was that we were in a fool's paradise; we carried out a lot of training, but our tactics fell far short of the 'Home' Divisions and this, later, led to a considerable number of casualties that could have been avoided. We should have done far more training in the use of weapons in conjunction with the use of ground. It is true that it was not easy to do in the time available.

Monty sensed an element of uncertainty amongst the 'Home' Divisions, and if that was the case it must have been heartening for them to find themselves fighting alongside us in battle. Inevitably the knowledge that they had been brought back to lend substance to the Home Army imposed an additional strain on those returning Divisions. In the first place there was a tendency to accord them superhuman qualities, and second, they themselves were conscious of having fought in many hard engagements and many had begun to wonder how long their luck was going to last. The 50th Division, which, after a long spell in the desert, came back to become an Assault Division, was burnt out by the end of 1944. Therefore when the story of the early weeks in Normandy unfolded it was discovered that the Home Divisions had an élan which carried all before them and which the 'battle-tried' Divisions did not emulate. This élan combined with the higher state of their training led to a series of successes, which in turn led to the development of a high morale. I would not say they felt they were more effective than the Divisions which had been in the Middle East, but at least they knew that they could hold their own if comparisons were to be made.

There was another factor, which I think should be recorded. Douglas Wimberley moved heaven and earth to ensure that the Highland Division, as far as it was possible to do so, was entirely composed of Scotsmen, and refused to accept everyone who might turn up in new drafts. He personally visited other formations and units to see if he could winkle out any Scotsmen they might have. When we were overseas he made it clear that the Highland Division was the natural home for all Scotsmen. Needless to say this policy was very unpopular with both the War Office and 'A' Staffs generally, but he pursued it quite openly and unrepentantly as long as he was in command. Whether it was actually stated or whether it was only inferred I do not know, but the Jocks got it into their heads that if they were evacuated they would be returned to the Division and nowhere else. This conviction was confirmed when it became known that staff officers from the Division combed the reinforcement camps for Scotsmen and took them away from where they found them. In September 1943 the situation at Salerno was critical and Army Headquarters was forced to scrape together all the reinforcements they could lay their hands on, which included a considerable number from the Highland Division previously wounded in Sicily. They were all swept up into other units and the Jocks were furious, because they considered that a promise had been broken. The upshot was that they refused to go into action at Salerno; in fact they mutinied.

The abler commanders in the bridgehead talked to these men in such a way that they finally agreed to fight, on the understanding that they would be allowed to return to the Highland Division when the crisis had passed and this promise was kept; others refused and were later court-martialled. These men, rightly or wrongly, considered that a promise had not been kept. Some time later I met General 'Ginger' Hawkesworth. He was one of the commanders who induced the Highlanders sent to him to go into battle, and fight they certainly did. When it was all over and the time came for the men to be sent back to the 51st, which was still in Sicily, many decided that on second thoughts they would prefer to stay with the 4th Division with General Hawkesworth, who could not resist passing this on to me.

A group of us were selected to give lectures on the Sicilian Campaign. Our audiences were the Home Divisions and the Home Guard. The latter had, by now, expanded beyond all knowledge and were very enthusiastic. Interspersed were the usual pre-invasion visits, most of which took place during March and early April. The first to come was Monty, who had returned from Italy to take over command of the 21st Army Group from General Sir Bernard Paget. On this occasion the men were lined up facing inwards and down the space in between paced Monty, very slowly, pausing from time to time to have a word with an NCO or man as the fancy came to him. There had been a number of changes both in the officers and the men, so there were many there who had not seen him before and this was the opportunity for them to do so. When he had completed his tour he moved to a Jeep, called the men around him and gave them a talk. It was a more sober speech than usual, although interspersed with a number of cracks and it made a deep impression on all. The whole parade lasted little over half an hour when he then moved on to others. He was full of vitality and good humour and it was quite a tonic, which he intended.

The next visit was by the triumvirate, General Eisenhower, Air Chief Marshal Sir Arthur Tedder and Monty. There were no speeches as the purpose of the trip was for as many as possible to see these great men and for them to see whatever training was likely to be of interest. They stayed with us for the better part of the day culminating in the playing of Retreat by the massed pipers of the Division. I met General Eisenhower on this day for the first time. He had a great personal charm and it was impossible not to take to him as his warmth and sincerity were so patent. He was just as much as home speaking to British as he was to American soldiers. Somehow when he talked to anybody that person felt that he mattered and this was done in the simplest and most straightforward way. His Headquarters, comprising officers and men from all three services of the nations involved, remained harmonious at all times, and he ensured that it did so throughout the campaign. He went to such lengths, especially in respect of the British, that some Americans said that he was the best General the British had. Behind all this lurked a very strong and determined character, as was shown when he took the decision to invade on the 6th of June in the face of grave difficulties and mounting hazards. He was blessed with an understanding heart and whatever might be said concerning his strategic or tactical skills, I can think of nobody who could have filled his position with anything like the same ability or success.

Towards the end of February the King, dressed as the Colonel-in-Chief of the Cameron Highlanders, visited us. He came alone and spent the day watching training of various kinds, being joined by the Queen and the two princesses in the late afternoon when the Divisional pipers played Retreat. The day therefore was made more interesting for him than had been possible when he came to see us before we went to the Middle East in 1942. When visiting one of the battalions he watched some small exercises to do with the use of explosives and one of these was attaching a 'bee-hive' to a tree in order to bring it down. When the preparation was completed the party moved on, but about 300 yards away there was a loud explosion and down crashed the tree. The King was taken by surprise as he thought it had only been a 'dummy' run. When he saw the tree fall he let out a grunt and said 'I would not be allowed to do that on any of my estates.' We hurried on to the next demonstration. At the end of the day we all turned up for the playing of Retreat, and saw the two princesses. I suppose that Princess Elizabeth would be about eighteen at the time and the group looked quite delightful.

It was not until March that the senior officers were informed of the complete Normandy plan. We went to a conference when Monty told us the thinking behind it. He was very much aware of the beach defences on the coast of Normandy, which were daily becoming more formidable under the drive of Field Marshal Rommel. The method by which these were to be neutralised had been the special study by the 79th Division under General Hobart. We were not concerned with them. What did matter was that we should penetrate inland to as great a depth as we could, and this presupposed taking risks. Monty knew little about Scotland, nevertheless he took the famous quotation from Montrose as his key to the task which lay ahead:

He either fears his fate too much or his deserts are small,
Who dares not put it to the touch, to win or lose it all.

Few of us had any doubt that Normandy would make far greater demands upon us all than any of the previous battles had done.

Sometime during April 1944 I had the privilege of being present at St Paul's School, Army Group Headquarters, when two days were spent by commanders down to the rank of Major General and a few others, to study certain aspects of the overall plan. I was still a Brigadier but I believe that I was let in because I might have to understudy our Divisional Commander, if anything happened to him. I did not go on the first day when the King and the Prime Minister attended, but only on the second. This was devoted to the study of certain specific problems framed by Monty, who was the overall land commander at this stage. The purpose was to consider what might go wrong, particularly on the boundary between 21st Army Group and the Americans, and the actions required to put it right.

The problems would be put and we would troop off into adjoining rooms to think out the solutions. This made people like myself really think through the opening stages. In the event two of these theoretical situations did in fact arise, as well as one or two others. When time was up we trooped back into the main conference room and selected officers were invited to give solutions. All went well until a problem arose affecting the Americans and General Omar Bradley was invited to produce his solution. His answer was not given in a particularly convincing manner, but it seemed to be unfolding sensibly, when he was brusquely interrupted by Monty who exclaimed, 'No, no Bradley, that is no good, no good at all. It would be quite useless.' There was a gasp from all the Americans there, but before anything else could be done or said Eisenhower jumped up quickly and said, 'No, Monty. You can't do that. Sit down General Bradley. Now Monty, let us go on to the next problem.' Omar Bradley, looking a little flushed, sat down, the other Americans just sat there and glowered, but great damage had been done. The next speaker was General Collins, an Irishman if ever there was one, and made of different stuff. He was later to become Chief of Staff of the American Army (Staff) in Washington. The problem (if such and such a Division has been driven back to the beaches, what will you do and what will you do with it) provoked the reply, 'As this Division will in no circumstances be driven back onto the beaches, the question is purely hypothetical' and sat down. There was a roar of laughter, particularly from the Americans. These exercises were undoubtedly of great value and demonstrated Monty's genius in the tactical field, but his relationship with the American commanders, never very good, suffered severely from this conference.

This and similar incidents led to Generals Bradley and Patton deliberately thwarting Monty, particularly when the latter proposed to break through into the Ruhr in September 1944. Another by-product was the question of the command of the ground troops. To start with, a single commander was needed, but as the size of the American effort increased, so did the pressure from the American side, both military and political, for a separate commander for all American troops in the theatre.

When we were having lunch that day at St Paul's School I was sitting with Douglas Graham. Monty stopped to have a word with us. He said that he was to be the overall ground commander, and added, 'The Americans don't like it, but there is nothing they can

Nap on far left with his brothers and sisters in 1908. The Editor's mother is on the right.

Nap's mother in her 70s.

Newly commissioned into the
Cameron Highlanders.

With 'Uncle' Ferrers and the Cameronians in China, 1927.

Troopship at Hong Kong, 1927.

Flying to Palestine in the Vickers bomber with Sandy Galloway and Dick O'Connor. All three were destined to become generals.

Nap training with the Wehrmacht in 1937.

With 'Bear Leader' in Germany, 1937.

With the Duke of Gloucester and other Cameron Highlanders.

Introducing Gordon Highlander officers to Prime Minister Churchill before El Alamein.

Highland Division on the move, North Africa, 1943.

A near miss in the desert.

Advancing through Sicily, 1943.

Monty and Mountbatten in Sicily, 1943.

Requisitioned donkey in Sicily, 1943.

Gun line in action, Sicily, 1943.

The Brigade Commander,
Sicily, 1943.

With King George VI before Normandy.

Queen Elizabeth takes the salute during the pre-Normandy visit.

Montgomery talking to a piper during his visit to Nap's brigade before OVERLORD.

Nap with Eisenhower and Monty, May 1944.

The great Armada bound for Normandy, 6 June 1944.

General Horrocks, 1944.

Generals Patton, Bradley and Montgomery, Normandy 1944.

The dreaded *Nebelwerfer*.

The devastation that was Caen, 1944.

Harsh Northern
Italian winter
conditions, 1944.

The horrors of Monte Battaglia, 1944.

Nap with
Generals Mark
Clark and
Sidney Kirkman,
Commander
XIII Corps, Italy,
1944.

6th Armoured
Division on the
move in
Northern Italy,
1945.

Crossing the
River Po,
April 1945.

6th Armoured Division river crossing, 1945.

Surrendered Cossack and German weapons and equipment.

With Field Marshal Alexander, the Supreme Commander Mediterranean, and Lieutenant General Dick McCreery, Commander 8th Army, during the advance through Italy, early 1945.

6th Armoured Division tank at Poggio, Northern Italy, 1945.

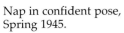

Argenta 1945.

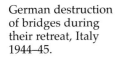

Nap in confident pose,
Spring 1945.

German destruction
of bridges during
their retreat, Italy
1944–45.

General Freyburg sorting out Tito's partisans.

In London after the war, Nap having collected his CB.

Final message to 6th Armoured Division, May 1945.

The King and Queen of Denmark with their daughters, Monty and Nap.

Eightsome reel in the Royal Palace, Copenhagen, 1961.

With the King of Norway.

51st Highland Division Commanders with Monty at the disbandment of the Division, North Inch, Perth – October 1967. From left to right: Brigadier 'Jumbo' Stirling, DSO; Brigadier Lorne Campbell VC, DSO; Major General Douglas Graham, CB, DSO, MC; Lieutenant General Douglas Lang, KCB, DSO, MC; Major General 'Freddie' Graham, CB, DSO; Major General Edward Maitland-Makgill-Crichton, OBE; Major General Douglas Wimberley, CB, DSO, MC; Field Marshal Montgomery, KG, GCB, KCB, CB, DSO; Major General Roy Urquhart, CB, DSO; General 'Babe' MacMillan, KCB, KCVO, CBE, DSO, MC; General 'Nap' Murray, GCB, KBE, DSO; Major General J Scott-Elliot, CB, DSO; Major General Ian Robertson, MBE; Brigadier James Oliver, CB, CBE, DSO.

do about it.' He seemed very pleased about this and it clearly did not enter his head that a change might be made later. The dislike of Monty ensured that in the end this happened. It was a great pity and led to Eisenhower having no overall ground commander, or even a deputy to himself, to coordinate the operations of the Army groups. At this exercise I met, for the first time, our Corps Commander, General Sir John Crocker.

In the early part of the year I met a number of civilians who were openly critical of Monty and his methods, and clearly hoped that we would give them some support. In particular that his Orders of the Day, issued before battles, were bombastic and theatrical. None of us gave these birds of prey any encouragement. In the first place Monty won his battles, and whilst his Orders of the Day might appear to be theatrical when read in the comfort of a London Club, they had a different impact to men about to go into battle. We were rather distressed to find such a campaign in progress, but some members of the armed forces were not without blame as a result of disaffection consequent upon his ruthlessness. Whether they liked it or not, the fact remained that he was a highly successful commander in the field, and had the overwhelming confidence of all ranks under his command.

In April we left Buckinghamshire and moved across into Essex and Brigade Headquarters was installed in Braintree. Whilst we were there one or two of us were invited over to dinner with Mr R.A.B. Butler who was then the Minister of Education in the National Government, and he and his wife were most kind. He had a miniature billiard table tucked into his library upon which we played. We carried out one or two exercises near Newmarket at this time and it was fun having long runs over the heath. It also gave me the opportunity to call in on my old Commanding Officer of Egypt days in 1931, Lieutenant Colonel Hyde-Smith, who lived near Bury St Edmunds (he was visibly relieved when we assured him that we had our own provisions and were not looking for a meal; rationing was still very strict at this time).

When we got into May we were gradually drafted into special camps, surrounded by barbed wire, in the vicinity of Tilbury, which was to be our port of embarkation when the time came. We amused ourselves as best we could and amongst other things learnt to play 'soft-ball', introduced by some Canadian officers who were attached to us. A Horse Artillery Regiment, which formed part of the 9th Armoured Division, ran our camp and did a splendid job. They had been originally included in the 21st Army Group, but had to make room for the Polish Armoured Division primarily for political reasons. I much admired the way they took their disappointment which they refused to allow to affect the humdrum role they were called to fill.

We then briefed all ranks on the plan and the role they would be required to play. As we were a follow-up Division, the information was not as concrete as it had been on previous occasions; although 153 Brigade would be the leading Brigade, it was not expected to land on D-Day.

It was early June and I decided to take the battalion commanders to London, have an evening there and return in the small hours. We borrowed a car and arrived in London and had tea at the Waldorf, which enabled the husbands to have a last word with their wives by telephone. We saw *Sweet and Low* with Hermione Gingold and then walked across the road and had a first-class dinner in the 'Ivy'. As we were finishing dinner who should arrive but my brother-in-law, Terence Donovan. He of course saw nothing exceptional in finding us there, having no idea how near the invasion was, and we accepted the glass of brandy he kindly offered with gratitude.

We got back soon after midnight and early in the morning went aboard our respective ships. On this occasion I was in an LST (Landing Ship Tank), which had a much larger displacement than the LSI which took us to Sicily the year before. After breakfast we went over the ship. It had two decks, each of which was packed with vehicles of all shapes and sizes and which were shackled to the deck. It was as well that they were because once we got into the Channel the ship rolled quite a lot and the strain on the shackles was considerable. I cannot think how we employed ourselves during the day and it came as a great disappointment when we learned that the invasion had been postponed by twenty-four hours. However, later that day Eisenhower decided that he would make no further postponement and so it was that about the same time as the assault troops sailed off to attack the beaches in Normandy, we also sailed down the Thames from Tilbury and out into the English Channel. We were off.

Chapter Fifteen

Normandy

We passed through the Strait of Dover, feeling a little apprehensive, knowing the size and scale of the German guns located in the area of Calais. After an hour or so we breathed a little more freely as we drew clear of the Strait. Apparently later convoys taking this route were not quite so lucky. It was a clear morning and the visibility almost too good; on the other hand there was a strong swell coming up from the Atlantic, which did not augur well for the landing and was to be the precursor of heavy seas at the beachheads. This swell was not such as to seriously inconvenience us, but the effect on the vehicles was almost hilarious. As each roller swept under the ship the vehicles would sway far down, remain poised there for a few seconds and then commence the return journey with the utmost dignity only to dip down in a similar manner on the other side. Occasionally they would retain an upright stance for a little, and then the procedure would be repeated. They all kept time together beautifully and Walt Disney would have done justice to them in another version of *Fantasia*.

Towards the middle of the afternoon we changed course and moved in a SSW direction, as we were by now approaching the dispersal area for the run-in; our destination was 'Sword' beach, which was just west of the River Orne near Ouisterhem. During the afternoon we passed streams of craft heading north towards England, having presumably landed their loads of men and vehicles successfully. At this stage the sea was swarming with ships of every kind, including warships and it was another demonstration of the impact of air power in amphibious operations. I cannot remember that we were inconvenienced from the air throughout the whole of the crossing. As the ships travelling south passed those going north there were none of the usual catcalls which such occasions invite; the business afoot was too serious. The plan had assumed that the LSTs (Landing Ship Tanks) being faster would close the beaches before the LSI (Landing Ship Infantry), which were smaller and slower and carried the marching infantry. In the event the latter arrived first and having less draft, could get closer inshore. The Commanding Officers at once asked permission to land straight away and this was granted. These troops were to have been preceded by the recce parties of the Brigade, travelling in the Command ship of the 3rd Canadian Division, but this latter ship also had been prevented from getting its personnel ashore, consequently the infantry had to go ahead with their own disembarkation as best they could. It was much safer to be on land than to be swinging about a few hundred yards off shore, presenting a very vulnerable target. Therefore the only people in the Brigade to get ashore on 'D' Day were the infantry, with their personal weapons only. The landing was difficult as the sea was rising and big waves were breaking on the shore and it was fortunate that only two men were drowned.

On landing (7th June 1944), we (153rd Brigade) were to move from the beaches and march south to Ranville which adjoins the Pegasus Bridge on the east side of the River Orne and which had been captured the day before by the advanced guard of the 1st Airborne Division. We were forced, however, to lie at anchor about 3,000 yards off shore and during the night the whole of the landing area was bombed by the German air force. They did not achieve a great deal, although it was unpleasant while it lasted. The following morning the sea was still running high and it was impossible to get close to the shore and start unloading, but the Commanding Officers being ashore, Chick Thomson (5th Black Watch), 'Scrappy' Hay (1st Gordon Highlanders) and Bill Stevenson (2nd Seaforth Highlanders) could not be allowed to fend for themselves indefinitely, so I got the ship's Captain to launch an assault craft and taking one or two members of Brigade Headquarters with me, made for the shore. It was not obvious where a suitable landing place was at the water's edge because it was cluttered up with wreckage. We just jumped into the sea where it was not too deep and waded ashore. I was at least drier than I had been for the landing in Sicily, but the water was much colder with little prospect of drying out immediately. There was a small Beach Group

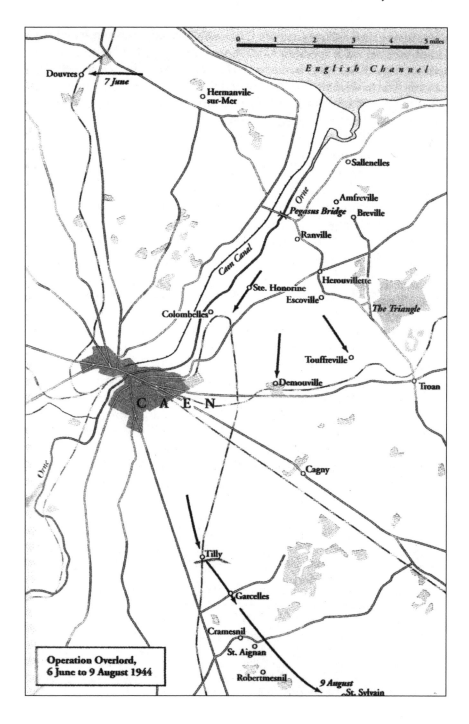

English Channel

Douvres
7 June
Hermanvile-sur-Mer
Sallenelles
Orne
Amfreville
Pegasus Bridge
Breville
Ranville
Caen Canal
Ste. Honorine
Herouvillette
Escoville
The Triangle
Colombelles
Touffreville
Troan
Demouville
C A E N
Orne
Cagny
Tilly
Garcelles
Cramesnil
St. Aignan
Robertmesnil
9 August
St. Sylvain

**Operation Overlord,
6 June to 9 August 1944**

organisation where we landed and they directed us up a lane, which had been taped, and which was free of mines. We were soon clear of the beach and then we moved over some sand dunes towards the road. There was a squadron of 'DD' Tanks* amongst the dunes, potting away at some centre of resistance, still holding out further inland. We finally reached the road leading to Ranville on the left hand bank of the River Orne which we crossed.

On our way there we ran into a sergeant in the 1st Gordons travelling in an 'acquired' van who picked us up and took us on to the Brigade area. Although it was to be some hours before we could hope to see our supporting artillery, the 5th Black Watch was already preparing to carry out an attack against the Radar Station at Douvres la Deliverande, (some 5 miles west of the landing beaches), which appeared to be heavily defended. A plan was made, but no artillery support could be provided, so it had to be postponed. However, there were one or two Naval Monitors** and other naval craft, which might enable the attack to go in the following morning, so it was laid on again. This naval support, however, was required elsewhere, so it was to be several days before we were sufficiently strong in artillery to carry out the coordinated attack on the radar station. The subsequent attack by the 5th Black Watch was repulsed by the very strong German garrison which made it impossible for the Black Watch to move forward, such was the strength of the enemy fire, and the battalion was ordered to withdraw to rejoin the brigade which entailed the re-crossing of the River Orne via the Pegasus bridge. (Ultimately it took a heavy naval bombardment plus two Brigades to capture that radar station, not a Battalion.)

[Editor's Note: Unfortunately the remaining twenty-seven pages of manuscript comprising this important chapter are missing. The Editor has attempted to substitute the missing pages with a narrative describing the

*Duplex Drive Tanks, six-wheel-drive amphibious trucks, designed by General Motors Corporation and used in a number of World War Two landings.
** Naval Monitors were essentially floating artillery spotters, out of range from German shore guns, which transmitted radio requests for supporting fire from our troops on the ground to either warships or fighter bombers at sea or bases in England. They were of particular value to the 51st Highland Division who were up against the crack German 21st Panzer Division, having inadequate tank support themselves.

events which took place between 7 June 1944 and early August 1944 from what 'Nap' told him and original sources in The National Archives and The Imperial War Museum Library, together with quotes from Salmond, *History of the 51st Division; So Few Got Through*, Lindsay; *The Spirit of Angus*, McGregor; and *None Bolder, The Highland Division*, Delaforce. In addition the Editor has transferred some of 'Nap' Murray's own words from 'Reflections' a later chapter of the memoirs which specifically refers to Normandy.

'Nap' told the family after the War that the Normandy Campaign was the most difficult experience in his fighting career. We believed that he refused to obey an order from his Divisional Commander to attack; the latter then requested Montgomery to decide who was right, he or his Brigadier on the battlefield. Montgomery assessing the situation on the ground decided 'Nap' was right and the General wrong. It is, however, clear from the records that this was not quite the case. The defeats and difficulties in Normandy of the 51st Highland Division were exemplified by the failed attack by his Brigade on a huge factory situated at Colombelles on the outskirts of Caen in July 1944. 'Nap' did object to the plan but was over-ruled by his GOC. The attack did take place with disastrous results. It is the Editor's belief that the subsequent unfair criticism of Colonel Thomson and his Black Watch Battalion together with the poor intelligence of Divisional Command on the strength of the factory's defences might have been the breaking point in his relations with the GOC and possibly led him to say as much either to the Corps or Army Commander.]

From 'Reflections':

'*From the start of the invasion the Highland Division in Normandy were under constant pressure from 1st Corps, (General Crocker) to carry out small attacks of limited scope in order to expand the Orne bridgehead and generally contain the enemy on our front. The attacks that we made were very expensive and unavailing and accordingly any success we had sapped the strength of the bridgehead and the Division. The former was invaluable as demonstrated in late July 1944 when three Armoured Divisions (7th, 11th and Guards) went through it supported by two Infantry Divisions. It was for such a purpose that the bridgehead was intended, not for penny packet stuff.*

'*The Highland Division was not an assault Division in the invasion of Normandy but a "follow up", landing in Normandy on 7 June 1944, a day after D-Day. This in itself*

*was unfortunate as the Division was accustomed to leading
major operations. It was fed in over a period of a couple of
days piecemeal and not as a composite Division. The
Divisional Brigades were under the temporary command of
different Divisions, for example my Brigade (153) was under
the temporary command of the 6th Airborne Division, then
moved to 1st Corps and certain Battalions received their
commands from other Brigades, (e.g. the 5th Cameron
Highlanders were attached later to 153 Brigade from
152 Brigade). My Brigade comprising the 1st Gordon
Highlanders, the 5th Black Watch and the 2nd Seaforth Highlanders and led in the landings in support of the 3rd Canadian
Division, then sidestepped to the east to support the British
3rd Division and re-crossed the River Orne to support the 6th
Airborne Division during July 1944. My Brigade was the first
to cross the Orne and in due course others followed. The 6th
Airborne under General Gale was as good a Division as the
war produced, but they were very thin on the ground and
whilst we carried out a series of local operations which were
helpful in consolidating their bridgehead, they were extremely
costly in terms of troops and material, mainly owing to the
indifferent minor tactics of the "Jocks". The Airborne soldiers
were most unimpressed by the 51st Division in these early
days, but this was to some extent inevitable because the 6th
Airborne had been trained in England for at least two years
before the invasion whereas we had not.'*

The fortunes of the 51st Highland Division were not happy ones
during the first six weeks of the invasion. The failed attack on the
radar station did not augur well for future operations. The advance
into Normandy was marked by constant underestimation of
German defences (starting with the failed attack on the radar
station) and subsequently advancing south-east towards Caen on
the east bank of the River Orne. There, in wooded rolling country
ideally suited for defence, 'Nap's' Brigade 153 ran into fierce opposition from the 21st Panzer Division, the only Panzer Division in
Normandy at that time, together with its crack 121st battle group
led by the formidable Hans Von Luck.

[**Editor's Note:** An example of this resistance took place a week after the Landings when the 1st Black Watch was ambushed advancing towards Breville and its leading company was decimated in a defensive ambush some 2 miles from the Landings and where some captured Jocks were shot in cold blood by the Germans. It was not until June 18th that the village of St Honorine, only 3 miles south-east of Breville was finally recaptured after being retaken by the Germans in continuous close-quarter fighting. It is worth recalling here that the timetable for the 21st Army Group was to have captured Caen, 25 miles south-east of the beaches, on D-Day.*]

'Nap' wrote later (from 'Reflections'):

'Thereafter in the later weeks of June and all of July 1944, the 51st Highland Division fought at a great disadvantage. First, we could not properly deploy the Division because the bridge-head over the River Orne was contained in a small area (the "Triangle") to allow for the Divisional Artillery to move into it. Divisional supporting fire therefore had to be directed from an angle west of the river, limiting its effectiveness whilst we ourselves were exposed to fire from three sides and our casualties from artillery and mortar fire were very high indeed.'

A view endorsed by Dr Yellowlees, then MO of the 5th Camerons, who still recalls the horror of the Nebelwerfer attacks in the 'Triangle' when the 51st Highland Division were in orchard country, close to St Honorine and subjected to this mortar/rocket fire, which was designed to create maximum effect by having the warhead halfway down the rocket so as to detonate on impact, but above ground. Its distinctive whining noise and very loud explosion distinguished it from the conventional artillery attacks, and with a range of over 4 miles and probably being directed from the German observation post set in the Colombelles factory chimneys a few miles away, it was horribly effective.

At that time all three Brigades of the Division were enclosed in a salient on the east side on the River Orne known as the 'Triangle' measuring 300 yards at the base by 800 yards on the sides, attacked on two sides by strong German forces, lacking artillery support and being subjected to constant enemy artillery and mortar fire from

*Doherty, p. 160 quoting from The National Archives.

German multi-barrelled mortars whilst fighting in wooded country ideally suited for surprise attack. Such a surprise attack took place in late June 1944 when 'Nap' lost half his Brigade HQ in a sudden 'stonk' of mortar/artillery fire from an unexpected direction lasting only a matter of minutes at an 'O' group in an orchard at Benouville close to the Pegasus bridge a few miles south of 'Sword' beaches. An event vividly described by Colonel Sir Martin Lindsay, second-in-command of 1st Gordon Highlanders:

> *'The Brigade HQ consisting of a few caravans, tents and slit trenches was in an orchard near Benouville. The Brigadier, "Nap" Murray, a Cameron Highlander, had just begun to talk to me when there was a sudden swish and a bang and a shell landed right in the middle of the orchard, causing nine casualties. Every three or four minutes for the next half hour something landed pretty close. "God almighty," I thought to myself, "if this is a rest area, how can I ever stand the real thing"'*

Shortly after this attack, Montgomery sent 'Nap' a handwritten note regarding the officers he now needed to replace those who had been killed or wounded at Benouville:

> *'Dear Nap... I have requested these officers to be sent over to replace your casualties'* (27 June 1944)

At that time 'Nap' wrote to Bill McFarlan MC (a Gordon Highlander who had been with him at El Alamein and who wanted to rejoin the regiment):

> *'We have had four to five working days of the stickiest and most tricky fighting I can remember. Casualties were not light. You will be sorry to hear that Charles Thun was killed and Jim Robertson wounded...we could ill afford to lose them. The weather considering it is summer is atrocious, it rains like hell. We are settling down conditions pretty well and the chaps have more than held their own in the battles we have had so far. The Boche is nevertheless very good indeed and we cannot treat him lightly at any time.'*

A few days later he wrote again...

'We have had a stiffish time here; nevertheless things are going pretty well, the conditions are completely different from any we have been required to compete with hitherto... and it took us a day or two to get used to them. Both Harry Gordon and Jim Robertson were injured, but not badly... Yours ever H Murray'

Differences between 153 Brigade and Divisional Command had started in June when 'Nap' had expressed concern at the dismissal of Brigadier Harvey-Haugh CO, 151 Brigade in late June and some Battalion COs who had been replaced earlier.* In early July his Brigade were ordered to attack a huge factory at Colombelles on the outskirts of Caen on the east side of the River Orne. The purpose of this attack was to deprive the Germans of very high observation posts set both in the factory and its chimneys and which overlooked the entire Orne bridgehead. At a Divisional Conference on the 28th July 1944, the proposed attack was discussed and the minutes record the objection of 'Nap' Murray to the plan, arguing that it would be better that his Brigade attack the Toufferville brickworks to the east of Colombelles owing to their previous knowledge of that area, but to no effect. It may have been after that meeting his GSO3 Harry Gordon said to him:

'Well Sir, we didn't learn much from that meeting', to which he replied: *'Yes we did, we learnt how not to do it.'*

His objection having been overridden, the attack took place at night on 10/11 July. The attack failed because of underestimation of German defences and poor intelligence which failed to reveal that the Germans had their new powerful heavy tanks (Panzer Mark VI) in readiness for such an attack.

Those tanks destroyed ten out of the eleven Brigade Shermans resulting in 'Nap' being forced to withdraw both the 5th Black

*Minutes of 51st Highland Division Conference, 28 June 1944, The National Archives.

Watch and 1st Gordons under a heavy smokescreen to avoid destruction. Very heavy casualties resulted and after the failure of the attack divisional criticism was levied against the Brigade and in particular the 5th Black Watch. This was rebutted by both 'Nap' and Colonel Thomson, who concluded in his report to Division that his battalion had fought very gallantly against 'impossible odds in an impossible situation occasioned by an impossible plan'. 'Nap' Murray wrote to Thomson at the same time (17 July) that he (Murray) had been at fault, in that he had agreed to carry out the operation, which was fundamentally unsound and his only regret was that the operation should ever have been considered necessary.*

These rebuttals did not receive any acknowledgement from Divisional HQ. The later revelation, however, that Divisional Intelligence had underestimated the strength of German defences at Colombelles (probably from Montgomery's Liaison Officers), led directly to Montgomery's diary comment on the 15th July:

> 'that the 51st Highland Division was not battle worthy. The Division is down and will not fight; we shall have to get a new Divisional Commander. It is very regrettable that this fine Division has sunk to such a level.' (Montgomery's diaries, Imperial War Museum Library, July 1944.)

General Bullen-Smith was subsequently relieved of his command on the 26th July 1944, being replaced by General Tom Rennie, an event vividly described by Delaforce in Monty's Highlanders:

> On the 26th July Montgomery interviewed Bullen-Smith, (an emotional scene as reported by Dawney, Monty's LO), 'You must go, the men won't fight for you and you will go home now.' Charles came down with tears pouring down his face. Monty, deeply moved, said, 'If I don't remove you Charles, men will be killed unnecessarily, you must go. That is all.'

---

*From 5th Black Watch War Diary July 1944 and The Spirit of Angus, McGregor, pp. 129–130. The futility of this attack was underlined by the fact that the Germans themselves pulled down the Colombelles chimneys only two days later.

From 'Reflections':

'The Highland Division had been sent home in Nov 1943 from Sicily to take part in the planned invasion in Normandy in 1944. The troops were quite certain that this was the inevitable outcome of the successful campaigns in North Africa and Sicily, but to me it was quite incredible that we were on our way home in that year 1943. Our return synchronised too with a change of command.

'Douglas Wimberley, our revered Commander, had been chosen to be Commandant of the Staff College and his successor Charles Bullen-Smith had until then been in command of the 15th Scottish Division, which had been training at home for three years and therefore knew all that was required to be known on land warfare in Europe.' (He had also served with 'Nap' in Montgomery's 3rd Division in 1942.)

'Unfortunately our new Commander failed to realise the splendid opportunity, which our experience and his training provided. Instead of taking firm command of the Division and leading them into another form of land warfare, (in which he had so much to offer, and all the necessary training), he assumed that we, having been fighting for over a year in North Africa and Sicily, knew all the answers.

'Needless to say the Highland Division was only too happy to be accepted on this evaluation and it was very difficult indeed to induce our Battalion Commanders to carry out realistic training.

'The result was that there was not only a few weeks to carry out training in the spring of 1944, but it was not as ruthless as it should have been. A very heavy price was exacted for this shortcoming in the early days of the Normandy invasion.

'It is easy to be wise after the event, but the trouble was that it was difficult to approach the problem of Normandy with the same degree of humility, which had characterised our approach to the problem of desert warfare two years ago.

'There was no mood to go back to the square one of 1942. It might have been possible to have done so if more ruthlessness had been shown by the Divisional Commander and

although everyone was happy to be home again, the cry arose "Who else is fighting this war'" a remark echoed by Richard Doherty. "The six-month period in England for training softened, rather than hardened the Division for the trials ahead." *

'It was not easy to be at the receiving end for weeks on end without relief. However, the strategy of the battle commenced to pay off in late July, early August when the Americans broke out on the western flank some 20 miles west of Caen at St Lo and we (52 HD) attacked with the Canadians east of Caen towards Falaise joining up with the Americans in the Pocket by mid August 1944.'

The fortunes of the Highland Division greatly improved both under General Rennie and from their move from the 1st British Corps to the 2nd Canadian Corps under the command of Lieutenant General Guy Simonds. 'Nap' Murray had been at Staff College with Simonds in 1937 and fought alongside his forces in Sicily six months before and had a very high regard of his qualities. It is significant that the Canadians were not under the direct command of the 21st Army Group, being Dominion not British forces. Simonds showed great imagination in his methods of attack, e.g. the use of searchlights to enable tanks to advance at night by reflecting their light off clouds and by stripping self-propelled gun carriages and replacing the guns with infantrymen to get them forward, fresh and fit.

This offensive, code name 'Totalize', took place in the bocage country east of Caen close to Colombelles in August 1944 and was preceded by a massive aerial attack by both the American and British Air Forces involving over 3,000 bombers with devastating effect on German defence, tanks and morale.

'Totalize' in conjunction with Montgomery's 'Goodwood' offensive broke the German lines of defence and enabled the Highland Division to advance south to Caen which, after huge artillery bombardment, was finally captured on July 10th. Thereafter the Germans were driven south towards Falaise at which point the two Allied armies, the American 1st Army advancing from St Lo and the 21st Army Group from Caen joined, thus creating the Falaise

None Bolder, by Richard Doherty.

Pocket which destroyed the effectiveness of the German army in Normandy.

Days before these events, far to the south in Italy, Major General Templer had succeeded General Evelegh (see next chapter) as GOC 6th Armoured Division and whilst travelling south of Florence he was badly injured in a freak accident on 5 August 1944 caused by a grand piano falling on his back, invaliding him out of the War altogether (but not from the Army, later becoming CIGS and a close friend of 'Nap'). A week after that accident 'Nap' was on his way to Italy from Normandy to take over command. It was a complete leap into the unknown for him and one certainly made on Montgomery's recommendation. The choice of 'Nap', however, was vindicated by the striking success that Division experienced in Italy and Austria between August 1944 and May 1945.

> '*It (Normandy) was the most trying experience I had during the War or any other time. The main difficulty was to maintain morale, as it was not easy to be at the receiving end for weeks on end without relief.*
>
> '*I had not seen eye to eye with my Divisional Commander who had gone home a couple of weeks previously and promotion was the last thing I expected. Nevertheless I left France with a comforting thought, that after this sticky start, the Highland Division was itself again under its new Commander, Tom Rennie.*'

> '*It was on this day, 12th August, news arrived that the ever-cheerful and highly-experienced Brigadier 'Nap' Murray had been given command of a Division in Italy where he was destined still further to enhance his reputation . . . but the 51st HD was indeed sorry to see him go. He had led the Brigade with great skill and during the early days in Normandy had maintained morale despite the difficulties of having his three Battalions under other people's command. He was succeeded as 153 Brigade Commander by Roddy Sinclair, later Lord Caithness.*'*

*From Salmond, *51st Highland Division* and McGregor, *Spirit of Angus*.

Chapter Sixteen

Italy and Austria

We arrived at an officers' reception unit in Portsmouth about breakfast time and it was a very dusty and untidy-looking Brigadier who put in an appearance there. I met the Commanding Officer who was very circumspect in his enquiries. It emerged that quite a number of officers were passing through the unit from Normandy for the widest of reasons. The opening remarks were, 'Hope you had a good trip. Where are you bound for' Can I help in any way?' No attempt to enquire into circumstances leading to my appearance there. I did, however, ask for a railway warrant to London as I had an appointment with the Military Secretary on Monday morning. This eased the tension somewhat, and we then had a good breakfast and went off down to the railway station to catch a train. I rang up Winchester and found quite a part of the family was there so planned to spend the rest of Sunday with them, going on to London the following day. I do not quite know how they managed it, but there was a car to meet me and I went out to Harestock. There was the Donovan family, my sister and Ma.

It was a very hot day and I remember the Donovan children jumping in and out of a ridiculously small pool in the garden, with my mother watching them all from a deck chair. After lunch I suddenly felt very tired, stretched myself out on the lawn and went fast to sleep.

The following morning I went on to London, called on the Military Secretary, got confirmation that I was to take over command of the 6th Armoured Division and that I would be required to fly out to Italy the following Friday. It happened that there was a previous commander of the 6th Armoured Division in London at the time, Major General Vivian Evelegh, and I went over to Whitehall to meet him. He had assumed command of the

166

Division the previous spring and had led it throughout the spring and summer in the battles of Cassino, the Liri Valley and the pursuit up the length of Italy. Previously he had commanded the 78th Division, which was his real love; as well it might be as it was one of the outstanding Infantry divisions of the war. It was particularly interesting to meet him because he was basically an infantry soldier and his experiences could not fail to be of value to me. He had been succeeded by Major General Gerald Templer only a couple of months before, but I had to wait until I got out to Italy before I was to find out why I was needed so soon after Evelegh left.

I went down by train to an airfield in the West Country on the following Friday and exactly a week after giving up command of 153 Infantry Brigade I found myself in the air heading for Gibraltar. We landed at Gibraltar at 7 a.m. the following morning and two of us were taken off in a car to the residence of the Governor, General 'Rusty' Eastwood, where we were to stay. We had an excellent breakfast and were then taken on a tour of the Rock. This was particularly interesting because until Sicily fell in 1943 the place had been in a state of siege. From 1939 onwards they had burrowed away into the Rock creating headquarters, hospitals, store places, workshops and all that was needed to provide complete overhead protection for the garrison. We spent the better part of the morning visiting one place after another and there seemed to be little doubt that Gibraltar would have been a very hard nut to crack. We went back to the 'Convent', had lunch and then flew on to Algiers. We arrived there in the early evening and drove to our hotel.

We stayed in Algiers for the night and flew on to Naples the following morning, only staying there for an hour or two before leaving for Rome. We flew too high for it to be possible to distinguish much on the ground connected with the spring battles, although it was a pleasant thought to consider that it was only a year since we had completed the conquest of Sicily and that we were now on the southern outskirts of Florence.

We landed in Rome in the middle of the afternoon, and there I was met by the GSO1, Guy Peyton and the A/Q, Quentin Hoare.

The following morning I set out to Florence by road, being accompanied by Guy Peyton. It emerged that he was about to hand

over to Lieutenant Colonel P.H. Labouchere ('Labby') of the 3rd
Hussars, but he had been with the Division throughout the year
and could therefore give me the background I badly needed. It
appeared that my predecessor, Major General Gerald Templer, had
been the unfortunate victim of a road accident of an unusual kind.
He was a very able officer, and it came as no surprise to any of us
that he finally became CIGS and a Field Marshal. During the
summer he had been commanding the 56th (London) Division,
which I had got to know in North Africa and had been given
command of the 6th Armoured at about the time that the Division
was approaching Florence. It was considered that those who might
be considered for command of a Corps needed first to have had
experience in commanding both an Infantry division and an
Armoured division, hence the appointment. Early in August he had
gone forward to visit one of the leading regiments, had arrived at
a point where a bridge had been blown and proceeded to drop
down one bank in order to cross over. As the Jeep took the descent
a 3-ton lorry came down the other way and the two vehicles arrived
at the bottom at about the same time. It may be that the driver of
the lorry was slightly unnerved by the sight of the Divisional
Commander and his flag, and that he made evasive action on a
sufficient scale to unsettle the load he was carrying. There was a
rending sound and, freed from its bonds, a grand piano plunged
over the tailboard and pinned the Divisional Commander in his
seat. The impact cracked his spine and he was evacuated back to
hospital and took no further active part in the campaign. It is
alleged that when one of the men climbed out of the lorry to inspect
the situation his first exclamation was, 'Blimey Bill, look at the
grand piano.' These were the circumstances which led to me
becoming a Major General, and show to what extent the element
of chance affects a career in the Armed Forces, particularly in war.

Guy Peyton went on to explain the overall military situation in
Italy. After the fall of Rome and when the Fifth American Army
and the Eighth British were in full cry in pursuit of Kesselring, a
decision was taken that substantial forces would have to be withdrawn in order to invade the South of France in the operation
known as 'Anvil'! It appeared that Alex had opposed this with all
his might as he was convinced that the strategic aim was to carry
the war into Yugoslavia, liquidating the German forces in Italy in

the process, but France was deemed to be the decisive theatre and thither went about ten Divisions including the French with their mountain troops.

This operation had been launched only five days previously. The plan before the withdrawal of these ten divisions to invade Southern France was to break through the Apennines in the centre, but it was now for consideration whether it would be preferable to attack first on the eastern coastal plain and then drive through the mountains when the opposition had been weakened. This plan was accepted and on the same day as 'Anvil' started, the Eighth Army started to move across to the coast; as we drove north this move was in full swing and would be complete by the 22nd of August. The XIII Corps of the Eighth Army, however, would remain up in the mountains and come under the Fifth American Army commanded by General Mark Clark, which meant that the 6th Armoured Division would remain in the mountains as well. It was not easy to see what purpose an armoured division would serve in the Apennines but at that stage there was nothing to be done about it. The immediate role of the 6th Armoured Division would be passive until the American Fifth Army got into motion which would not be for two or three weeks. The attack of the Eighth Army started on the 25th of August.

We went on to discuss the Division itself. It had been more or less continuously in action since April and the battle for Rome. I had last seen the Division at Enfidaville in May of the previous year, but it had not been employed again in 1943, having taken no part in the campaign in Sicily or the landings in Italy. In 1944, however, it had been in action continuously for nearly five months. The Division had its Armoured Brigade (26th) of three armoured regiments under Brigadier Neville Mitchell and an Armoured Reconnaissance Regiment, the Derbyshire Yeomanry; the 1st Guards Brigade commanded by Brigadier Andrew Montague Douglas-Scott, and the 61st Infantry Brigade commanded by Brigadier Adrian Gore, consisting of three battalions of the Rifle Brigade. The latter was something of a luxury for an Armoured division as the normal complement is only one motor battalion, but it was brought about by the Supreme Commander Middle East, Field Marshal Sir Henry Wilson, who, having served in the Rifle Brigade, decided that these three battalions should be grouped together under another Rifleman. At a later stage we were to benefit from this arrangement, which enabled each Armoured regiment to have its own motor battalion.

There appears to have been a considerable amount of speculation as to who would succeed Gerald Templer and the selection of an infantry Brigadier from Normandy crossed nobody's mind. As we drove along it occurred to me that I had one advantage in not being too closely identified with these three main elements: Field Marshal Alexander obviously took a great deal of interest in the Guardsmen, Field Marshal Wilson in the Green Jackets and General Sir George Clark in the Armoured Regiments. It looked like a collection of small private armies and the need was primarily for an impartial umpire. I was not certain that I necessarily had the required qualifications, but it made my debut simpler. The road journey took up most of the day and we started to move through some of the battle areas such as Perugia and Arezzo, upon which Guy Peyton was illuminating.

It was an incredibly hot day and it was a relief when we finally arrived at Divisional Headquarters close to Florence. I spent the first two or three days going around the Headquarters and meeting the Staff. I wore a balmoral at all times, a very suitable form of headgear, particularly in a tank. At an early stage it became obvious that the Headquarters was highly professional, and communications on a different plane altogether from those of an Infantry division. From the Headquarters I moved out to meet the Regiments; although we were up to the River Arno and on the outskirts of Florence, whilst we were not in close contact with the enemy we could move about freely. As I went around I was trying to make up my mind what the next few weeks would have to offer. There would be little scope for the Armoured Regiments, not much for the Rifle battalions, but quite an amount for the Guardsmen. None were trained for fighting in mountainous country so the main hope would be that we would break through the Apennines before the winter really set in and have the opportunity of a mobile battle in the valley of the River Po thereafter.

While I was engaged in this survey the Eighth Army, on August 25th, started their attack on the coast. When they had attracted the main reserves onto their front we too started to come in and it was a relief to discover that the main attacks of the American Fifth Army would be made by Infantry divisions initially, with the 6th Armoured providing flank protection.

In the event the American Fifth Army did not attack until September the 12th, although they closed up to what became known as the Gothic Line in some preliminary operations. By the end of August there was a hope that we might get through the line before winter set in.

I went along to see the Ayrshire Yeomanry. This Regiment had been horsed in 1939, but when it became obvious that their chances of getting into the War on a horsed basis were nil, they agreed to be converted into a Field Regiment Royal Artillery. The interesting thing was that this Regiment was affiliated to the Guards Brigade who would not move anywhere without them. During my visit I asked one of the troop commanders the name of the Commander of the Guards Battalion he supported and was rather taken aback when the question elicited no answer. As the individual looked rather embarrassed I went on to talk to one of the other officers. At the end of the visit the Acting Commanding Officer confided to me that the troop commander knew perfectly well who the Commanding Officer was, but as he was always known as 'Uncle Teddy Bear', his real name escaped him. I was relieved to hear this, because the tie-up between the infantry and the artillery was taken for granted and was a 'battle-winning' factor.

Later that day I was joined in my caravan by the Commander Royal Artillery and Brigadier Clive Usher. The problem was the command of the Ayrshire Yeomanry. The Regiment really felt that the time had come for one of their own officers to assume command and they had, in Major Hamilton Campbell, just the chap. Furthermore, this officer's father had commanded before him during the days when the Regiment had been mounted on horses, and it would give the Regiment special satisfaction to see him get it. Clive Usher, however, informed me that the Director of Royal Artillery for the Eighth Army had decided that command should pass to another 'professional', on the understanding that he would remain with the Regiment for not more than six months, when Hamilton Campbell would be appointed. This seemed to be reasonable and Clive added that the 'professional' was coming in to lunch and I would have an opportunity of meeting him. We had our mess in a marquee, pitched amongst some trees and on going in I saw Geoff Bourne, who had been at the Staff College at the same time, although a year senior to me and who had been in 'Plans' in the War Office when I was in Staff Duties. 'Hullo Professor,' he shouted. 'What the hell are you doing here?' Pins don't drop easily in a marquee but might well have been heard to do so, such was the paralysing silence that followed. I laughed, he looked on my shoulder and we had a drink together. He was much senior to me in the Army in a substantive rank, and had come down from Brigadier in order to get experience of the command of a Field Regiment in the field. In fact this was the 'professional' who was to take over the Ayrshire Yeomanry. He was a remarkable officer, who had lost an arm twenty years before but this disability did not prevent him from reaching high position in the Army, finally going into the House of Lords as a life peer. Mungo Hamilton Campbell, at the end of the year, achieved his ambition in getting command, so all was well in the end.

I met Mark Clark soon after my arrival. He made the usual polite gestures, which are a feature of such occasions, and then went on to unfold his plan. It soon became clear that the attack was really designed as an all-American affair. It seemed to me that Mark Clark determined that it would be American soldiers who would break out onto the plain and capture Bologna; he had a weakness for that sort of thing. The 'eye-wiping' stage of the War was apparently still with us. The Americans fought a splendid battle but the ground, and later the weather, proved too much for them and they were finally halted some miles short of the plain. As the battle developed we got more and more involved and I was forced to employ the tank crews as infantry. We remained in the Apennines for six months and were only finally withdrawn in February 1945. I did not see much of Mark Clark until some weeks later as he was taken up with directing the main Fifth Army attack.

Our Corps Commander was Lieutenant General Sir Sidney Kirkman, a Gunner, and I went to his Headquarters for lunch one day when he was entertaining Sir James Grigg, then Secretary of State for War. In the course of conversation it emerged that I had been recently serving with the Highland Division in Normandy and he volunteered the comment that the Division had not been doing very well recently. It was odd that a Secretary of State for War should have taken time out to make a derogatory remark about a Division in the field in another theatre, but he obviously enjoyed making it.

We watched the progress of the Eighth Army with intense interest. It may be that the physical difficulties over on the coast had been underestimated, because all one heard of was the passage of one river line after another, although this did not matter so much as the summer was still with us and the rivers dry. It was at the beginning of September when we heard that an attempt to put the 1st Armoured Division through had failed and, because they suffered losses on such a scale, later that year it was broken up. This was the first sign that we might find ourselves involved in a protracted battle and that a breakthrough in the immediate future was unlikely. Compared with the central mass of the Apennines, the coastal strip appeared to offer good opportunities for offensive action, but the foothills which ran down to the sea were some hundreds of feet high and were quite close together, being separated by the rivers flowing down from the hinterland. On the 12th of September the attack of the American Fifth Army went in, at the same time as a powerful attack by the Eighth Army. The infantry fought with great gallantry and with powerful artillery and air support and drove a deep wedge in the centre, which carried them to within 12 miles of Bologna.

I think we might have avoided the gruelling winter campaign which we were about to conduct had the weather not broken towards the end of September. Torrential rain soon turned the rivers into raging torrents and made movement over the mountains a very slow and laborious business. The temperature dropped, the rain turned to snow and certain parts of the front saw conditions which resembled the War on the Western Front in World War One. Operating on the flank we edged our way forward with limited attacks and patrolling. Once we came across a poor blow in the road, we moved an Armoured Regiment up and bounced through for 3 miles before another bridge went up. Soon after this we handed over the whole of this flank to the Armoured Brigade, who dismounted the tank crews and operated as infantry. The reason for this was that the Infantry divisions in the centre had suffered very heavy casualties, and reinforcements in Italy were hard to come by. Consequently the Guards Brigade and the 61st Infantry Brigade were transferred across to Castel Benito in order to relieve some American regiments. The Armoured Regiments remained as infantry for some weeks with quite a degree of skill in a defensive role.

The 1st Guards Brigade finally relieved the Americans on Monte Battaglia*. Both sides occupied only the ground which dominated roads and communications, leaving some ground unoccupied, but the feature, which included Monte Battaglia, was vital, crowned by a stunted ruined castle dominating the valleys of Senio and Santerno, being 2,000 feet high. The approach was a minor road, which had been designed to meet the needs of local traffic, but now with its bridges blown away and the surface scarred with shell-holes, the road had completely collapsed. This became typical of all the mountain tracks as the winter wore on, and it was only by turning out gunners who had no role, such as the anti-tank regiments and the Anti-Aircraft Regiment to augment the resources of the Royal Engineers, that the roads were kept in. There was always a point beyond which the transport could not move, and this was 5 miles from the 'Main Road' so far as Battaglia was concerned. Here the troops would dismount and would proceed onwards with porters and mule trains. As the rains continued these tracks became liquid mud and then the bottom fell out of them. Men's boots, even when tightly laced, could be pulled off their feet; fully-loaded mules would belly and often had to be shot where they were. If a man got sucked in it might take an hour to dig him out. Although it was only 3 miles to the top, the return journey would take ten hours to cover. An Indian muleteer expressed what many thought when he said, 'Mule tired me very unhappy.'

The following four months were physically the most unpleasant I have ever experienced, although the experiences of the forward troops beggared description. Many of the positions were so exposed that the dead of both sides remained unburied for some time. What with mortaring and shelling, day and night, combined with incessant rain, the lot of the troops was almost intolerable. The rain filled the slit trenches but the slit trench was the only place where a man could find shelter from shellfire. Permanently soaked to the skin and permanently in danger, he would spend his day in the bleak

*See map Northern Italy, south of Bologna, trig point 1190.

surroundings of stunted and decapitated trees, hundreds of water-logged shell-holes, unburied corpses, sopping blankets and empty ration tins. In spite of all that the main enemy remained the mud. A vital consideration was the evacuation of casualties. The men were prepared to accept the inevitable operational risks, but it was essential that arrangements for the evacuation of casualties should be of the highest order. To fail here would have had the most adverse effect on morale. In the case of Battaglia a chain of medical posts was organised, each about 400 yards apart and by means of it casualties were got back to 'Jeep head' in three and a half hours, a remarkable achievement when the tracks were so awful.

With the major offensive shifted elsewhere, the operations were reduced to small local attacks and raids combined with patrolling. We did not have the resources to stage anything more ambitious and the conditions in any case were against major operations. We then started to take risks. It was obvious that the campaign in the Apennines was going to drag on into the winter. The Eighth Army, from time to time, crossed yet another river line, in spite of the appalling conditions imposed by the Romagna, but the number remaining to be crossed seemed to be legion. The Fifth Army inched its way from one hill to another, but progress was increasingly on a diminishing scale. So when we were getting into late October, we started to pull out battalions in succession and send them back to the vicinity of Florence, which was only 50 miles away, for three, four or five days at a time. As we only had six battalions, we never allowed more than three out at a time. Had we not done this we would rapidly have become unfit for battle. We were now in the centre of the American Fifth Army, General Mark Clark visited us quite often and always marched straight into the Operations Room and stared at our dispositions with apprehension. 'You know, General Murray,' he would say, 'your division gives me great concern as you are so thin on the ground. It always took a whole infantry division of nine battalions or more to hold this area, and here you are with only six.' Of course the conditions had changed so much in previous weeks that a smaller force could have done the job. But what he would have said had he discovered that there were no more than four battalions, I shudder to think. We always knew when he was likely to come, and therefore always had a special map ready for him. I think my Corps Commander suspected what we were up to, but left us alone. We carried on in this way for at least two months without being found out either by the enemy or higher authority. We were to spend nearly five months in the Apennines before we were finally withdrawn and would have been good for nothing at the end of that time if we had not conserved the officers and men in this way.

I think it was General Eisenhower who decreed that, whatever the cost, pressure on the Germans would be kept up during the winter in Europe and this applied to the Armies in Italy. Whereas the conditions were entirely unsuitable for offensive operations, we nevertheless launched two or three on our front which were very expensive both in lives and matériel, and which achieved practically nothing. Whilst there could be no suggestion of breaking off the campaign and going into winter quarters, we would have been equally effective merely by maintaining our positions. All we were doing was to reduce our capacity for offensive operations. It was not until late December that it was finally decided to go over to the defensive, a decision that was not taken out of any consideration for the condition of the troops, but because there was suddenly a shortage of artillery ammunition and the danger existed that there would not be enough for the spring offensive. We were just grateful that at last the proper decision was taken. We stayed on in the line until the end of January when we withdrew to the vicinity of Florence.

For me the year 1944 was one long continuous slog. From June until August we were fighting in the bridgehead in Normandy and just when we were about to break out, I was transferred to Italy, when the big chase up through Italy was over and the autumn and winter campaigns in the Apennines were about to commence. Although I had been given command of an Armoured Division my first six months were to do with fighting infantry battles. Those months in the second half of 1944 saw an Armoured Division committed to war in the mountains, for which they were neither equipped nor trained, but it only demonstrated that one frequently has to fight wars as we must and not as we would like to do. Nevertheless it seemed to me to be extraordinary that so little attention was given to the urgent need to employ all Mountain Divisions in Italy instead of wasting them elsewhere. The thought of the 52nd Lowland Division specially trained in such warfare going into action at Walcheren, below sea level, struck us as the height of stupidity. It was not until the New Year of 1945 that the Americans made the 10th (US) Mountain Division available to the Fifth Army and their impact was terrific. If these two divisions had been made available in the autumn of 1944, I am quite certain we should have penetrated into the Po Valley at a very early stage.

In January 1945 the Corps Commander, Lieutenant General Kirkman, went home on leave and I temporarily took over command of XIII Corps as an acting Lieutenant General, although on the Army List I was still shown as a Major in the Cameron Highlanders. In February we finally withdrew from the Apennines and after a couple of weeks in the vicinity of Florence moved across to Catholica on the coastal plain and rejoined the Eighth Army. It was a glorious spring, with a warm to hot sun and suddenly the Apennines receded into a squalid muddy memory, never to be repeated. To walk down roads and actually hear the sound of your feet was delightful.

By now it was early March and we discovered that the spring campaign was due to start in early April, so there was no time to lose. A certain amount of reorganisation ensued, including the replacement of the Coldstream Guards by a battalion of the Welch Regiment in the Guards Brigade, and a battalion of the KRRC in the 61st Infantry Brigade. I could never help being prejudiced in favour of these riflemen because of the memory I always retained of the pre-1914 days when I saw them in all their glory. We trained as much as we could although this part of Italy is so intensely culti-vated that we were apt to do a certain amount of damage to orchards and vineyards. This was the time to have study periods and decide upon the technique we would employ if the opportunity came our way for armoured action. The final discussion was called 'Razor Blade' and was so-called because it cut both ways, in that we worked solidly at the various issues we needed to settle. We decided that, as we had three motor battalions, we would operate in three regimental groups; these would each consist of an armoured regiment, a motor battalion, a battery of artillery and some Sappers. The Guards Brigade would be in reserve to punch holes if required and the Derbyshire Yeomanry provided a reserve of armour for use as the situation demanded.

In the plan, the 6th Armoured Division constituted the sole reserve left in the hands of the Commander of the Eighth Army, General Sir Richard McCreery. He was one of the most knowledgeable and experienced armoured commanders in the war, and his Regiment had been the 12th Lancers. He was determined that the Division would be used in an armoured role, but only when the circumstances were favourable to its use in this way. It presupposed breaking out through the infantry when the latter had softened up the opposition and the battle was on the verge of becoming fluid. Such situations are difficult to read and the conclusion we came to was that we would have to be prepared to fight our own way out if needs be. We knew also that there was little likelihood of breaking out on a broad front. It was essential to make our battle groups as flexible as possible.

The spring offensive started on the 8th of April and the Eighth Army opened the proceedings by clearing up the right flank including Lake Commachio. To give some idea of the weight of support available in these closing days of the war, these early operations were supported by 1,500 guns of various calibres, 800 heavy bombers and 1,000 medium fighter bombers. After what appeared to be an interminable series of water obstacles, all that stood before the Eighth Army eight months after they commenced their attacks in August 1944, were four major and four minor river obstacles, in addition to the usual network of dykes, deep ditches and flooded fields. In spite of all these physical difficulties, we were extremely fortunate that we enjoyed an exceptionally dry, hot spring. The general direction of the advance of the Eighth Army was towards Argenta, which, once gained, opened the door to mobile operations on a reasonable scale. The main hope of employing the 6th Armoured Division in an armoured role largely depended upon breaking through what became called the Argenta Gap and it was there that our thoughts were directed.

The battle moved steadily forward; the American Fifth Army did not intervene at this stage, but waited for the Eighth Army to attract in its direction sufficient of the enemy reserves to warrant the breakout from the hills. It was important to watch closely the progress of the forward divisions because in a relatively short space of time we were 40 or 50 miles behind the leading divisions. I went to Army Headquarters daily to meet Major General Sir

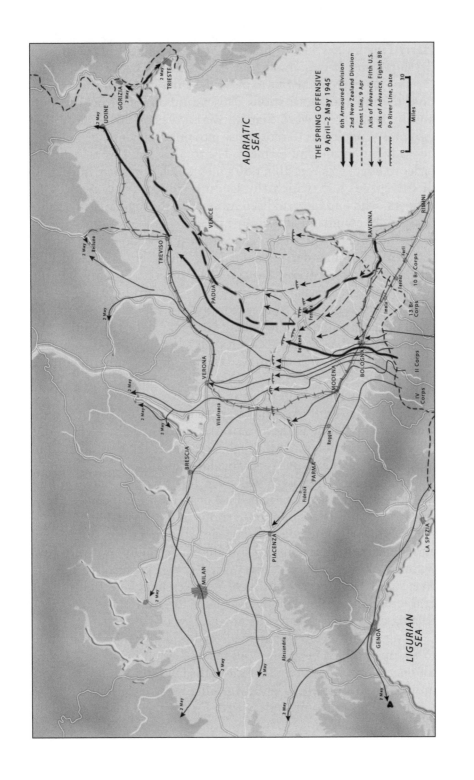

THE SPRING OFFENSIVE
9 April–2 May 1945

6th Armoured Division
2nd New Zealand Division
Front Line, 9 Apr
Axis of Advance, Fifth U.S.
Axis of Advance, Eighth BR
Po River Line, Date

0   Miles   30

ADRIATIC SEA

LIGURIAN SEA

UDINE   GORIZIA   TRIESTE
2 May   2 May   2 May

Belluno
2 May

VENICE

TREVISO

PADUA

RAVENNA

RIMINI

Forlì
Faenza
Imola
Castel Bolognese

10 Br Corps

13 Br Corps

VERONA

Villafranca

MODENA

BOLOGNA

II Corps

IV Corps

Reggio

PARMA

Fidenza

PIACENZA

BRESCIA
2 May

2 May

2 May

2 May

MILAN

2 May

Alessandria
2 May

2 May

2 May

GENOA

LA SPEZIA

2 May

Harry Floyd, the Chief of Staff, in order to be kept in touch with developments. It was about four days after the battle started that the time appeared to be ripe to move the Division north and to close up with the leading formations. This we did on the 14th/15th April and went so far forward that we were occasionally shelled. This move also enabled us to reorganise into our regimental groups and be ready for instant employment. The total distance we travelled in order to effect this was about 50 miles which was some indication of the speed with which the leading troops drew away. Our gunners, who had hitherto been supporting the Eighth Army, came back under command at the same time.

On the 18th of April, I was called to Army Headquarters to meet the Army Commander (General Dick McCreery). He said that all the indications were that we had captured Argenta but the reports were somewhat conflicting. He was not prepared to say whether it was possible to break through there, but he wanted me to go forward and meet Lieutenant General Charles Keightley, the Commander of V Corps, to see for myself what the position was and report back to him what were my impressions. I put the Division on six hours' notice to move and went forward. Charles Keightley clearly thought the way was clear, but I went on to see Major General Keith Arbuthnott, commanding the 78th Division which was operating in the area of Argenta. It had always been our hope we would break out through Argenta, as the ground beyond appeared to be the most favourable for armour.

Unfortunately the 'gap' was even less obvious than we had thought, but two factors decided me in accepting this challenge. In the first place the opposing troops must have had quite a hammering in the previous ten days since the operation commenced and might well be seriously disorganised. Secondly, we were now within striking distance of the River Po, and in this area the 6th Armoured Division would have its last chance of fighting an armoured battle. We would never have forgiven ourselves if that fleeting chance had escaped us: it was now or never.

I rang up the Army Commander and told him that I was ready to go, upon which he at once put me under command of V Corps for operations. I also got on the air to the Division and by the afternoon the Armoured Brigade Commander, together with the regimental group commanders were forward and making contact with the commanders of the 78th Division on the ground. The Division was to move forward at first light the following day, passing through the 78th by the early afternoon. The Armoured Commanders looked a little distrait after their reconnaissances, as they did not get anything like the amount of information they had hoped to get, and felt that they would be forced to fight their way out. One of them was foolish enough to say that we were to go about the business in exactly the way we said we never would. He got the broadside his remark called for, but I never reminded him of it.

The day's operations nevertheless were disappointing, mainly because the great charge which some had hoped for, even expected, never looked like materialising. It is true that we moved out beyond the 78th Division, but the total penetration was not much more than a mile or two in front of both the leading regimental groups. It was disappointing, but not altogether unexpected after a winter spent operating defensively in hills. The main advantage was that we were now out on our own, and had the ball in our court. I was not altogether satisfied that there was a sufficient sense of urgency forward in a situation which required boldness, so I ordered a light aircraft to be lined up to enable me to fly down the front to see for myself.

I was about to leave when up drove Charles Keightley, who appeared to be in a towering rage, or if not, a well-simulated one. He jumped up the steps of the caravan, threw his hat into the far corner and more or less shouted, 'This is no way for an armoured division to operate, in twenty-four hours you have made practically no advance at all.' He then produced a map, pointed to an open piece of ground and said, 'Look, there is a splendid tank run, why don't you use it?' Well, good tank runs are a little too obvious, as the Eighth Army had discovered to its cost on many previous occasions, as they are also ideal for anti-tank defence. I told him that the Division had its orders for the day, which was to penetrate forward on as wide a front as possible and enable me to use the reserve as the situation demanded. I agreed with him that somehow the advance had to be speeded up, but I could only do this within the framework of the existing plan. With that he had to be satisfied, but it was tiresome to be confronted in this way by one's superior commander, particularly as we had given far more thought to our problems than he could hope to do. He went off, clearly far from satisfied, but somewhat mollified by the possibility that things might be on the move. I then went off to the airstrip and did a first-class piece of snooping. We flew at a couple of hundred feet and I could see individual tanks and headquarters with the greatest of ease, and for the most part they appeared to be immobile. I was back at my Headquarters within the hour and could order one regiment to cross a bridge in front of them straight away as it was unguarded and invite others to move into areas which they appeared only to have under observation. This resulted in crossing one canal that day and closing up onto a second in time for a night crossing by the Guardsmen.

The following day, the 21st of April, we regrouped with the Armoured Brigade Commander commanding the left wing with two armoured regimental groups, while I commanded the right wing and the reserves. The same day the leading regimental group on the left, the 17th/21st Lancers, broke through and was later followed by the 16th/5th Lancers. This breakout was made possible by good map-reading. It looked as if the Fossa Cambelina emptied itself into the River Reno but was, in fact, separated from it by a bund about 30 yards wide, virtually a ready-made bridge. The first attempt to cross was thwarted by a Tiger tank with its 88mm gun. However, by this time in the battle aircraft were available on quite a scale for the direct support of infantry and a flight of rocket-firing aircraft soon liquidated the tank. Through went the 17th/21st and before last light the 16th/5th had moved through, and then round to the right ready to operate at dawn. I at once released the third armoured group, the Lothian and Border Horse, and at first light they went through and extended the front still further to the right so that by mid morning on the 22nd we had all three armoured groups travelling north-west in line heading for the River Panaro and cutting right across the lines of communication of the German Parachute Corps. Away to the east the Derbyshire Yeomanry availed them of the bridgehead, which had been created by the Guardsmen, and started to move over in order to protect the flank and rear of the Armoured Brigade from the direction of Ferrara. This operation was particularly impressive. The 'Fossa Cambelina' was 20 yards wide, but protected by high levees on both banks. The Sappers came along, blew in the levee on the near side, threw a number of fascines into the canal bed, ran a Churchill tank on top of them, thereby providing a bridge and blew a gap in the levee on the far side, thus making a complete passage. All this was very well done, but would have been a complete waste of time and effort had the drivers of the tanks and vehicles following up been unable to avail themselves of it. This famous old Yeomanry regiment did not fail us. One after another the tanks lined up, drove forward over the near levee, crept down onto the Churchill tank, which was only just wide enough to take them, emerged at the other end, roared up the slope and away to their mission. It was highly professional and an indication of the quality of the Regiment in a crisis. I was enchanted with this performance and possibly stayed too long to watch it; it was only with the greatest of difficulty that I could drag myself away. And so, into the afternoon with all attention now directed onto the Lothian and Border Horse, on the River Panaro very close to the Po, the outside right closing on Bondeno in the north, with the hope of capturing the bridge there intact, thus completing the enemy discomfiture.

The approach was made through a series of orchards which were alive with anti-tank weapons fired by infantrymen, but the Riflemen who were travelling along with the tanks jumped off and liquidated them as fast as they appeared. It was getting on to dusk when the leading troop got within a few hundred yards of the bridge and on orders from the Squadron Commander put spurs to their tanks and crashed over the bridge, firing everything they had while doing so. Just as they disappeared in a cloud of dust, a Tiger tank emerged from its hideout nearby, waddled over the bridge behind our people, and then the bridge went up. Our tank crews fought on for a bit, then were forced to surrender, but we re-captured them within the week and I was delighted to meet them all when they returned. During the night, a series of enemy columns came up from the south heading for the bridge, all of which went straight into the bag.

The following day was a day of mopping-up because our task was completed south of the River Po, and at this point there were no other missions in prospect. In an action which had lasted only three or four days we had captured 3,000 prisoners, driven another 6,000 prisoners into the arms of the American Fifth Army, destroyed II Parachute Corps and created a gap of 20 miles through which the 2nd New Zealand Division marched the following day. It was the last armoured action the 6th Armoured Division was to fight, and although it was of relatively short duration it was highly satisfactory and a splendid postscript to all that had gone before in North Africa and onwards over a period of three years.

On the 23rd, while we were taking stock and sending detachments north to the River Po, Charles Keightley appeared. He shook me warmly by the hand and congratulated me and the Division on the outcome of the operation. I think his ire of the 20th of April may well have been caused by an intense desire to see the 6th Armoured Division, which he had commanded in North Africa, shine in Italy. I think he did not necessarily appreciate the tactical problems in Italy in the use of armour as we did. Also it is always a delicate affair when a formation you yourself have previously commanded returns commanded by somebody else. The difficulty of giving the new commander his head is very real.

We set up our Headquarters about 5 miles from the River Po, being satisfied that now that we had opened the door, others would fall over themselves passing through. The first arrivals were the 2nd New Zealand Division who went straight up to the river on the 23rd and commenced to prepare for a crossing. We watched their movements and activities with interest and complete detachment. Later in the day, we were informed that we had ceased to be under command of V Corps and would now come under command of General Sir John Harding and XIII Corps.

That evening both General McCreery and General Harding appeared together at my caravan, and the former said what a splendid thing it would be if an Armoured division carried out the crossing of the River Po. I think I looked at him with an expression of complete disbelief, only to discover that he meant what he said. Through my mind ran the names of all those magnificent Infantry divisions of the Eighth Army, such as 56th (London), the 78th, the 8th and 10th Indian, and all those Poles who should have been just the people for the job. Naturally this was no time to enquire after their health and the arrival of a mass of amphibian 'experts' established that we were 'for it'.

Before night fell a Warning Order went out to the 1st Guards Brigade to be prepared to cross the River Po on the night of the 25th/26th April – in two days' time. The following morning, the 24th, we had a conference at Divisional Headquarters and Brigadier Gerald Verney went off to plan with his battalion commanders. It was discovered that the New Zealanders would go over the same night as we would, but their attack would be under cover of a powerful artillery barrage, as was their normal custom. It occurred to us that as we would not be able to put more than the Guards Brigade over initially so it would be better to make a silent crossing, consequently we cut down reconnaissance on the river line to the absolute minimum.

The New Zealanders comprised a special if not private army, and I learned a lot from Bernard Freyburg on how such a hand should be played. It was on the afternoon of the 24th that the Army Commander and the Corps Commander arrived forward and there was the hint of a suggestion that we should go over that night. At once Bernard Freyburg went into action, while I held a listening role, in which the grave difficulties of the operation were stressed, including the statement that the river was running at 9 knots. This shook his hearers considerably and then he expanded on the responsibilities that rested on his shoulders vis-à-vis the New Zealand Government, in respect of the men under his command and other matters. I listened to this with the greatest of attention, but just when Bernard was warming to his subject one of his staff officers pulled him aside to tell him that some enterprising New Zealanders had, in fact, got across and found there was practically no opposition. It was marvellous to see the change of front which Bernard adopted and at once he was all action and determined that he would go over that night and vanished. I went over to the 1st Guards Brigade and Gerald Verney's response to the possibility of going over twenty-four hours early was splendid. He said that they had expected it and were ready to go. It happened that there was a good launching area for the DUKWS and further downstream a good landing beach, which was well placed no matter what the speed of the current was.

The plan was that as soon as a bridgehead was formed we would start building rafts for vehicles and possibly tanks. We had no bridging equipment and would be dependent upon the bridge the New Zealanders were to build. Nevertheless, it was a somewhat risky affair to be dependent on rafts and DUKWs. The Po there was at least 400 yards wide; it may not have been flowing at 9 knots but it was very swift, with the water coming down off the mountains in the spring thaw. If the opposition was on any scale the whole operation was fraught with great peril. It was about midnight that the boats pushed off in complete silence, with a terrific cannonade away to the left where the New Zealanders were crossing. One or two mortar bombs fell near the DUKWs but casualties were nil. The business of turning around the DUKWs for further echelons was agonisingly slow, but by first light the Grenadiers were over and to be followed by the Welsh Guards. In the early hours of the morning the Sappers started to build their rafts and by midday we seemed to be well established.

Apparently we had surprised the enemy who were in the middle of a relief. In the meantime our artillery, which had been deployed on the south bank, came into action and their defensive fire saw off the inevitable counter-attacks. When the rafts were finally built we started to get supporting arms over to the infantry, but the turnaround was desperately slow and very little had got over that first day.

Fortunately for us the German Army had been virtually destroyed south of the River Po and the enemy had relatively few heavy weapons or tanks to oppose us on the other side, consequently, weak as we were, we could take risks regarding our flanks. The New Zealanders kindly gave us time on their bridge periodically, which was a great boon. By the 28th we had reached the Adige river, and were in the process of planning a further advance when we received orders to stay where we were, on the grounds that it was only possible to support one Division north of the Adige at that stage. Once more the War appeared to be over so far as we were concerned, but in any case we had really outmarched our resources. The Armoured Brigade had been left south of the River Po and could fend for itself. The rest of the Division, consisting of the Guardsmen, Riflemen, Artillery and the Derbyshire Yeomanry, was spreadeagled over at least three river lines with no bridges. The 27th Lancers, an armoured car regiment, suddenly turned up and asked if they could use some of our rafts; we gave them some vacancies and it was lucky that we did, as subsequent events were to show.

On the 29th of April I decided that I would go forward to see how the New Zealanders were getting along and to pay my respects to General Freyburg. The road north to Padua was absolutely crammed with the transport of the New Zealanders and it was just as well that we had not been required to share it with them. On my way up the column I periodically enquired where the General was to be found and got the inevitable response, 'Right up forward, Sir.' The original Order of March had been typical. The column was led by a squadron of the 12th Lancers, armoured cars, and then came the Tactical Headquarters of the Division, including Bernard Freyburg in a Jeep.

On this particular day there was also a convoy of lorries well forward which were required when the time came to 'liberate' Venice. I finally arrived at the outskirts of Padua and discovered that a bit of a battle was going on with heavy rifle fire and a certain amount of mortaring. On the right of the road I found General Freyburg with a small staff. He appeared glad to see me and, although as cool as a cucumber, always seemed to have plenty of time at his disposal, speaking in a slow, measured way as if to underline his complete detachment. He told me that he was temporarily held up, as there seemed to be a private war going on in the town between the 'partizani' and others with whom they appeared to have some scores to settle. If it went on much longer he was intending to intervene, as he wanted to get on down the road towards Venice and later Trieste.

It was about this time that he ran into odd pockets of Yugoslavs, all dressed in uniform with a Red Star on their hats, who were trying to dissuade him from proceeding any further. They were in small parties and although they were armed, seemed to have no higher organisation. It was a very remarkable organisational feat on the part of President Tito to have thrust them so far into Italy at such an early stage. Bernard met them, listened as best he could to what they had to say, and then, very politely, asked them to lead him to their commander so that they could discuss the matter. He would go down the road, followed by the rest of the Division and, needless to say, went on going in the absence of anybody of standing to talk to.

We had a battalion of the Grenadier Guards in the Division, in which Bernard's only son Paul was serving. A day or so previously we received the news that Paul had been awarded the Military Cross, and it gave me great pleasure to pass this on to him. It

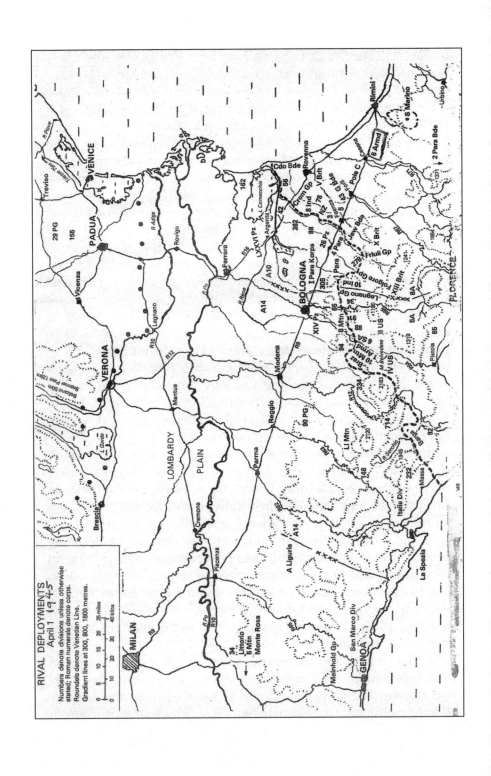

RIVAL DEPLOYMENTS
April 1 1945

Numbers denote divisions unless otherwise
stated; Roman numerals denote corps.
Roundels denote Venetian Line.
Gradient lines at 300, 900, 1800 metres.

seemed to me to be poetic that Paul had been awarded the only military decoration to have eluded Bernard. The latter was the holder of the Victoria Cross, the Distinguished Service Order with three bars, but not a Military Cross. Bernard was absolutely thrilled, seized me by the arm and said, 'As a father, you will understand what this means to me.' I could well understand his pride, but I was not a father myself – I was not even married and told him so. He looked at me in complete astonishment and obviously could hardly believe his ears, although I should not have thought it was all that surprising. Still holding my arm, he led me out of the house and onto the main road, which ran past it leading into the centre of Padua, and for the next half an hour we paced slowly backwards and forwards while he lectured me upon the blessings of married life. There were quite a few bullets whistling through the air, while some of the mortar bombs fell uncomfortably close and I could not but be aware of them. These noises off might never have existed so far as Bernard Freyburg was concerned and we might have been pacing up and down Birdcage Walk for all the impression they made on him. As the New Zealand historian Major General Kippenburger once remarked, his idea of danger was purely relative. Warming to his subject he instanced cases of New Zealanders marrying on a 'whisker' and the bliss which married life inevitably brought in its train. It was not unfunny as I was much more aware of the stray bullets than the theme of his discourse. I got the impression he thought it was a pity that it was not possible to marry me off straight away in Padua, but that my deficiency was sufficiently urgent to warrant immediate action as soon as circumstances allowed.

Just when I wondered what further arguments he would bring forward in support of the theme, a staff officer came running up the road with a message, which required his return. We retraced our footsteps in a leisurely manner and parted on the doorstep of the Headquarters. He went inside, I moved back to my Jeep and set out again for Lendinara; there were more risks to be found in Padua than I had bargained for, not least being married off with little compunction to some unsuspecting female.

When I got back to the Headquarters plans for 'Rest and Recreation' were far advanced, and the usual poker and bridge schools were getting organised. It was drinking time when I got back, and I was just reaching out for something when the GSO1, 'Labby', came smartly in and said laconically, 'Well Sir, it looks as if we shall have to take to the road again.' He was 'too right' as the Australians say. The message was a peremptory order to move at first light through Padua and travel north as hard as we could, make first for Udine and then Tarvisio and Austria. We went straight around to the command vehicle and sent out the necessary orders. As time was not on our side I told the operator to send them out in 'Clear'. At first he almost flatly refused to do so, so ingrained was security in the Royal Corps of Signals. It took some minutes to explain to the signallers that the enemy interception organisation had been broken up and that in any event even if they picked up the messages they would not be able to make use of the information. So I finally had my way and then jumped into my Jeep and went back to Corps Headquarters for more detailed information. The Corps Commander (General Keightley) explained that there was increasing evidence of an attempt on the part of Yugoslavia to try and occupy as much territory in Italy and Austria as possible in the hope of having bargaining counters when the War was finally over. Bernard Freyburg and his New Zealanders were being directed on Venice and Trieste, and we were to make for Austria. That was all I wanted to know and I returned to Lendinara, to find the arrangements for the move far advanced. The most mobile portion of the Division was the 61st Brigade of Riflemen and they shot off at first light. Our generosity in making our rafts available to the 27th Lancers paid off, because they were placed under my command and we soon got them right forward. The Guardsmen and Derbyshire Yeomanry followed along later. I was sorry for the 26th Armoured Brigade, marooned south of the River Po, and could only be thankful that they had not been denied their final run through the Argenta Gap ten days previously.

We were still, as Napoleon would have put it, 'En flagrant délit de concentration', straddled over three rivers. The chances of fighting a prolonged battle were small and risks had to be taken. Things were now really moving because when I took the road the following morning, the 30th of April, the New Zealanders had almost completely disappeared and the firing in Padua had ceased. We soon got through Padua and made for Udine. The crossing of the

River Brenta was exciting as there was no bridge, but only a causeway. There were still odd packets of opposition and we nearly ran into an ambush by a small party which the forward troops had overlooked. Luckily they gave themselves away and it was simple to recall a company of Riflemen who bounced them out from the rear. We passed several small groups of Yugoslavs setting themselves up in the villages and it was clear that they were going to become quite a problem. They always hoisted the Yugoslav flag, but it was noticeable that an Italian flag went up beside them. By the time we got to Udine we were beginning to outrun our supplies and in addition we were incurring an increasing number of operational commitments. We set up a temporary Headquarters in an imposing-looking building and it was there that an astonishing group of men with long beards called, travelling in a Ford 'T' car, which I did not remember having seen since before the War. They luckily had an interpreter with them and it transpired that in front of us was the Cabinet of the Chetniks, those Yugoslavs who were opposed to Tito and had finally sided with the Germans. The only absentee was Mihailovich, the leader or Prime Minister, who stayed behind in Yugoslavia, was captured by Tito and subsequently executed. These men were seeking asylum, having slipped out of Yugoslavia ahead of Tito's men, with the help of the Germans with whom they were operating.

I went back down the road with them into Gorizia where the Chetniks were located. One was bound to be very sympathetic towards them, as I well remembered the excitement caused in 1941 when they rose against Hitler and sparked off a national rising, which seriously affected Hitler's plans for that year, including the invasion of Russia. As the war progressed the Communists under Tito became an increasing threat to their concept of the Yugoslav way of life, until they finally sided with the Germans. We sat around a table with interpreters mainly supplied by them and we could not fail to be impressed by the quality of these men who had risked everything and lost. Outside we could see thousands of the Chetniks milling about. Their uniforms were ragged and torn; they had a few automatics but were mostly armed with rifles; there were one or two ancient-looking guns, but the whole army was on a horse-drawn basis. Their families, women and children were there and they had cattle on the hoof for slaughtering. Their transport consisted of a motley collection of carts of every description, mostly in an advanced state of disintegration. When we went out it was clear that they were convinced that their only hope of survival rested with us. This was the sort of situation which is best dealt with on a low level, otherwise political considerations are apt to intervene, which is not necessarily practical. We brought down some tanks of the Derbyshire Yeomanry and some of the Riflemen, and deployed them further to the east. They were apt to sit on bridges in such a way that it was difficult for others to get over, the roads also receiving special attention, and we ensured that there was nobody who understood a word of the Yugoslav language. When this deployment was completed the Chetniks moved away to the west, finally coming to rest far to the rear at Palmanova. All of this took up a couple of days in which time the 27th Lancers and other infantry elements moved on north towards Tarvisio.

From Udine to the north the road became increasingly difficult and we started to flush out many of the Germans who had been driven into the foothills in large numbers. It was something of a relief that opposition was unorganised and slight. On the other hand the Yugoslavs constituted a continuous menace to our security and provided a whole series of local problems, which took up both time and troops, both of which were in short supply.

One particular instance took place at Cividale. Here the Partizani, who had been a thorn in the side of the Germans for at least a year and who operated from the nearby mountains, had liberated the town amidst scenes of wild rejoicing as families were again re-united. Then, almost from nowhere, in marched a Yugoslav battalion, allocated themselves all the public buildings, raised the Yugoslav flag and requisitioned everything they pleased. Feeling was beginning to rise when the Grenadier Guards arrived and they made it clear that they were there purely for the maintenance of law and order, and these political considerations were nothing to do with them. This did not prevent the Yugoslavs putting up a manifesto requisitioning food supplies, clothing and military equipment, and attempting to assume military control. This was all a little breathtaking considering that the population of the town was 90 per cent Italian. The plans for 'liberation' must have been made months before. Luckily the Italians completely ignored this manifesto. In the evening the Corps of Drums of the

Grenadier Guards arrived, stepped out of their lorries, adjusted their belts, formed up in the main street and marched and counter-marched for over half an hour with the dignity and precision to be expected from this famous regiment. This performance had a sobering effect on both sides and led to the Guardsmen assuming complete control until the political differences were settled.

In the meantime, at Caserta, the terms of the surrender of all German forces in Italy was being decided, which meant that when we arrived at the Austrian frontier at Tarvisio, the poles were up and we swept into Austria. The 27th Lancers had orders to travel as fast as they could to the east and they were given all the petrol we could scrape together for the purpose. Divisional Headquarters followed on through Villach, past the Woerter-see and so on to Klagenfurt. I kept with the armoured cars as far as Klagenfurt but they went straight on towards Vienna meeting the Russians at Judenburg. I think the Russians were somewhat taken aback by the speed of these cars and the distance they covered in the short time available. It was just after we had passed the Woerter-see that I caught up with Regimental Headquarters and I was having a word with the Commanding Officer, Andrew Horsbrugh Porter, when I was suddenly surrounded by a mass of excited soldiery in ill-fitting battle dress and very long hair. They appeared to be unarmed. For a moment I wondered how such a situation could arise and where these people had come from, but when I heard them speaking there was no doubt that they were New Zealanders and that we had overrun a prisoner-of-war camp in which they had been, in some cases, for four years having been captured for the most part either in Greece or Crete.

When I went home that summer of 1945 for a short leave I visited the Royal Overseas League Club and a New Zealander came up to me, having recognised the Divisional Sign on my shoulder, and introduced himself. He had been one of the men I met on that hot and dusty morning in Austria and he never would forget that day when he and others saw that cloud of dust coming up from the west, with the certainty that, after all they would be released by the British and not the Russians. They could not believe their luck, hence the excitement.

I went on into Klagenfurt and took the surrender of the German Commander (General von Loehr). I was soon joined by the Riflemen and the Derbyshire Yeomanry. In the matter of this surrender we had special instructions regarding the SS, otherwise the mass of prisoners were merely herded into areas without any special precautions.

Klagenfurt is situated near to the Loibl Pass check from Austria into Yugoslavia and it was through this pass that the German forces operating against Tito were in the process of withdrawing. I went down to the south of the town to find out what the situation was. The Commanding Officer of a Rifle Brigade Battalion told me that he was in the process of coming to some arrangement with the German Commander when a force of Yugoslavs appeared and insisted that they alone should take this surrender, and would the British be so good as to withdraw. We had no instructions on such a matter and it was really not a matter of major importance who took the surrender so long as it was achieved. This Yugoslav force, in some incredible way, had a troop of light Honey tanks. These tanks obviously had prestige value, but had ceased to have real significance in an armoured engagement as their armour was thin and their guns feeble. In fact they were obsolescent. The Riflemen withdrew to a distance and were reinforced by a squadron of the Derbyshire Yeomanry.

Quite what happened in the opening exchanges of fire we never discovered, but at an early stage all the Honey tanks were destroyed and the Yugoslavs retired somewhat precipitously. We then met the German Commander, a type I knew only too well and highly professional, with whom the surrender was speedily effected. The manner of their surrender was simple: they moved through us, throwing their personal weapons into a field we indicated and parking their tanks, which were Mark IVs, formidable even at that late stage in the War, in a field beyond.

The piles of weapons, equipment, transport and armoured vehicles assumed enormous proportions and one could not help thinking of the futility of it all. When this was in the process of being executed I suddenly realised that those Mark IVs constituted something of a threat. Each was armed with a 75mm gun and were quite a match for the Shermans of the Derbyshire Yeomanry. It was not unimportant that these tanks should be neutralised before they got into the wrong hands. I had a word with the Squadron Commander of the Yeomanry and suggested that at long last the opportunity presented itself to test the penetrative qualities of our tank ammunition. A gleam came into his eyes and I departed. Later in the day, I heard, with relief, that the destructive powers of our tank guns, admittedly at the relatively short range of 300 yards, had been most reassuring. What mattered was that these Mark IVs were no longer operational, having been reduced to shells. The same treatment was also meted out to some 88s (artillery) which were too effective to be allowed to survive. It would have been maddening to see these weapons turned against us, which could well have happened. When I got back up the hill I heard the thudding of guns and later a plume of smoke followed. That was the end of the Mark IVs but not the end of the story. The Yugoslavs returned later and, as expected, claimed all the captured weapons. They were highly indignant when they saw the condition of the tanks and guns. They did not leave the matter there and for some weeks complaints trickled back from our own Foreign Office enquiring into the circumstances of this affair. Nothing, however, could restore the tanks and guns into any form of serviceability and the debate finally petered out for want of purpose.

Coming down from the north-east we took another surrender, and it took the form of a Cossack Corps, all mounted on horses, with horse-drawn guns and transport, and with mounted bands at intervals down a seemingly endless column. The Corps was almost entirely officered by Germans, and it was therefore a straightforward affair to arrange places where all arms would be dumped, and the areas into which the troops should move, dispose of their horses and pass into captivity. The morale of this force was amazingly high and they frequently burst out into some of their National songs. A few days later we received orders in respect of them, to the effect that by agreement between the 'High Contracting Powers', the whole Corps was to be marched to certain railway sidings and sent back to Russia. There was nothing in the orders requiring us to ensure that every officer and man was to be returned safely to Russia, and in any case no mention was made of the fate of the German officers. I sent for the senior German officers and read them my instructions.

[**Editor's Note:** This was written by 'Nap' Murray before the great controversy concerning the forced repatriation of Cossacks/Yugoslavs who fought for Germany, when Solzhenitsyn gave his interview with the BBC

Russian Service in 1974. At that time 'Nap' wrote to *The Times* repeating what he wrote in his memoirs, namely that he gave the Cossacks twenty-four hours' grace before closing the gates of their compound in contradiction to the orders he received from Army HQ. This action did not have the anticipated consequences he had hoped, with many of the Cossacks staying where they were. It doesn't detract, however, from the moral courage he displayed, then and earlier, in questioning orders that he thought were of dubious nature, e.g. Mark Clark's orders in northern Italy in 1944, Bullen-Smith's orders in Normandy, and earlier battle situations in North Africa and Sicily.

Some of the subsequent commentators who wrote books on this subject did not take on board the fact that he had been an Army interpreter speaking fluent German, and the fact that fewer prisoners were forcibly returned by the 6th Armoured Division than any other in the Eighth Army at that time.

It was not surprising that during the last years of his life he was invited to be present at the unveiling of the memorial by Angela Conner to these Cossacks, which stands in Thurloe Gardens, close to the V&A.

Later in the 1970s he said on the BBC television documentary *Prisoners of Yalta*:

Every man mattered and I refused to deal with captured troops en masse, allowing some 1,500 to escape. I gave them all the benefit of the doubt, but anyone who stayed behind after the twenty-four-hour warning stayed behind at their own risk.]

They obviously had expected something of the sort, but sat there with completely expressionless faces, and only a flicker passed over their faces when I said that the Staff would be down at midday the following day to make the necessary arrangements. I told the Staff that there was to be no move to the camps before midday and I then closed the conference.

The next day the German officers and some of the Cossacks had time to say goodbye and vanished. We made no attempt to trace them. At midday when we took over it was astonishing to see how many there were waiting to go back to their home country. We had been given the usual assurances that they would be fairly dealt with on their return, but it was difficult to believe that these promises would be kept. The men marched down to the sidings later in the day and in due course were herded into cattle trucks and steamed away to the east. There was a touching resignation on the faces of the men, caught up in events which had proved too much for them as they returned to Russia for whatever might befall them there. It was a sad end for them and we could only hope that their fate was not as bad as we feared it would be.

Gradually the political temperature perceptively dropped and we came to terms with the Yugoslavs. The soldiers were somewhat perplexed to find that our Ally was not as cooperative as they should be and sought instructions as to the action they should take against aggressive Yugoslav convoys or looting soldiers, or even the physical protection of the inhabitants against violence. It led to a powerful Order of the Day by Field Marshal Alexander, coupled with a personal telegram to President Tito. From then on we became more and more an Army of Occupation, with an increasing amount of time on our hands. Had we been asked what sort of recreation we would prefer when the War was over, we found all those things in abundance in Austria. On the Worter-see were speedboats and yachts, as many horses as we could possibly deal with, fishing, shooting, golf and tennis. There were a number of first-class hotels around the Worter-see, all of which were allotted to Regiments and Brigades as recreation hostels. Previously these had been used by the Germans as convalescent hotels and suited us admirably.

The temptations were enormous and some were not quite strong enough to resist the opportunity to make a little hay. The Army Commander, General Sir Richard McCreery, however, was quite ruthless in dealing with such as overstepped the mark. It is to be feared that this sort of thing happens 'even in the best regulated families'. Even in the matter of the distribution of sporting facilities there was a lack of responsibility and a determination to hold on to whatever came the way of a Regiment or individual as if it were an inalienable right. Many thought back to their frame of mind in later years and found it difficult to believe that they could have behaved as they did.

At the beginning of June a small parade was held in Klagenfurt at which some of us received American decorations. The Army Commander was invested with the Distinguished Service Cross and I with the Legion of Merit, Degree of Commander. In my citation, (read out with great solemnity), I felt laughter bubbling up within when I thought that as a result of conserving soldiers I was receiving this award. (The citation reads 'he displayed a great tactical skill in accomplishing his missions even at times when his command was unavoidably under strength . . .'.)

In June the Division started to change its shape. The first to go were the 1st Guards Brigade and this was a real wrench. They had fought with great distinction throughout the North African Campaign, the length of Italy and were in at the finish in Austria. The presence of such high-grade infantry in this famous Armoured Division was quite invaluable, and they proved their quality in every action they fought. There were two operations while I was in command which I thought were of outstanding merit. The first was the long-drawn-out defensive battle at Monte Battaglia where they gave much more than they got in almost indescribable conditions; the second was the crossing of the River Po at twenty-four hours' notice with a hastily collected gaggle of DUKWs and very little else. This latter operation required steady nerves and first-class planning, and in both they were not found wanting. The next to go were our Territorial Yeomanry regiments. The Lothian and Border Horse disappeared over to Milan, the Ayreshire Yeomanry was gradually run down and the Derbyshire Yeomanry started to get ready for a move to Egypt.

I managed to slip home at the end of July for a couple of weeks and I was actually in London for 'VJ' day. It was just a jaunt but it was nice to see the family again. My absence enabled Army Headquarters to get us out of the Schloss Tentschach and down to a comfortable house on the shore of the Worter-see. We did not stay there long as we were then ordered to move back to Padua. When we got back to Italy we went through the motions of training, but it was all a bit unrealistic.

We celebrated Christmas in style and in the middle of it I received an order to report back to London and the War Office to take up the appointment of Director of Personnel Services. I had no idea what the duties of this Directorate were except that it came under the Adjutant General. Before the year was out I was in a train travelling slowly across Italy, through France and so back home again. My travels were over for the time being. The 'purple patch' of 1945 was probably the most exciting and fulfilling year of the whole of my service.

Part 3

Generalship 1946–1989

Chapter Seventeen

The Victory Parade

The War Office was a very inflated affair at this time and was to continue to be so for some years owing to the continuation of National Service and considerable overseas commitments. I cannot say that I was looking forward to another spell there after an interval of only six years, but clearly there was a great deal to be learnt.

So it was back to the Staff with a vengeance, although I could hardly complain as I had had nearly four years in command in the field, covering the command of a Battalion, a Brigade and finally a Division. I could not help thinking how fortunate I had been in having served such a long apprenticeship in the Cameronians (Scottish Rifles). Perhaps twelve years as a subaltern was a bit on the long side, but the Regiment always gave younger officers plenty of scope and encouraged them to take on responsibilities much beyond their rank. There was the additional advantage that we were always encouraged to be outward-looking, out into the Army as a whole, out into the other services and to run for the Staff College. It was only when I met other Regiments that I realised how broad-minded our own senior officers were. The War meant that many of us were ready to take such chances that came our way and it provided opportunities on a considerable scale. Nevertheless it was interesting to reflect on the extent that chance affected one's career. First, getting command of a Battalion about to go overseas on Active Service, the chance wounding of a divisional commander giving me my Brigade, and finally becoming a Major General as a result of a grand piano sliding out of a lorry and incapacitating another.

My new appointment carried with it four major responsibilities, namely Discipline, Ceremonial, Dress and Pay. It then emerged that it had been decided to appoint a Director who had had battle experience as being more likely to be in tune with the soldier. This proved to be another instance of luck as I was still only a substantive Major, halfway down the list of Majors in the Queen's Own Cameron Highlanders, but this appointment, which carried with it the rank of Major General, enabled me to retain my rank until, with the passage of time, I picked my way forward in substantive rank. It meant that whilst other officers in the higher ranks were required to drop one or possibly two ranks when the War was over, I never did so and remained a General for the rest of my career, a total period of seventeen years.

My predecessor was Major General Gurney and he introduced me to the work. Thereafter we saw extraordinarily little of each other. Although problems connected with discipline, ceremonial, pay and dress jostled their way onto my table, it was the organisation of the Victory March which took first place in the first few weeks. The overall responsibility for public parades of this sort rests with the Home Secretary; in 1946 this was Mr Chuter Ede, and a splendid Chairman he proved to be. His stories relating to the vicissitudes in the life of a schoolmaster were excruciatingly funny, but they were never allowed to impede the work in hand. At the first meeting, held in the Cabinet Office, Mr Ede outlined the requirement. It was to be held in June and all our Allies would be represented on it, all three services, the Dominions and Colonies, Civil Defence Workers, the Women's Services and all vital war workers including the miners. He added that it was the wish of the Prime Minister, Mr Attlee, that the march should take place in the blitzed areas in the East End. Armed with this we withdrew back to Eaton Square to provide an outline plan. There were two Brigadiers working under me: Brigadier George Bradshaw, who was responsible for ceremonial matters and the other Brigadier George Burns who looked after the disciplinary side. We searched through the War Office files to find a precedent from the First World War Victory March but all we found was a photograph of King George V standing on a saluting base outside Buckingham Palace. In a way perhaps we were fortunate not to be bothered with precedent because we would certainly have a considerable number of mechanised vehicles in the parade, whereas the 1919 parade was entirely marching personnel.

When it came to routes it became obvious that Infantry could not be called upon to march for hours around the East End of London, so we got out of the difficulty by having two columns, with a mechanised column going all the way around the East End and a marching column which would not have to march more than 8 or 9 miles on an inner circle embracing Oxford Street, Charing Cross Road, the Embankment, Parliament Square, Whitehall, the Mall and so back to Kensington Gardens. It would take two or three hours and was quite enough.

All went well until we had to explain where the marshalling areas would be and the time they would have to be set up; as we had troops coming in from all over the world two camps were needed for two months or more. When one or two of the members of the Committee heard this they were most indignant – surely, they said, a few days was all that was necessary and in any case those taking part could be herded off into air-raid shelters on the outskirts of London. The debate raged for a considerable time and Mr Ede was able to keep the temperature down in the most remarkable way. Gradually they accepted the concept that we should have to ensure that contingents from overseas, including our Allies, would expect to stay in the country for some time, in order to make the journey worthwhile. The debate ended with us having our way, provided, in the case of Kensington Gardens, that the children continued to have access to the Round Pond.

It was only later that I discovered that one of our most outspoken critics himself lived in Millionaires' Row and had a personal interest in the outcome of this debate. Just as we had cleared this up Mr Ede said that it was the Prime Minister's wish that the Chiefs of Staff should be in the march and we agreed that they and the 'Supremos' should travel in separate cars ahead of the mechanised column.

Detailed planning reached the stage for the Home Secretary to take the whole plan to Buckingham Palace for the approval of the King. In the plan we had arranged for the King, the Queen and the two princesses to drive out of Buckingham Palace, presumably in an open landau, to the saluting base. The King at once took exception to this arrangement and allegedly said to Mr Ede, 'I do not know who made this suggestion, but as I have not ridden around my capital since my coronation, I intend to do so on this occasion.

Tell those responsible that I will drive ahead of the Marching Column.' A deputation from the Home Office duly arrived at Eaton Square to discuss the implication of this. We had already planned for three columns and here was a fourth. Actually it was rather fun to think that the King was prepared to take a decision of this sort, and it only remained to solve it.

We decided that we would have to reshape the whole plan. Then we found that the King would have to wait on the saluting base for about twenty minutes before the mechanised column put in an appearance and we filled this in by arranging for the Massed Pipe Bands of the 51st Highland and the 52nd Lowland Divisions to play up and down the Mall.

The Home Office delegation withdrew, much relieved, reported back to Buckingham Palace, secured the approval of the King and we were in the clear. In the process we had to speed up the column containing the Chiefs of Staff to make sure that they got to the saluting base before the King did. There was no doubt in my mind that this alteration vastly improved the whole affair and the close look that thousands had of the Royal Family pretty well stole the show. The sight of this excellent family sitting together in an open carriage, a family that had shared all the dangers of a six-year war, was very moving.

The way now seemed clear to hand over the whole plan to the General Officer Commanding London District, General Sir Henry Lloyd, under whose command all the troops on parade would be, and we were in the process of doing so when there came a rumble from the Admiralty. In the Chiefs of Staff group were six individuals. These were the three Chiefs of Staff, Alanbrooke, Cunningham and Portal; the other three were Alexander, Mountbatten and Wilson. We had managed to procure three or four open cars and the plan was that each car should contain two of these. The rumble from the Admiralty stemmed from the First Sea Lord, who considered that, as the Chiefs of Staff had been forged into a highly successful team, they should travel around the mechanised route in the same vehicle. Of course this would unbalance the party. But Lord Cunningham was not to be put off by this, took the question to the Chiefs of Staff Committee at their next meeting and I got a peremptory order to carry out his request. Then a real chase started, because we had to have an open car wide enough to take three sizeable officers of high rank. During the war no cars were made of the type we wanted, preferably a Rolls-Royce, and we had to hawk around individual owners to see what could be found. We finally found a Rolls-Royce, which had a roof, folded up partially at the back, but which left the cab enclosed. As it was the only one we could get, it meant that the situation was going to arise which I had wanted to avoid, whereby one officer would have to drive around the route by himself. I sought an interview with Alanbrooke to see if it would be possible to include a seventh VIP to keep the party balanced. He stared at me and said, 'Certainly not, things are difficult enough as they are, without any further complications.'

On the day, the three Chiefs of Staff piled into the first car, the Rolls, which was a pretty tight squeeze. Then Alexander and Mountbatten very quickly got into the second leaving 'Jumbo' Wilson to roll along in solitary state in the third car creating the very situation I had hoped to avoid.

The mechanised column started off from Regents Park on its long drive through the East End of London preceded by the Chiefs of Staff. At much the same time the Royal Family set out from the Palace at the trot, went up Constitution Hill, Park Lane then to Marble Arch before turning off down Oxford Street, being followed by the marching column streaming out of Hyde Park. By 10 o'clock the whole machine was in motion. I had no part to play in the parade myself but managed to get a seat in a window in the War Office with one of my nephews.

The march past began at about 11 o'clock and lasted an hour, being concluded by a fly past of aircraft, which was spoilt as the weather finally broke and the rain came down. I turned away from the window with a sigh of relief that it all seemed to have passed off successfully. Organisers on this sort of occasion have very little to win, but a great deal to lose. It was a very moving spectacle, but somehow it seemed to be dated and its like will not, I believe, be seen again.

A week or so later a Government reception was held at Hampton Court at which the King and Queen were to be present and to which all those who had been concerned with the Victory celebrations were invited. At a certain stage in the evening some of us were presented and when my turn came, there was a twinkle in the King's eye as he turned to the Queen and, moving his hands across each other, said, 'Oh! This is the chap who went like this with the Victory March.' We all laughed and I passed on to make room for the others. I could not tell him how much the Victory March owed to the change of plan he called for.

It was while all this planning was going forward that I began seriously to wonder whether the time might not be ripe to retire. On one hand I was still only a substantive Major and therefore could not hope to get much of a pension, but against that I was still only in my early forties and probably employable. It was about this time that I once again met General Sir John Crocker, then GOC-in-C Southern Command. He felt very strongly that there were too many restless officers about at this time contemplating retirement, and he was concerned that there might be a run-out, which the Army could not afford and tried to dissuade as many as he could from going. So I thought over the situation as the months went past and finally put aside all thoughts of retiring, although as it happened, it was much easier for officers retiring from the Army to get good employment in the 1940s.

While the Victory March was being planned we had quite a lot of trouble from discontented soldiers. Under my Department came all the military prisons and detention barracks, and through our hands passed all the papers to do with courts martial. The Judge Advocate General was Sir Henry MacGeagh and he was always most helpful when we found ourselves in difficulties, as we often did. The initial unrest was to do with releases from the forces. An excellent scheme had been drawn up in which length of service and age were used in order to assess the group into which a man would be placed in deciding when he would be finally released; a few had been released before the end of 1945, but thereafter the groups tended to get bigger and the tempo slowed down a bit. The troops knew which groups they were in, but were disappointed at the slowing-down process. There were some disturbances abroad, particularly in India and the Middle East, and such was the atmosphere in the House of Commons in 1946 that Members started to refer to 'strikes' in the services; it was only when we had a mutiny on our hands that they suddenly realised that by using such words in relation to the Armed Forces they were playing with fire.

The first real mutiny took place in the Far East and had nothing to do with demobilisation. It was more a question of bad man management. There was a Parachute Battalion stationed in Malaya having recently returned from active service in the Dutch East Indies. The Battalion went into a camp which was located by the sea, and which was not as well provided for as might have been wished. The Commanding Officer decided that the time had come to go over straight away to a peacetime footing, which entailed a number of restrictions. Amongst the latter was an order that lance corporals would not go out with soldiers when off duty. One evening the Orderly Officer went down to the Canteen to see that all was well there and because there was nothing unusual to be noted at all the officer left the Canteen and returned to the officers' lines. A short time after this the lights in the Canteen suddenly went out and a voice came out of the darkness saying, 'Are you all ready to stand by what we agreed upon?' This was greeted by some shouts of 'Yes', whistles and catcalls. Then just as suddenly all the lights went on again.

The following morning what appeared to be the greater part of the Battalion was loitering about on the sea wall refusing to do duty. Whatever the shortcomings of the Commanding Officer might have been up to this point, he now acted with commendable speed. He went down to the sea wall and ordered everybody to go into the Dining Hall where he would address them. They did as they were told and he talked to them. His speech was conciliatory but firm. He realised something had gone wrong and they would have to put it right. On the other hand collective insubordination was mutiny and they were in a state of mutiny at that moment. His speech was met in stony silence, and nobody moved or spoke. The Commanding Officer then moved forward and spoke to two or three men in the front row and asked them what the trouble was. One of them piped up and explained how difficult it was to get ready for morning inspections owing to the mud. One said that there were not enough water points in the camp and washing and shaving were sometimes almost impossible, when there was a shout from the back, 'Come on out all of you, we are getting nowhere.' Upon this the whole assembly jumped to its feet, poured out through the door and back to the sea wall.

There was nothing more to be done except to report the incident to higher command. Brigade Headquarters at once paraded a

Battalion of infantry, which was marched down to the camp, and all the mutineers were put under close arrest.

A General Court Martial was ordered, the President being a Brigadier. We were kept informed of events as they unfolded, but at this stage could not intervene. It created a considerable amount of public concern, as the Parachutists were held in very high regard. Questions were raised in the House. I went across once or twice to see the Secretary of State for War, who was Mr Lawson. He came from Durham and was particularly concerned regarding the sort of sentences which could be meted out. I could only advise that the War Office had considerable powers, which could be used in mitigation if the circumstances warranted it.

The trial was a mass trial and there were 238 accused. The case for the prosecution was a fairly straightforward affair, as the circumstances were hardly in dispute, although it was important to identify each man as being concerned in the mutiny.

The defence then opened and one after another, the men went into the witness box and gave their evidence. Each man gave an individual account of his part in the proceedings, was cross-examined by the Prosecuting Counsel and then was replaced by the next man to take his stand. Some fifteen cases were tried in this way with well over 200 to come, when the Defending Counsel rose to his feet and addressed the Court. 'If the Court was prepared to try the men in batches, owing to the great length of time which would be required if each man gave evidence personally, it would considerably shorten the proceedings.' The thought of hearing another 200 witnesses was a little daunting and the Judge Advocate, who sat in with them, said that from a legal point of view there was no objection to this procedure.

Later the trial recommenced and the proceedings came to a conclusion remarkably quickly. We were rather surprised to receive a cable informing us that the trials had been completed and that a Staff officer was flying home with the papers. The staff officer arrived and was at once taken over to the Judge Advocate General who had decided that he would see the papers himself without further delay. The following morning I had an urgent telephone call from Sir Henry MacGeagh informing me that he would be forced to advise the Secretary of State to quash the whole proceedings. This was something we had not expected, but within twenty-four hours we had in front of us the detailed opinion and recommendations of the Judge Advocate General. His main reason for making the recommendation to quash the proceedings was that the men in the batches on trial, who were not the spokesmen, had been deprived of the basic right of all British citizens to speak in their own defence. A closer examination of the papers also revealed that when the men had been tried individually there was a considerable divergence in the degree of guilt and the punishments awarded. There was nothing for it but to recommend to the Secretary of State to quash the whole proceedings, which he was more than happy to do.

There were other excitements of a similar nature, including the refusal of men to embark for service overseas, to occupy some of our time in 1946, but these were dwarfed by the revolt which took place at the detention barracks in Aldershot. Our difficulty was that we held a great number of men with long criminal records, who had had no intention of fighting in the War. These men assumed, wrongly, that there would be an amnesty as soon as the War was over to enable them to be released to follow their normal pursuits. Superimposed on them were men who had committed military offences, but who were in no sense of the word criminals. In the early months of 1946 we were in the process of separating the sheep from the goats, but the explosion in Aldershot upset our plans.

At a later stage in the mutiny the Commander-in-Chief of the Southern Command, General Sir John Crocker arrived at Aldershot. He spoke to some of the officers who were in charge of the containing operation, ordered the doors to be opened and went inside. His imperturbability and calmness seemed somehow to produce a complete silence. He told them that no purpose could be served by continuing in a state of revolt and that the sooner the mutineers surrendered the better. He promised that their grievances would be looked into and where possible remedies applied. When he finished a great iron stove came hurtling down from above which only missed him by a narrow margin, but there was a howl of rage from some of the men above who dealt with the thrower in a way which neutralised him for the rest of the time. It helped to cool the temperature and within an hour the whole lot had been paraded outside and marched off to pastures new. This revolt was a blessing in disguise. The 'Aldershot Glass House' could now be written off forever, and a later study of conditions within these establishments finally brought them into line with modern thinking on the subject.

The conditions of service in the Navy, Army and Air Force were widely different and the Treasury moved heaven and earth to bring them all into line. One particular concession consequent was free leave travel, a purely wartime innovation which the Treasury was determined to eliminate altogether. In 1946, just before I left the War Office, Mr Emanuel Shinwell became Secretary of State for War. The latter had been in the Ministry of Fuel and Power and carried far more guns than his predecessors. After being duly briefed he set out for the Chancellor's meeting, and the item on the agenda was reached which called for the reduction of free leave passes from three to two. Mr Shinwell thereupon exploded, banged the table and said, 'You cannot do it, man. What do you think the Army will say when a concession is taken away from them as soon as I arrive? You cannot do it.' What we liked about Mr Shinwell was his readiness to fight our battles, which he did, completely identifying himself with our problems.

It was early 1947 that I was informed I had been selected to take over command of the 1st Division in Palestine from General Sir Richard Gale, whom I had last seen in the bridgehead near Caen three years before. The War Office grinds slow but exceeding sure, and is an impressive machine if allowed to work normally. Only in one direction did I find matters irksome and that was when some officer or another would arrive in the War Office with a fixation on some particular subject and would flog it to death. One could see them from a long way off and when a given file turned up more frequently than it should it was getting into the 'worrying' phase. When a file got into this condition I always put it under the carpet. After a couple of days my Private Secretary, the long-suffering Mr Price, would come in, look through the trays of files, have a look in the cupboards and depart. Later he would come in and say that a certain file was missing, that it had been marked to us, but he could not find it anywhere. I invited him to search anywhere he liked, and this he did. A few days later there might be another spasm of searching and then the hunt would die down. At this stage the time was ripe for incineration and after the clerks had retired for the night into the fire it went and that was the end of it. Really quite an expeditious method of bowling skittles over.

I made my bow at the end of September 1947 and thereafter only entered the War Office on business, and normally by invitation. At the beginning of December I went along to the Victoria Terminus in order to fly out to Cairo, on my way to Palestine and the 1st Division.

Chapter Eighteen

Palestine and the Mediterranean

The actual move to Egypt and Palestine had a humorous side. While waiting to be called forward at the Victoria Air Terminus I found a copy of Carola Oman's book on Nelson on the bookstall and the temptation to buy it was too strong for me when an announcement was made that the flight had been postponed but that arrangements were being made to put us all up at a nearby hotel. Although the air company paid for the hotel bill, there were some additional expenses, which suddenly left me short of cash. We took off the following morning in good time and that evening arrived in Cairo. Here again I had to spend the night, but managed to get a railway warrant to take me up to Ismailia. I gave the porter at the Cairo railway station all the money that remained and although one can never give an Egyptian porter enough, I think his expression of disapproval on this occasion had some substance. I arrived at Ismailia at the end of the morning and another porter picked up the bags and took them.

Luckily I found a car waiting for me to take me down the road to GHQ Middle East, which was located at Fayid near the Great Bitter Lake. The Headquarters at Fayid had sprung out of the desert near the Great Bitter Lake when we finally evacuated Cairo after the War. The Mess was very comfortable and I at once made arrangements for the trip to Palestine. The railway was still in at the end of 1947, but there were a number of light aircraft available at Fayid; one was booked to fly me up to Lydda the following morning and a telegram was sent to HQ 1st Division announcing the probable time of my arrival. In the early afternoon, however, a car arrived with an ADC and I was taken off to spend the night with the Commander-in-Chief, General Sir John Crocker, who had gone out some months before on the retirement of General Sir Miles Dempsey.

The timing of my appearance was interesting, as only a few days before the Attlee Government had announced its intention of relinquishing the Mandate the following May. This meant that all the problems to do with British troops in Palestine would take on a completely different complexion. The following morning I went out to the airfield and flew off up over the Sinai Peninsula. These light aircraft normally fly very low and so it was fun to retrace the route we had followed in 1930 when we went on that tour in a Vickers Vimy bomber.

I landed at Lydda at about midday and then realised that it was just five years since I had passed that way in an ambulance on my way to Suez and possibly South Africa. I was met by Robin Leigh Pemberton travelling in the Straight 8 Horch, which the 6th Armoured Division had 'acquired' in Austria two years or more before. The 6th Armoured Division by this time had ceased to exist and had been replaced by the 1st, although it came to life again two or three years later when the Russians started creating problems in Europe. The car had been passed on to the 1st Division and it was delightful to be greeted by this old relic. We drove on up the road to the Headquarters at Tel Levinsky. Fighting between Jews and Arabs had not yet broken out, but the decks were already being cleared against the day of our departure. Richard Gale was going on down to Egypt to become GOC British Troops. All camps were fortresses, including our own, which we shared with an Infantry battalion. There was a barbed-wire fence all around which was patrolled and the entrance was completely wired in with a dug-in post within 30 yards covering it with fire. At this stage we suffered few raids, they were to come later.

I believe that the decision of the British Government to pull out was taken in the hope that it would force both sides to get together and hammer out a solution. This hope was speedily dispelled with Jews and Arabs alike prepared to make no concessions. The Arabs in Palestine at this time numbered about a million and a quarter, as against half a million Jews, and they were convinced that with such superiority they were bound to have their way. Even at this stage they were determined to drive every Jew into the Mediterranean and said so in the most forceful language imaginable.

The British Government was having a particularly difficult task in holding the ring by denying the thousands of Jewish immigrants, mostly from Europe, entry into the country in the face of strong pressure from the United States. This meant that the 6th Airborne Division up in the north was very largely deployed to prevent illegal entries by ship. The Royal Navy intercepted these ships and when caught they were escorted across to Cyprus and the passengers offloaded there. Some, however, were turned back to their ports of origin and the despair which must have seized them when they found themselves travelling west again must have been dreadful. Nevertheless it was not very funny to see these refugees run up the Union Jack with an enormous swastika painted on it. At this time one could not help but sympathise with these people. This sympathy, however, tended to become weaker with the passage of time when their efforts to create a Jewish state were deemed to justify almost any measure.

Our main responsibility was the maintenance of law and order as long as we continued to hold the Mandate and to evacuate the country when the time came with a minimum loss. The future of Palestine remained a political question, which was not the business of soldiers. It was in the hills that the Arabs seemed most secure, particularly as there they would expect support from Jordan. The Jews were initially more concerned with the coastal plain and the access it gave to the sea. Arms were being smuggled in on quite a scale in spite of all attempts to hold it in check. Both sides were short of weapons of all natures but especially heavy weapons and armour, which were virtually non-existent. In all this it was obvious that the Arabs were completely unorganised, whereas with the Jews it was quite otherwise. I remembered that there had been a Jewish brigade in Italy during the last year of the War which had been equipped and trained by ourselves. Based on the experience they gained over a two- or three-year period during the War they were busily engaged in creating a small field army. They had even gone as far as creating a battle school near Nathaniah. This battle school was within 2 or 3 miles of our own Divisional Battle School and no doubt a certain amount of liaison took place, as ours was commanded by an officer in the Lincolnshire Regiment and the Jewish commander had also served in that Regiment during the War. The Jewish extremists gradually stepped up their efforts to get weapons and ammunition and it was a help to our people in

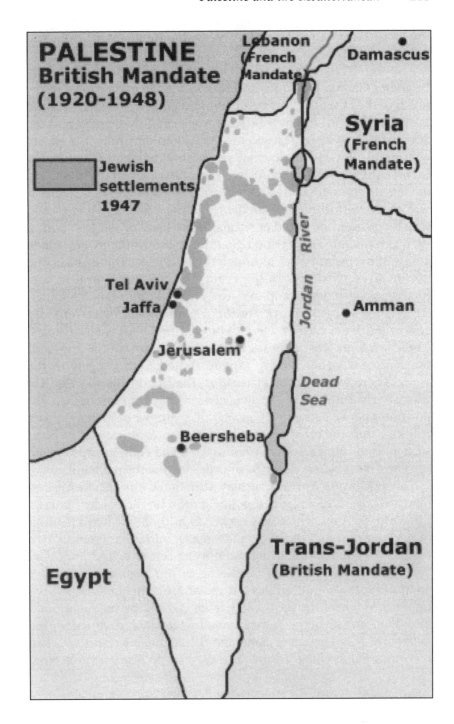

the battle school to be tipped off when the Irgun Zwei Leumi had a raid in mind.

The 1st Division included the 1st Guards Brigade, under Brigadier George Johnston, and was located in open camps in the north of the Divisional area and adjoining that of the 6th Airborne Division. The 3rd Infantry Brigade was near Tel Levinsky and the 2nd Brigade was in Jerusalem itself, coming under the direct command of GHQ Palestine, the Commander-in-Chief being Lieutenant General Sir Gordon MacMillan of MacMillan. All movement from now onwards was an operation of war, whether it was to do with the roads or the railways. I had my own escort, which consisted of a soldier sitting in the back of the Jeep with a Bren gun mounted on a tripod. So far as I know nobody ever made a pass at me personally,* although there were occasions when one got involved in affrays in the road. The road to Jerusalem was finally provided with stand-in patrols from the anti-tank regiment. Ambushes became more frequent and mines electronically controlled from nearby were exploded under passing vehicles. These incidents were almost exclusively the work of the Jews and the sympathy of the soldier rapidly shifted from the Jew to the Arab. There were two main reasons, the first being that the Jew was utterly ruthless in the measures he took to strengthen his position and we suffered a considerable number of casualties as a result of this; the other reason was that the Arab seemed to be at such a disadvantage both in organisation and equipment, so much so that a few soldiers deserted in order to give them a hand.

The Jews were apt to overplay their hands as their successes increased. We had a fortified police station on the border between Jaffa and Tel Aviv, which was known as Jaffoon. We had a platoon of infantry in it and the station acted as a buffer between the two towns, although all the firing came from Tel Aviv. The Jews then commenced some systematic sniping of our post and we lost a couple of men. We solved this particular problem quite simply. We established where the shots came from and during the night put a bazooka into one of the houses, camouflaged it, and waited for the next shot. Sure enough it came and the bazooka's retort wrecked the room from which it came and we had no more trouble from

---

* Nevertheless Mentioned in Despatches at this time.

that quarter. Jewish propaganda was very ably handled and much of it we found highly diverting, so little had it to do with reality.

Although all camps were 'fortified' it was certain that, if you dropped your guard at all, advantage would be taken of it. And indeed, on one occasion, a Regiment was surprised. Their camp was overlooked by a high water tower, from which a continuous and close watch of the camp could be maintained. One morning, at about 7 a.m., a small convoy of vehicles moved down the road towards the entrance, the leading vehicle belonging to the Palestine Police Force and containing men dressed in Palestinian policemen's uniform. The leading vehicle stopped, a man got out and before the sentry realised what was afoot found a pistol shoved into the pit of his stomach and told to stay where he was. A party then descended from the vehicle, moved towards the guardroom, made them face downwards on the floor and forced the safe. The rest of the convoy then drove in. Men poured out of the trucks, held up the two men in the armoury and started straight away to load weapons of every sort into the lorries as fast as they could. It happened that the Orderly Room was not far away, and the Regimental Sergeant Major went out to see what was going on, to be greeted with a round of Tommy-gun fire. He threw himself to the ground and shouted, 'We are being raided.' The Commanding Officer took the situation in at a glance and realised that his only hope of thwarting the raiders was to get across the road and summon help. He did so, was shot down in the middle of the road and died instantly. The raiding party vanished as quickly as they had come, but the richer by at least 200 rifles. It was the worst raid we had, but it was typical of many other attempts.

General MacMillan decided that his mission was to ensure the evacuation of all troops and stores without undue loss of life or material. In his own words, he did not wish to declare war on either side. It gave the Jews rather more scope than they could otherwise have hoped for and, when an Arab village was destroyed, the massacre of its inhabitants went unpunished. The Arabs were always needling away, but for the most part left us alone. We were fair game so far as the Jews were concerned.

As spring approached, guerrillas from Jordan, Syria and Iraq started to trickle into Palestine, but they operated in small groups and appeared to have no higher organisation. An ugly situation developed in Jerusalem where some renegade Palestine policemen blew up a building there and escaped. It caused many casualties and the troops had a very difficult time with the Jews for some days until the perpetrators were named.

Matters came to a head in Haifa towards the end of March and the beginning of April. The difficulty in Haifa was that the Arab and Jewish communities there were intermingled and affrays were constantly occurring, causing a number of casualties including quite a few British. The local Jewish commander called upon the GOC of the 6th Airborne Division and suggested that it was in the best interests of all concerned if the Jews and Arabs had a 'show-down', and what did he think about it? The General thought it over and sent for the Arab leader, put the proposition to him and awaited his reactions. Needless to say, the Arab, being an Arab, accepted the challenge with alacrity, being well satisfied that numbers would settle the whole thing in their favour. It only remained to get the three parties together and to agree upon procedure.

The first requirement was that the British should evacuate their posts in the town and withdraw to the periphery where they could ensure that there was no interference from outside. Then the time and date when the seconds would leave the ring and the referee, the General, could call 'Time'.

If there had existed any doubts regarding Jewish organisation and ability these were speedily dispelled. Within an hour the Arabs were pouring out of the town and down to the quayside, prepared to pay astronomical sums to their fellow Muslims to ferry them over the bay to the safety of Acre. There was a great outcry at home suggesting that the Arabs had been 'sacrificed', and fuel was added to the fire when it was alleged that the British handicapped the Arabs by holding the ring and thus preventing an unknown number of Arab irregulars joining in the fray. It all died down after a time, but the fact remained that Haifa was Jewish from that time onwards. Perhaps it was unwise of the General to abdicate responsibility, which was his of maintaining law and order; thereafter he remained only nominally in control.

There was quite a lot of correspondence in *The Times* regarding the circumstances, which led the Arabs to flee from Palestine. One group contended that the Arabs were forced out by Jewish terrorism, and the other group argued that the Arabs had with-drawn on instructions from their own leaders. I can only speak for the southern half of Palestine, where the 1st Division was deployed, and there is no doubt that the Jews pursued a systematic policy of terrorism. They moved about at night and with the aid of a few mortars shelled villages, ensuring their immediate evacuation. The pattern was too obvious for it not to have been part of the overall plan.

It reached a climax in the middle of April when the Jews turned their attention to Jaffa. This problem was utterly dissimilar from that of Haifa in that the two communities lived quite separately, the Arabs in Jaffa and the Jews in Tel Aviv. The firing from Tel Aviv was stepped up and for the first time the Haganah took part. I was forced to deploy some tanks in the vicinity of Jaffoon, and they were very effective in neutralising an attempt to penetrate into Jaffa itself. There was a pause after this setback, and then the Jewish mortars started up and commenced a systematic bombard-ment of Jaffa. I sent for the Liaison Officer we had with the Jews in Tel Aviv, who was Mr Ben Gurion Junior. I told him that the mortaring would have to stop as there was no fire coming back, and the action was purely provocative. He was dressed in the equiv-alent of battledress except that he wore very short shorts and looked very businesslike in the military sense of the word. He was somewhat evasive and said that he could not give orders, although he would try and see what could be done, and then departed. It was soon obvious that he would do very little about it, so I ordered the CRA of the Division, William Stirling, to deploy a battery of 25-pounders in the vicinity of Sarafand and to be prepared to shell Tel Aviv. We had a look at the map of Tel Aviv and agreed which were the most likely mortar sites. There was a good OP in Jaffoon and within an hour the Gunners reported that they were ready to fire. In the meantime there had been no slackening of the mortar fire, so I gave the order for five rounds gunfire and this was later repeated. The effect was electric, and all mortar-firing ceased. There was a long pause and then in came Mr Ben Gurion with the astonishing request that they wanted a truce. He looked a little distressed and was very sooty which made me wonder where he had been when the shelling took place. I explained that I was responsible for law and order and could not very well share it with anybody else. So long as they continued to fire on Jaffa, we would continue to shell Tel Aviv and it was as simple as that. 'Oh,' he said, 'I don't think they will accept that.' And I could only say that the choice was entirely up to them and no other conditions would be acceptable.

It must have been most unpleasant to experience being shelled in the confined space of a town and it certainly had the desired effect and there was no more mortaring at all. Nevertheless, the Jews achieved their aim, which was the evacuation of Jaffa by all the Arabs in it. They knew that so long as we remained there was some hope of survival, but not afterwards.

Early the next morning we heard that an exodus was taking place, and we went up the road to see what the form was.

Some distance from the town we started to move through a stream of Arabs of both sexes, men, women and children, mostly on foot, but some in cars and lorries, all moving desperately towards the south away from it all. All conditions of people were there from well-dressed women carrying their handbags and wearing high-heeled shoes, down to the poorer classes and all had fear in their eyes. No Arab leader had anything to do with this mass evacuation, because these people were desperate and actuated by the one motive of placing as great a distance between themselves and Jaffa as they could.

As the day wore on it became increasingly obvious that we could not leave Jaffa unprotected and we put some troops into the town. Jaffa was now a city of the dead, as if the Pied Piper had been that way and swept everybody into oblivion. This was a town which had previously contained 30,000 inhabitants, and now it was empty. Doors of houses were wide open showing interiors depicting panic departures, with food still on the table and fires burning. Shops full of wares of all description were waiting for somebody to come along and help themselves. The Jews occupied Jaffa at their leisure and the previous citizens departed for the Gaza Strip where they are to this day.

Most of us arrived in Palestine with considerable sympathy for the Jews and their ambitions, after the terrible experiences so many of them had had during the War at the hands of Hitler. Nevertheless it became increasingly apparent that, in their desperation, they were utterly ruthless in the matter of creating the Jewish

State and their methods approximated to those from which they had themselves fled. They had no mercy on the Arabs and brushed aside their claims to equal rights contemptuously. From the end of the War onwards, whether we were holding the Mandate, or in the process of giving it up, their policy was based on the use of terrorism as a political weapon.

There were one or two lighter aspects of life at this time. The Second-in-Command Mediterranean was Vice Admiral Sir Thomas Troubridge, the last of the line of the distinguished Admirals that family produced. He came in at Haifa, flew down to Ramallah, was met by General MacMillan and went on down to Jerusalem by road. There was an area on the road which was disputed territory and on this occasion there was an action in progress between the Jews and Arabs, and a certain number of mortar bombs fell nearby. The General apologised for this discourtesy, but the retort came back, 'I heard only nine bombs go off and I am entitled, as a Vice Admiral, to fifteen.'

On another day, when going up to Jerusalem, we ran through a Jewish convoy which was being shot up by Arabs. There was a burst of automatic fire which sprayed the side of the road without injuring us so we wirelessed back for the nearest patrol to come on up to sort it out. I then found that my driver was livid with rage and he rushed up to me and said, 'Look at this Sir.' I looked and saw that he had a lump of mud on his sleeve. Just before we left he deserted to the Jews, taking with him one of the Headquarters vehicles. The Jews were offering large sums of money in return for military vehicles or heavy equipment. In fact the Armoured Regiment lost a tank one night, when one of them was suddenly started up, charged through the wire and vanished complete with two troopers.

While all these alarums and excursions were in full play we were concerned with our re-deployment. The plans in 1948 visualised that the garrison of Egypt would be transferred to Cyrenaica and that a large station would be built there, consequently I arranged that our Headquarters should go on up to Tripoli.

In the meantime the 6th Airborne Division had gone home and the 1st Guards Brigade took their place in Haifa. The plan was for the rest of the Division to withdraw back into Egypt, moving across the roads of the Sinai Peninsula over a period of two or three days. We had some trouble with the troops when we left some of the camps, particularly Sarafand, where they tried to set light to the buildings rather than see it fall into the hands of the Jews as soon as we had departed. It was an indication of the feelings of the soldiers who are usually undemonstrative.

I flew out on the first day of the withdrawal in an Air OP which enabled me to coordinate the movement of the two columns towards the main crossing place over the canal at Kantara. It was a full day and was not made any easier when the Egyptian Air Force strafed some of our airfields. They did not do a great deal of damage, but made us a little more circumspect. We asked GHQ Middle East to invite them to lay off, as their map-reading appeared to be somewhat faulty. I spent the night at Rafah and flew off the following morning to supervise the last lap before preceding the columns to the Canal to ensure that arrangements for our reception were complete. It was now only thirty-one years since Allenby had conducted his Palestine Campaign and entered Jerusalem. I remembered how excited we were at the time and it certainly never occurred to me that I would be required to conduct a somewhat inglorious withdrawal in my lifetime.

On the second day of the withdrawal, an Egyptian army advancing from Egypt into Palestine passed our own. They were very unimpressive, being unkempt, dirty and, I thought, somewhat dispirited. They were not to realise it at the time, but in May 1948 they had the opportunity of liquidating the Jewish problem which has not come their way since.

I stayed in the Officers' Club in Moascar for a few days. It had been considerably expanded since I was last in that part of the world in 1930 and it was very comfortable. I went around seeing the various commanders then left for home in order to go on a Land/Air Course at Old Sarum. I did this not only for the interest of such courses, but also to get out of the way of the Staff who profit from the absence of the Commander on such occasions. George Collingwood happened to be on the same course. He was then a Brigadier commanding an area in Scotland.

While on the course I ran into a senior officer who asked me what I thought of the Palestinian affair. I replied that I would not have missed it for anything. He replied, 'Whose side were you on?' – I suppose one of the stupidest remarks ever made by one soldier to another. It was an experience to find oneself in really challenging circumstances, but it was made the more worthwhile to witness the outstanding quality of those National Servicemen, who had been for the most part too young for the War, conducting themselves in the midst of chaos and great danger like veterans. Most of them were children in 1940.

I flew back to Tripoli after a couple of weeks in England. While we were at home we heard the echoes of the Palestinian War. As expected the Jews soon dominated the coastal plain and the Egyptian Army made very little impression on them in spite of much superior equipment. On the other hand the Jews failed to make any real impression other than carrying out operations into the Judean Hills and Jerusalem remained in the hands of the Palestinian Arabs. This was largely due to the intervention of Jordan, with its artillery and tanks. At this time there were still a considerable number of British officers seconded to the Jordanian Army, and the Jordanian Artillery was handled by professionals. The Israeli Army suffered heavy casualties, sufficient to cause concern to their Government. There were some angry scenes in Parliament when some Jewish MPs accused the Government of intervening on the side of the Arabs in the Palestinian War. The Foreign Secretary refused to budge and said that we had commitments with our Allies, which it was essential to us to honour.

Tripoli and the Mediterranean

The transition from the semi-warlike nature of Palestine to the North African coast which had at the time few political problems, came as something of a relief. When the Eighth Army went through five years before they were followed by AMGOT, which stood for Allied Military Government of Occupied Territories, and these civilian organisations were still in being when we arrived. There was one covering Tripolitania and another in Libya, with its offices in Benghazi. These were staffed from our own Diplomatic and Colonial Services, and included district commissioners, engineers, and a complete administrative staff. In Tripoli we had, as the head of the Mission, Mr Travers Blackley. When it came to political matters, of course, Mr Blackley was the authority and his grasp of affairs in his domain was total. At about the time of our arrival there was a certain amount of unrest and Mr Blackley thought it would be a good idea to have a parade of the 1st Guards Brigade and a march past.

The Guardsmen, of course, were immaculately turned out in khaki drill and they made an impression on the local populace. This was the summer of 1948 and although this ex-Italian colony was hoping to get complete independence, matters were still in a state of uncertainty which was to be resolved before I left.

We launched all sorts of projects and had full support from GHQ at Fayid, particularly from the Engineer-in-Chief, Tubby Broomhall. We were not allowed to build anything new, but could improve on or expand any existing buildings particularly for married families. The War was now three years away and there was a feeling that, on Army terms, there was no reason why the restrictions and privations of the War would be extended indefinitely. Some had seen nothing of their wives for a year or more. The subsequent developments became a tug-of-war between Tubby Broomhall and me on the one side, and the Command Secretary and my own 'Q' Staff on the other.

I visited the various Regiments in turn and at an early stage went up to Sabratha where the 4th/7th Royal Dragoon Guards were stationed. Their barracks, like the others, had been built by the Italians in between the Wars and were quite reasonable. The road out to Sabratha was in remarkably good order and the journey took us well under an hour. This regiment was 'clued up' and always had a couple of wireless sets out down the road reporting our progress. Therefore, when we arrived, there was the Commanding Officer, Lieutenant Colonel Tom Moulton Barrett, with his Second-in-Command and Adjutant standing at the foot of the steps of the building which served as his Orderly Room.

We swept in through the gate, bent off to the right and in a very short space of time were well bogged down in a foot of soft sand, a situation that was almost inevitable and from their point of view eminently desirable. It did not actually need a demonstration of that sort to make the point, but it did not go unheeded and one of our first tasks was to get them a tarmac road. Tom, who was a bachelor and a descendant of the family in the play *The Barretts of*

Wimpole Street, decided that he was not prepared to continue to serve in such conditions and left the Army by the end of the year. He was a first-class regimental officer and much that was wrong in Sabratha had been put right by him before he finally retired.

It was about this time that measures were being taken to improve the lot of the soldier and the CIGS, Field Marshal Montgomery, was anxious to ensure that each soldier had his own bedside lamp. Situated as we were with power faults the rule rather than the exception, particularly in the outstations, bedside lamps were out, but another innovation was the issue of pyjamas to the soldiers, and I well remember that when they were issued, the men went to bed early to enjoy the 'luxury' without any further waste of time.

The next trip was to go down to Homs and the 6th Field Regiment Royal Artillery. They were much better off than the 4th/7th and in any case their ambitions were fewer. The barracks were only a couple of miles from the Leptis Magna. In their second year they laid on the 'Homs weekend' to which all and sundry were invited, and it became one of the more important of the social fixtures of the year. They had a marvellous station all to themselves and loved it.

Travelling through the country one could not fail to be impressed by the splendid job the original Italian settlers had done in reclaiming the land from the encroaching desert. I subsequently discovered that, had the Italians stayed on for only a little bit longer, the soil would have been sufficiently reclaimed to have stood up for decades, as in 1948 it was rapidly reverting to its original condition. There were also some very rich estates still being run by well-to-do Italians who were thriving under the protection we then provided, but once independence came their security was seriously jeopardised. We saw very little of the Italians who kept to themselves. Their great wish was that by some miracle opera would return to Tripoli, but this never happened in my time there.

The hinterland included a high range of hills about 30 miles inland and it was there that we carried out most of our training. We held our big exercises in the spring and these lasted a week or two. One early spring I flew in from Egypt to hear that there had been a snowstorm in Tripoli for the first time in living memory and the inhabitants had gazed in wonderment at the white flakes which melted in their hands. But the Commander Royal Artillery, Ted Colquhoun, was very concerned as up on the jebel were teams of Gunners surveying for the Artillery Practice Camp. They were completely cut off from us and from one another, and many must have perished but for the help and kindness of the local inhabitants. It took some days to rescue them and many were suffering from frostbite. I went and saw some of them when they went into hospital on their return. They thought that it was vital to tighten up the laces of their boots, presumably in order to keep the warmth in!

On my return we had a visit from an American task force, which included the aircraft carrier *Franklin Roosevelt*. The aircraft carrier was too big to get into the harbour. As this was the first visit of this type we decided to give a reception. When the fleet arrived the sea was running too high for me to go out in a barge so the American sailors sent a helicopter to Wheelus Field and in it I was conveyed out to the carrier, in which the Admiral was flying his flag. The Admiral and I went below and I invited him and his officers to a reception at the Ouddhan Club, which he was pleased to accept. I then got into my life jacket again, climbed into the helicopter and we swung over the side. When we were about 50 yards off we hovered over the running sea and I was given a thirteen-gun salute. This was the first time I had been honoured with a naval salute and the circumstances made it all the more memorable.

It was now time to return to the Suez Canal and see how the 2nd Brigade was faring. The whole of the Brigade Group was there, under the command of Brigadier Robert Poole, who had been in the same soccer side as I was in 1922 at Sandhurst. The situation in Palestine in the meantime had drifted into a stalemate, with the Arabs firmly established in the hills and the Jews along the coastal plain, with a few footholds on the high ground. This situation was to remain for nearly twenty years, until the outbreak of the 1967 War when the Jews finally occupied all the land west of Jordan.

In Tripoli the demands for independence grew and demonstrations, mainly of a non-violent character, took place, which increased in strength and intensity with the passage of time. The case of Libya, however, came before the United Nations and they won by a single vote. Apparently it was necessary to have a two-thirds vote in favour and history has it that the final vote, which came from Guatemala, decided the issue. From then onward the presence of British troops in any numbers would be unacceptable to the new ruler HE the Emir El Sayyid Muhammad Idris, although there were no changes before I left at the end of 1950.

In the spring of 1949 we were invited to carry out an amphibious exercise which was called ARCTURUS which meant a number of trips to Malta and the naval HQ of the Mediterranean Fleet (C-in-C Admiral Power).

Command of the 2nd Cruiser Squadron changed that summer and the new commander was Rear Admiral Earl Mountbatten of Burma who had just vacated the appointment of Viceroy of India. I duly called on him in his flagship the *Newcastle*, took the guard and then went below for a cup of coffee. His cabin was almost a museum with signed photographs of most members of the Royal Family on the walls, the sword presented to him by the City of London when he was made a Freeman was over the fireplace, a pile of photograph albums and some presentation swords and trophies. One of the trophies was a Japanese ceremonial sword. The blade of the latter is always kept in a special sheath and it was taken out for me to see. Of course it was a beautiful piece of steel and I could not resist the temptation to run my finger along the blade. As I expected it was just like a razor, but there was a gasp of dismay from the Admiral who immediately summoned the steward to remove the offending marks forthwith.

It happened that the visit of the 2nd Cruiser Squadron coincided with a visit from the CIGS who was now Field Marshal Sir William Slim and arrangements were made to ensure that the Field Marshal and the Admiral met. I invited the Guards Brigade to provide a Guard of Honour outside the Ouddhan Club and when I had done so I discovered that the Guardsmen never presented arms in such circumstances. There were numerous occasions when they did, but it was usually reserved for Heads of State, members of the Royal Family and other special ceremonial occasions. It seemed to me to be absurd that the First Soldier could not be granted this privilege and I asked the Brigadier to see whether he could not make this an exception. He said that he regretted that it was not possible, upon which I invited him to provide the Guard from the Queen's Own Cameron Highlanders. This order led to the Guardsmen agreeing to relax the rule and when Bill Slim arrived there was the King's Company of the Grenadier Guards looking quite magnificent, and giving him the salute the occasion called for. But on the balcony above the parade were a number of spectators, amongst whom was Rear Admiral Mountbatten and he knew far too much about such occasions as these. As soon as the inspection was over he came down to meet the Field Marshal, exclaiming that this was the first time he had known a guard to present arms in such circumstances, and would it not be a good idea to inform the King of it? Of course the Guardsmen were horrified and we quickly convinced the Admiral that this was a matter for the Brigadier and the Household Brigade, so the matter was dropped.

The political changes commenced to make themselves felt during my last twelve months in this spot in the sun. Libya had got its independence and the future of British troops there was in the balance. Although events were moving fast in Egypt there appeared to be no immediate crisis there, at least so I thought when I handed over to my successor, Major General Mark Mathews. These last two years in North Africa had been most interesting and, as it happened, turned out to be the lull before the storm.

It was in the autumn of 1950 that I was told that I would be going home at the end of the year to take over command of the 50th (Northumbrian) Division. My house in Tripoli belonged to the pre-war Italian Admiral, and was sited at the top of a cliff overlooking the Mediterranean. Down below was a beach of modest size where I bathed practically every morning. When Field Marshal Slim stayed at the house in 1949, he looked out over the balcony and said, 'This is wasted on a bachelor.' Actually it was ideal for the small Mess that I kept, although my successor, who was married, made other use of it. My time in North Africa had always been fully occupied. Three years has always seemed to me long enough for such appointments and, much as I enjoyed the challenges the previous years had provided, I was ready for home. I left late one evening in mid-December and had lunch the following day in my club.

Chapter Nineteen

Catterick

It was March 1951 when I put in an appearance at the Headquarters of the 50th Division, whose full title was the 50th Northumbrian Division and District. The Division was widely deployed and included Regiments as far afield as Sheffield in the south, York in the south-east and others on the Scottish border. In addition there were a number of regimental depots. The area included Westmorland, Northumberland, Durham and the North Riding of Yorkshire. The Headquarters had been in Darlington throughout the War and was still there, but was due to move across to Catterick that autumn and absorb Catterick Camp as well. The Officers' Mess was in a large building on the outskirts of the town, and had previously been an old folks' home. I decided I would live in, but did so in a manner not likely to embarrass the other members. The Headquarters were located on the same side of the town but nearer into the centre, and consisted of a group of houses which had previously been offices.

In 1953 the Division went down to Salisbury Plain and the last two days of the camp were taken up with a divisional exercise. This exercise was visited by a group of senior officers from NATO and they were sufficiently impressed with what they saw that they returned to Paris saying that this was no reserve Division but a front-line Division. It was very kind of them to say so, and very flattering, but it could not possibly be true. A Division carrying out a two-day exercise without a real enemy can be made to appear much better than they really are, and I gave this report no publicity. Nevertheless the 50th Division was quite outstanding in its own class.

The two and a half years I spent commanding the 50th Division gave me a very good insight into the workings of the Territorial Army. The divisional and regimental spirit was of a very high order, mainly because it had a first-class record in two World Wars and had the full support of the civil population.

I visited the various depots from time to time. They had plenty to do with constant intakes of National Servicemen doing their basic training. I went on one occasion to the Regimental Depot of the Green Howards which was located in Richmond, Yorkshire. A small Guard of Honour was paraded at the entrance to the barracks, consisting of some newly-joined Regular recruits. I asked the first man where he came from and the swift reply was 'Aberystwyth, Sir.' Somewhat surprised I put the same question to the second man who replied 'Swansea, Sir.' The third announced that he came from Cardiff. This intrigued me and I asked the third man why he had decided to go into a Yorkshire regiment. He said 'We tried for the Black Watch and were turned down, so we went for the Green Howards.' It was colour they were seeking and they settled for Yorkshire.

The next two years, from the autumn of 1951 until I departed in August 1953 were two of the most satisfying years of my career. Whereas before I had had to deal with the North of England and the 50th Division, some of it on a part-time basis, I now moved into Catterick Camp, which ensured that there were few gaps in the year's work. With the job went Scotton Hall, a lovely old Yorkshire country house. I had been aware of it on the two previous occasions I had been in Catterick, without having much idea what purpose it served or who lived in it. It was set on a knoll standing back from the main camp road and in the heart of that part of Catterick which had been dedicated to the Royal Corps of Signals since World War One. In fact the School of Signals was just over the fence at the back of the house. I had always had a high regard for the Royal Corps of Signals and was very happy to find myself living in their midst.

The Catterick of 1951 was very different from the Catterick of pre-war days, and the main distinction was the presence of the National Service soldier. The School of Signals was directly controlled by the War Office and, except that it had expanded considerably after the War, it retained its identity. Around it had sprung up the Signals Training Centre (or Brigade) which consisted of seven training Regiments, and on the other side of the camp was the Royal Armoured Corps Training Brigade, consisting also of a number of training Regiments. The total population of the camp was about 14,000 all told, including 2,000 officers. It took a little time to get round to all the headquarters and units.

Soon after I arrived an incident happened which proved beneficial to Catterick Camp in the long run. The training in Number 7 Regiment of the School of Signals was bound to be intensive as it is almost impossible to produce a trained soldier off the square in four weeks, and cover efficiently the ground to which the Infantry devote thirteen weeks. I went over on one occasion to be present when a draft of recruits arrived and watched the procedure followed in their induction. The men arrived at Richmond Station and, as they were being recruited into a corps, came from all over the British Isles. They were met at the station, piled into some open 3-ton lorries and were driven up the hill to the camp. They presented an astonishing cross-section of society including well-dressed young men, down the scale to honest labourers.

Inevitably a case arose where the squad instructor was one who lacked imagination, and who was so dissatisfied with the performance of his squad that, having given the whole squad some extra drills, told the assembled men that they were being held back because of the backsliding of one of their number and if they had any guts they would know what to do about it. Well, that was all they wanted to know and as soon as they could get back to the barrack room they fell upon the delinquent, stripped him naked, and applied dry scrubbers to his quivering flesh with the greatest of gusto. In those days there always seemed to be somebody about who was in touch with the press. I am not suggesting that he was necessarily a professional informant, but the fact remained that within a matter of hours we had been invaded by the press on quite a scale. The headlines of most of them the following day left little to the imagination. The word 'brutality' figured in all, and one went so far as to describe Catterick as the 'Belsen of the North'. I suppose there must have been a dearth of ordinary news, otherwise the joint outburst would not have been quite so hysterical. Courts martial are always held in open court, consequently when the men came up for trial the Court was packed, mainly with journalists. It happened that the 'victim' of this outrage cut a very poor figure, which did not surprise those who knew him, but which came as a bit of a surprise to the audience. The defendants, on the other hand, took their stand and could not have stated the case for the action they took more clearly or convincingly, but they were duly found 'guilty' and were each awarded twenty-eight days' Detention. The journalists moved out of the Court and found themselves in a bit of a quandary because all their sympathies by this time were with the accused. As the Reviewing Authority, I had considerable powers in respect of the mitigation of punishment, and later on I exercised them. This incident was valuable because the press, having been brought face to face with some of our problems, were much more discreet thereafter.

In between the Wars conditions improved considerably, but the stigma of the First War still remained forty years later. The programme of training in Catterick covered five to five and a half days each week, and the weekends were a bit of a headache. These conscripts had no free leave passes, such as the Regulars enjoyed, but they were at liberty, after they had been 'passed off the square', to take the weekend off at their own expense. Their pay amounted to very little and it was exceptional to find men in the ranks who could afford to travel any distance. My policy was to encourage as many as possible to get away, and I was not in the least concerned how they did it. The main need was to take the pressure off. At the stage when this plan was receiving all the encouragement we could give it, we received a letter from the War Office deprecating the practice on the part of the soldiers of 'thumbing' lifts; it was considered by higher authority that this should be discouraged in that it was damaging to the Army's 'image'. At this time it was customary for the soldiers seeking a break to get down to Catterick Bridge, which was then on the Great North Road, and thumb their way to practically every corner of the country. All these soldiers had to wear uniform and their identity therefore was unmistakable. Had they been prevented from continuing the practice of getting away our difficulties in Catterick would have been very much magnified. We proceeded to put forward a contrary point of view. In the first place there had been no complaints from the general public, and I deduced from that that most drivers, gazing upon these hapless young men, often saw the equivalent of their own sons standing there and were moved to concern themselves with them. Personally I admired the courage of these young men who were prepared to take a chance of getting where they might want to go to, and face the problem of the return journey which still made possible their appearance on parade first thing on Monday morning. It was the sort of exercise that had been encouraged during the War in order to build up the self-reliance and initiative of the individual, and had its place in character-building. We took a great deal of trouble to present our point of view, and thereafter we heard no more regarding the business of 'thumbing'.

The experience of seeing these National Servicemen (who preferred to be known as 'Conscripts') during the first few months of their two-year span was invaluable, and reinforced the high opinion I have always held in respect of the next generation. It helped me to understand their attitude to life, and no matter how long they grew their hair, and no matter how outrageous their manners and dress, I have never lost confidence in their ability to square up to things when it really mattered. Collectively I think they have displayed more real courage than was the case with my generation because they are prepared to think for themselves, and refused to be canalised as we were. At the same time I think many of them should give credit to their parents, more than they do, because it was the liberal ideas of their parents which gave them the freedom and scope that my generation never experienced. I continue to be surprised to find so many 'Squares' who are so intolerant of the next generation. Of course, on occasion, they appear to be outrageous, but, whether we like it or not, they are tomorrow, and the future is in their hands and not in ours. I have no doubt in my mind that they will handle the problems which will come their way with more realism than we see today. It is proving to be something of a humiliation to our present rulers that the young who are eligible to vote don't even bother to register.

Quite unexpectedly Field Marshal Montgomery decided that he would visit the 50th Division, as a result of a chance meeting with the Lord Mayor of Newcastle. He could only come over in the middle of the week, consequently it was not easy to get officers and men together in their drill halls for the purpose, and quite an amount of financial juggling was necessary in order to offset losses in earnings of many of the men. It was started off with an excellent dinner given by the Lord Mayor in City Chambers on the first night, which was to do with the City, and a second dinner the following night when the commanders of the brigades and units in the Division were the guests.

In the morning of the first day we visited regiments in Newcastle and the turnout was impressive, as many hundreds were there. We then drove down to Durham, where, at a luncheon given there by the City, the Field Marshal was presented with the Freedom of the City. After lunch we went up the hill to walk around the Cathedral and the Durham Battalion of the Cadet Force were on parade outside. Monty turned to me and said that this was not in the programme; well, he was quite right, but from the outset, I was determined that he should have a glimpse of the next generation in his programme. It later emerged that one of the cadets had attended the parade in spite of a direct order from his headmaster that no boy in school would be allowed off for that purpose. The result was that, the following morning, when he went back to school, he got a beating for his 'delinquency'. When he was asked about it, his face lit up and he said 'Oh! It was well worth it. I would not have missed that parade for anything.'

I went over to Paris on a couple of occasions because they were having discussions there at the time to do with the Russian threat, and three or four Territorial divisions had been earmarked for speedy reinforcement in emergency, of which the 50th was one. Joe Stalin was still alive and virtually anything was possible. On the second occasion, in the spring of 1952, it consisted of a week's study period, under the direction of General Eisenhower and conducted by Monty as his Deputy. The whole discussion was concluded by an address by General Eisenhower, which was very much to the point. At this time there were strong rumours that he was running for the Presidency as a Republican but nothing was said regarding this at the time publicly. Nevertheless within a matter of weeks he did, in fact, resign from the appointment of SACEUR, returned to the United States, and in no time at all he was in the race for the Presidency. I was therefore privileged to be present when he made one of his last speeches as a soldier. He was a man for whom I had the greatest regard. I do not believe there was any soldier alive at that time, of any nation, who could have welded NATO together in the way that he did in so short a time. All who served under him simply trusted him, and he also achieved the same success in producing a harmonious team which had characterised the integrated Headquarters he took over to Normandy in 1944.

It was the week before this exercise on Salisbury Plain started that Beatrice MacDermott (the mural painter, née Cuthbert) and I agreed to get married by special licence the week after exercises were over. A month before I had been nominated to succeed Major General 'Mike' West as the Commander of the Commonwealth Division in Korea, and it meant flying out at the end of September. I was not leaving Catterick until the end of August and a quick marriage would enable her to get a glimpse of the Army at home, which we felt was important. I needed a best man and wrote earlier in the week to my very old friend, Brigadier Cyril N. Barclay (who was the Editor of the *Army Quarterly* and who lived in London) to fill the role. We had arranged to be married at Caxton Hall the following Thursday which should have given him plenty of time to make the necessary arrangements. This letter was written in camp, and I gave it to my ADC, Jonathan Arnold, with instructions that it caught that day's post. He was going off into the nearest town with our pressure cooker which had developed internal trouble, and which was essential to my way of life in my caravan. He was so concerned with the pressure cooker that he forgot all about the letter and posted it surreptitiously when he found it in his mackintosh pocket two days later. The announcement was due to appear in *The Times* on the Friday morning, but it was leaked to the London evening papers on the Thursday evening, where Brigadier Barclay saw it, and there discovered the role he had been selected to play. In the meantime telegrams poured in offering congratulations. Jonathan Arnold could not make anything of these telegrams and kept asking what they meant, assuming that it might be a decoration of some sort. The exercise came to an end just before midday and then came the morning papers with the real news. Only then did Jonathan realise what an impact the pressure cooker had made on some of my arrangements.

Beatrice and I were married the following Thursday and travelled back to Catterick by road in a somewhat leisurely fashion, arriving on the Sunday. Beatrice managed to get round the camp and meet many of the wives, but it was not easy to come in as the wife of a Major General, and yet understand the succession of lower levels, all of which have a special significance of their own. The end of August duly arrived, together with my successor, Ted Colquhoun, who had been my CRA in Tripoli for nearly two years. We drove first of all down to the Headquarters and said goodbye to my faithful staff, but when we got back into the car the sergeants appeared from nowhere, armed with ropes, and proceeded to tow us away to the main road leading to London.

Leaving Catterick in 1953, I finally closed my association with it, after a period covering twenty-six years. When I left an article appeared in the *Yorkshire Post* on the 26th August 1953, to do with my term in command, with the heading 'Catterick Camp Gets the Human Touch'. I was well content with that.

Chapter Twenty

Korea

The month of September 1953 was taken up with inoculations and a short holiday down at Salcombe, where my mother joined us. We also paid a visit to Lady Reading, the Chairman of the Women's Royal Voluntary Service, as Beatrice rather hoped that she would be allowed to go out to Korea in a voluntary capacity. The reply was swift and uncompromising, and not at all the answer that Beatrice had hoped for. It appeared that this particular gambit had been played previously by wives of senior officers who wanted to join their husbands, but the privilege had been abused and Lady Reading did not encourage a further experiment in this field. This came as something of a relief to me, because to take over the Commonwealth Division as a husband of a few weeks' standing, surrounded by heavily married Canadians, Australians and New Zealanders, and to march in complete with wife where no wives were allowed, would have weakened my position to an extent which would have been quite unacceptable. It was a bit of a gamble going to Lady Reading, but it paid off and I finally departed in bachelor form. At the end of September I flew off to Korea, travelling by way of Canada, taking with me as ADC, Andrew Duncan* of the Cameron Highlanders.

One of the first things that General Eisenhower achieved on becoming President was to help bring about a 'Ceasefire' line in Korea, with a demilitarised zone separating North from South; so the war was, for the time being anyway, over. Apart from that the

---

* AD told the Editor that 'Nap' swapped his first-class ticket for two third-class as he thought it important that he should be educated in regard to Canada and the Canadian soldiers.

country in Korea was rugged, in parts mountainous, and on the whole unsuitable for the employment of armour. I spent a couple of days in Ottawa, and then flew on to Toronto where I met Major General Graham and later the newly-formed Rifle Regiment of Canada under Lieutenant Colonel Bill Mathews.

The following day we flew on to Vancouver and then emplaned to Tokyo. Flying with the sun and crossing the International Date Line explained why we left Canada one afternoon and reached Tokyo, some 5,000 miles away, the next morning. There, somewhat to my surprise, was a powerful reception party headed by Lieutenant General Sir Henry Wells, an Australian, who was the Commander-in-Chief of all Commonwealth Forces in the Far East, with his Headquarters in Kure; he was responsible to the Chiefs of Staff in Melbourne. The first thing I did was to call on the Commander-in-Chief of the United Nations Forces in the Far East, General Ed Hull. He must have had a tricky assignment living amongst the Japanese and being responsible to a considerable number of governments. I took the opportunity to visit some of the bases and installations. They had been there for three years or more and I was very impressed by the enormous amount of reserve ammunition. I finally left for Korea on the Saturday, and landed at Seoul that afternoon, being flown over in General Wells's personal aircraft.

On the airfield at Seoul I was met by General Mike West, whom I was succeeding, looking as buoyant and colourful as ever, and he took me over to inspect a Guard of Honour which was lined up for me. This guard was a very good introduction to my tour, consisting of a complete cross-section of the components of the Division, including Maoris and French Canadians.

We then drove across to the Headquarters of the Eighth Army in order to call on the Army Commander, General Maxwell Taylor. He came down from his Headquarters, which was tucked away in some low hills, and with him we took what the Americans call an Honor Guard. The Guard Commander reported the Guard ready for inspection, turned about, made for the near end of the Guard at a round pace and we were off! We travelled at what can only be termed a proper rifle pace; it was as much as we could do to keep up, let alone really discover much about the guard itself. Down the front line we went, roared up the other side and out. Gasping a little for breath we then left the parade ground and went up with General Maxwell Taylor to his office.

Maxwell Taylor was a General I never forgot. He was a dedicated soldier in the best sense of the word and was particularly well suited for this command as he had served much in the Far East and spoke Chinese fluently. He had commanded an American Airborne Division in France and parachuted back into his divisional area when Rundstedt staged his counter-offensive in the winter of 1944. He was quite charming to talk to and seemed to me to be a direct descendant of one of the Pilgrim Fathers; he spoke quietly and was austere, without being forbidding. He was clearly a master of his profession. At this time he was in the process of learning Korean, and every spare minute that he had was devoted to increasing his knowledge. He travelled much about the Army, which stretched the full length of the 38th Parallel, in a small helicopter known as a 'Bubble' as it could only take one passenger, and from time to time he would drop out of the sky onto a small helicopter pad which was just above the Headquarters. The helicopter would finally settle down in a cloud of flying dust, he would unstrap himself, climb out and greet you with 'How are you today, General Murray?' This, at first, I found disconcerting because I started to wonder how I did feel. Was I really well today? He was always most understanding regarding some of the problems which inevitably arise in a force composed of so many different elements. We would shake hands and he would strap himself in ready for departure. As soon as he was settled, out would come a pack of cards, all of which had a Korean word or phrase printed on them with the translation on the other side. He would gaze on the card and turn it over to see if he had got the answer right and if so it would be put to one side; if he got it wrong it would go to the bottom of the pack for further consideration.

The Commonwealth Division had been invited to give all the help we could to the South Koreans in the forward areas in reclaiming as many of their paddy fields as possible, many of them overgrown. It appeared that there was a great deal we could do in this matter, without seriously affecting our ability to fight. The only danger in this reclamation business was that it was impossible for a Westerner to distinguish a South Korean from a North Korean. Only a Korean knew and then only by the accent of the other. Therefore, although a great deal of reclamation was achieved in the next twelve months we could not allow it to penetrate into the forward area.

The other major work upon which the Americans were engaged was the creation of a South Korean army, in order to conserve United Nations forces as far as possible and make full use of the abundant Korean manpower. They were very happy to be used in this way, provided they were given something worthwhile to do. One regiment overplayed its hand and kept the men permanently on guard. They were surprised to find one morning that there were no guards left: the whole Korean contingent had gone and marched back to Rear Divisional Headquarters, deciding to 'soldier no more'.

This discussion with the Army Commander helped to give me some idea of the broader issues which confronted him and was an indication of the directions in which we could help him. We took our departure, went back to the airfield and climbed into a couple of light aircraft which were positioned there and took off over the hills to the Headquarters. The ground is flat in the vicinity of Seoul but in a very short time we were flying first over low hills, then higher ones, until we flew round Kamak San, a hill of 2,000 feet which dominated the whole of the divisional area and dropped down on the divisional airstrip which ran along the south bank of the River Imjin. The latter was quite an orderly stream at this time of the year, and not the fury it became in the summer during the heavy rains.

The Headquarters were in a gully that had steep sides and our caravans were dug into them, presenting a very small target to any snoopers from the air. At the bottom of the gully they had built a Mess, which was a two-storied affair built by the Sappers. The Headquarters included Brigadier Gregson, the AQ, Lieutenant Colonel Fishbourne and the CRE, Lieutenant Colonel Arthur Morris, who had been in my 6th Armoured Division six years before. The staff quarters were beyond and consisted of a series of lean-tos. It was a Saturday night and it was customary on this evening to play poker. Poker is not a game at which I have ever excelled and the only thing that struck me was that it was a game which needs to be controlled, even amongst friends. I remember my ADC in Italy getting out of his depth and being finally excused on the understanding that he never played in the Mess again as his brother officers were a bit too hot. The stakes on this first evening were occasionally high, but later it was possible for me to put on a piece of paper the highest amount anybody could lose in an evening, and this helped to bring the business under control.

The next day was Sunday which afforded a good opportunity to carry out a few reconnaissances, and Mike West and I flew out in a helicopter to have a look at the defences which we would man in the event of the war re-starting. The position was known as the Kansas Line. The weather in Korea in the autumn is quite excellent with a good strong sun, a light breeze and a cloudless sky. A great deal of nonsense had been talked about the weather in Korea because by and large it has the finest climate in the world. The spring and autumn are quite marvellous with continuous sun and the winter is very cold but dry, with the sun having sufficient strength to thaw ice in the middle of the day, much to the annoyance of the Canadians who had hoped to get in an unlimited amount of ice hockey during the winter months, and were thwarted by a thin layer of water on the ice which did not freeze until the light failed. There were two unpleasant months in the year, July and August, when the torrential rain and the water streams off the hills, dry waterbeds flood, and rivers become torrents and all but the most substantial bridges are swept away.

The Commonwealth troops had been working on the defences since July and they were in an advanced stage of development. There were complete dugouts in the first positions we visited which had 5 or 6 feet of overhead cover turning each into a little fortress with all-round defence. If attacked the defenders went below ground, sealed them off and called their own artillery fire down on themselves. The last battle before the armistice in July 1953 was known as the 'Battle of the Hook' and the amount of artillery ammunition used was on an enormous scale. This method was effective against the Chinese who must have suffered heavy casualties in attempting to break through. It appears that the Chinese always cleared the battlefield of their dead and wounded before first light, consequently the ordeal of the defenders was shortened to that extent.

Korea demonstrated that second-best ground is useless, as the attackers will always bypass it and throttle the defenders who have been outflanked. An interesting book was written about this time called *The River and the Gauntlet* and it set out the circumstances following the entry of China into the war, how they poured over

the high ground which was impassable and came down the other
side, cutting in on the roads to the rear and throttling those who
had been bypassed. This is what happened to the Gloucestershire
Regiment when the Chinese flooded through past Castle Hill where
they were deployed and took Kamuk San to their rear, carrying all
their close support weapons with them and finally appearing miles
to the rear on the Main Supply Route. So it was the United Nations
troops found themselves running the gauntlet and in constant
danger of being cut off as a result of being too road-bound.

The Gloucester Regiment had about 130 casualties, but 600 were
captured having lost the means of continuing the battle.
Nevertheless, looking at these defences on the Kansas Line I
thought how retrogressive the whole thing was; it was more akin
to the First World War than the Second. In its defence it could be
argued that our aim was to hold what we had knowing that it was
unlikely that the Eighth Army would receive further reinforcements
for anything more ambitious. The line of defence was the 38th
Parallel, and had the additional advantage of drawing the Chinese
Air Force into Korea where they could be got at, instead of being
forced to attack airfields in China. There was nothing, however, at
this stage to be said about these defences but it came as a relief to
fly over to the positions held by the Australian troops who, in addition to the fortresses, were digging open trenches from which
offensive operations could be carried out if necessary. The
Canadian Brigade was deployed north of the River Imjin and was
acting as the Covering Force to the Commonwealth Division, the
plan being that they would provide protection initially before withdrawing across the river and passing into reserve. They were also
responsible for the surveillance of the DMZ (Demilitarised Zone),
which separated us from the Chinese and North Koreans.

We flew back at the end of the morning, and then it emerged that
'A' Mess provided open house on Sunday mornings and always
produced a curry lunch. It was very popular and gave me the opportunity of meeting most of the Commanders and all the Brigadiers.
The Commander of the Canadian Brigade was Brigadier J.V.
Allard, a French Canadian of great ability who later became Chief
of Staff at Army Headquarters. The 28th Brigade, which consisted of two Australian battalions and two British, was
commanded by Brigadier John Wilton, who, in turn, became head

of the Defence Staff in Australia. The 29th Brigade was commanded by Brigadier Joe Kendrew, a very distinguished infantry commander, who had been awarded the DSO, to which he added three bars. He later became Governor of Western Australia where he was highly successful. I was therefore blessed with three Brigadiers of unusual ability. Mike West went off the following morning. General West was held in very high regard by all elements of the Division and revelled in the difficulties which Korea provided in such abundant measure during his tour of Command.

The following morning I went over to see Brigadier Allard and his Canadian Brigade north of the river, which also included a tour of the DMZ. It was while I was forward on this day that I became aware of the high state of readiness required by the Eighth Army. It was mandatory for 25 per cent of the infantry to be deployed in or immediately adjacent to their battle positions and the remainder capable of deploying within thirty minutes. One battery of each artillery regiment had to be on instant call and the remainder in action within twenty minutes. It seemed somewhat unreal as I could not believe that we could possibly have less than twenty-four hours warning if anything was likely to boil up, and it was the business of higher command watching the overall political situation to ensure that high states of readiness were only justified when an emergency was likely to arise.

My reaction was similar to those of the other Commanders in the Division and we agreed that these instructions would be ignored. It was the same experience as I had had in Italy and the last thing we wanted to see was a blunted weapon when the emergency really did arise. At the first opportunity I acquainted General Maxwell Taylor with my predicament and although he appreciated the position he was not prepared to withdraw the order. So we were in a state of stalemate with the onus resting on the Commonwealth Division to ensure that these arrangements were made. At this time of year the men spent most of the day working on the defensive positions and were about the healthiest troops I have ever seen.

One of the first considerations was to ensure that when off duty the men were as comfortable as we could make them, and to provide such other comforts and amenities as we could create. They lived in tents heated by petrol stoves – not only extravagant but dangerous. The strictest orders were necessary to keep them under control. We steadily developed a system of roadhouses, which augmented the canteen, two of which were used as theatres and also as cinemas and libraries as well as restaurants. It was too late in the year to do much for the officers, but we laid down plans to create two officers' clubs early in 1954, and by the spring, thanks to an almost unlimited labour force, we had them. These clubs provided a service which had previously been lacking in that they provided a meeting place for all officers in the Division, and it was good to see groups of Canadian, New Zealand, Australian and British officers grouped together making the word 'Commonwealth' mean something. (Field Marshal Wavell, in one of his pre-war lectures on 'Generals and Generalship', said that the soldier should be treated in much the same way as a thoroughbred hunter; he should be looked after in 'the stables' as if he were worth £500, but ridden in the field as if he were not worth half a crown. We did our best to follow this maxim.) We materially helped the Division to have a very high morale, which was very noticeable to those who visited us from time to time. Another factor in our favour was our system of reliefs whereby most Regiments were relieved as complete units as opposed to the steady turnover of so many men at intervals. The latter system was universal with the Americans and made their task of keeping up morale extremely difficult.

We were now getting into 1954 and we appealed finally for a decision one way or the other regarding the South Korean President's order that no Indian was to leave their camp at Munsan-ni so we could not entertain them in our camps. Our request was refused, as the President was not prepared to relax his order. We thereupon packed our lunch and drink into a couple of 3-ton lorries and, with suitable supporting cast of Brigadiers and proportional representation from the four Commonwealth countries, we shot off to Munsan-ni on the Sunday morning and entertained them in their own camp. It was the best we could do. They were quite touched by the effort we made, particularly as we took the Pipe Band of the Royal Scots for good measure. They departed back to India and the whole force had to be flown back by helicopter to Seoul. It seemed appropriate to do this, as this was the first time Indian troops had been employed outside their own country since gaining independence. They were delighted with this and in his speech of thanks Major General Thorat expressed their appreciation and paid tribute to the British Army saying that we 'taught them how to behave'.

Thanks to the fact that there was no war, we had an abundance of practice ammunition so we made pretty good use of it and in the wild unoccupied parts of Korea there was plenty of space to fire it off. There was little doubt that the Divisional Artillery was highly competent, which was not surprising as the artillery had been the dominating arm in the last battles of the war and the technique was established. It was quite another matter with the infantry whose shooting and tactical sense was incredibly low. We were right back where we were when General Sir Bernard Paget took over Home Forces in early 1942. To lend a little colour to an otherwise drab practical scene we had a series of marching and shooting competitions.

On our left flank on the Kansas position we had the 1st (US) Marine Division; we made an approach to the nearest Marine Brigade and suggested a visit. There was a long pause and then I received a formal invitation by the Divisional Commander, General Pate, to visit him at his Headquarters, which we were glad to accept and one or two staff officers went over with me. After a cup of coffee (they always had an early lunch if they had one at all) they made a 'presentation'. The presentation was the inevitable prelude to all such occasions and was devastating in its completeness, covering deployment of troops and weapons, the administrative 'set-up', the reserves of whatever nature and usually terminated by a sort of triumphant 'Any Questions?' more or less defying you to think of anything else.

It was during 1954 that the US Marine Division celebrated the raising of the Corps, and I was invited to go over for the dinner marking that occasion, given by the Divisional Commander. We knew it was a long drive and started reasonably early but nevertheless arrived about ten minutes late. We got rid of our coats and moved into the anteroom, only to find a large company standing with their backs towards us listening to somebody who was reciting something. We edged up and listened ourselves; to start with I had no idea what it was all about until I caught one phrase denouncing George III for 'ravaging their coasts' and then realised that I was listening to the Declaration of Independence which I had never read in my life. We listened with the greatest of interest and attention as the full tale of the horrors inflicted by us on the Americans unfolded, and it took quite a time. It finally reached its conclusion, the party broke up and the General came up and greeted us. I told him that I was glad to have arrived in time in order to discover what an awful chap George III must have been. He looked at me with a twinkle in his eye and said, 'Well, General Murray, that was the way they saw it, but perhaps today it has probably outlived its purpose.'

We also saw quite a bit of the Turks in Korea. On one occasion a party of us were invited over to the Turkish Headquarters. When we arrived we were greeted by their commander, Akurk, a magnificent figure of a man, who was obviously held in great awe by his officers and men alike. As far as I could see the Turkish Brigade were almost entirely dependent on the Americans for their clothing, equipment and weapons. They had of course their own code of discipline. There was no question as to who was commanding the Turkish Brigade and the Brigadier did not give any indication that he would be prepared to share it. The officers were terrified of him and one could only guess what his disciplinary powers might be. After lunch, we moved out of the mess and I noted that the guard outside the mess, who had come to present arms when we arrived, was still in that position. I had a horrible feeling that they had held on to that position throughout lunch to be on the safe side.

On to the study centre for the inevitable presentation. One interesting fact emerged, namely that the artillery support was provided by the Commonwealth Division Artillery and included a great number of defensive fire tasks which were given numbers for easier reference. Akurk looked at the artillery fire plan and said, 'But what do all these numbers mean?' It was explained that these numbers marked areas to which the opposing infantry might advance and by firing on them they might well be defeated before they reached our lines. With one sweeping movement of his hand he said, 'Take them all off the front; we fight with a bayonet and this plan will deprive us of our main purpose in battle; put them on the flank as you wish, but there must be no artillery defensive fire on the front.'

There was nothing more to be said and the Gunners withdrew.

We entertained the Brigadier and his officers later on, but a more important occasion was in April 1954 when the Australians and New Zealanders celebrated Anzac Day. Brigadier Ian Murdoch wanted me to make an appropriate speech on this occasion and brought over a draft, upon which we finally agreed. I set off for the parade, arriving in good time, to find that I had been preceded by the Turkish Brigadier, Akurk. The inspection was carried out, I returned to the saluting base and made my speech. I had hardly finished when Brigadier Akurk, with his interpreter, moved onto the saluting base and he then proceeded to make a stirring speech recalling the events of 1915 on the Gallipoli Peninsula and in what high regard the Turks held the Australians and New Zealanders. No Anzac Day is considered complete without Turkish representation. I imagine few would have thought such a thing possible.

In the late summer I was invited to attend the farewell parade of the Thunderbird Division. This was held some distance away and we took a little time to get there, finally arriving only just in time. General Maxwell Taylor himself took it, and although I did not realise it at the time, it was the first indication that there was to be a gradual rundown of the forces in Korea. The Division was drawn up in a very compact formation with the armour and artillery on the right, the infantry in the centre in great depth and the supporting services on the left. When the inspection was over the march past took place. The mechanised troops went past first driving steadily along at about 4 miles an hour, keeping station extremely well. Then came the infantry with a frontage of about fifty men, and a depth of a little more than that. This part of the parade was a complete eye-opener. It may be that this division was exceptional but only a small fraction of the men were white and the remainder coloured from yellow to black. I had never realised quite so clearly what an amazing cross section of humanity is to be found in the United States until that morning.

The hot and sticky summer of 1954 came to an end and the troops returned to their defences, although the regiments by now had been completely changed. Then it was that the scene changed because it was now over a year since the Armistice had been signed and it was decided to reduce the Field Army, the first warning of which came with the release of the Thunderbird Division. It happened at the time that the CIGS was holding his Annual Conference at the Staff College, attended by the Chiefs of Staff of the other Commonwealth countries; consequently a cable was sent home recommending that it would now be possible to reduce the Commonwealth effort from a Division to a brigade group. There was to be a British battalion, an Australian and a Canadian. The New Zealanders, who had had some difficulty in keeping their two units up to strength as the men were all volunteers (purely for service in Korea), were reduced to just a transport company. When I was still there battalions were beginning to disappear, so it was a very truncated division, which met my successor, Brigadier Geoffrey Musson, when he arrived in the middle of November to take over. Earlier that year I had been appointed Commander-in-Chief Scottish Command in succession to General 'Tiny' Barber, and would assume the appointment in March of the following year.

I had now been a Major General for ten years so promotion was more than welcome. I suppose it must have been almost a record in modern times to have commanded four Divisions of varying type and purpose, but I was glad to move on to another way of military life. (Slim's definition of divisional command was: 'It is good fun commanding a division anywhere . . . because it's the smallest formation that is a complete orchestra of war and the largest where every man knows you.' [**Editor's note:** From *Defeat into Victory*.]

My tour of duty in Korea came to an end in November. The operational side had never amounted to very much, but the opportunity of working along with Canadians, Australians and New Zealanders was welcome. When fighting divisional battles with higher command I had a very strong hand with four Prime Ministers behind me.

My departure took much the same form as my arrival and the day came when I said goodbye to my successor, my staff and the commanders, got into my aeroplane and flew down to Seoul. I said goodbye to General Maxwell Taylor, although I was to meet him again a few years later, and then got into General Wells's aircraft and flew back to Tokyo.

From Tokyo I flew to Port Darwin and then on to New Zealand

where I called in at Army Headquarters and addressed the officers there. It was a great pleasure to meet Major General Kippenburger, the New Zealand military historian, whose book *Infantry Brigadier* was a classic of its kind. I know that it was forbidden to keep diaries but in his case the records he kept were invaluable to later generations.

We left from there by plane to Sydney before going on by road to Queenscliffe where the Australian Chief of Staff (Lieutenant General Sir Sydney Rowell)* was holding a study period. To my great surprise I met Ian Campbell who had been a Staff College student at Camberley at the same time as I was, and who also played in the Staff College cricket side. He had taken an Australian battalion to the Middle East in 1939 and had been captured in Crete, spending the rest of the war as a prisoner-of-war. At this time he was the Commandant of Duntroon, the equivalent of our Sandhurst, and was also a Major General. He was quite overcome to find me in Australia, as I was the first of our course he had met there and the last.

After Queenscliffe I went on up to Canberra and stayed with the Governor General, Field Marshal Sir William Slim. The Field Marshal by this time was a very popular figure in Australia, although when he had first arrived two years previously his some-what blunt comments on aspects of Australian life had not been welcome. For instance, he told the Returned Soldiers League (the equivalent of the British Legion, except that it possessed consider-able political influence) that they were far too concerned with the past, and should be directing their attention more to the future. This was strongly resented at the time but in fact later became accepted. His delightful informality finally broke through and he became one of them. The story goes that on his way to some func-tion, dressed in uniform with his many decorations, he stopped off

---

* General Rowell wrote to 'Nap' on 8th September, 1954 and the following is part of his letter:

I trust you have enjoyed your time in command in this quite unique force. I suppose you are unhappy at the thought of not having had some operations with it. Nonetheless, I believe we have been fortunate in having had someone with your experience in command during a period in which Dominion troops perhaps might have become a bit restive. In fact, I said something to this effect at Camberley a fortnight ago.

to have a drink. There was a chap leaning up against the bar with his back to him, who slowly turned round to see who had come in. He gazed at the apparition, which was Bill Slim, and said, 'Jesus Christ'. 'No,' came the reply, 'only Bill Slim.' How true the story is history does not relate, but it was the sort of story which received wide currency and considerably increased his popularity. From Melbourne, where I called on the Governor of Victoria, General Sir Dallas Brookes, I continued by air, stopping at Darwin, Fiji, Honolulu, Seattle and Vancouver. I spent the night there and then flew out to Winnipeg, where we only stopped for about an hour; it was so cold that one's breath froze in one's nostrils. Then on to Ottawa until I finally took off on the last leg to the United Kingdom, arriving at Heathrow on a raw December evening a few days before Christmas 1955.

Chapter Twenty-one

Scottish Command

It must be the ambition of many who have served in Scottish regiments that one fine day they might find themselves Commander-in-Chief of Scotland, with Headquarters in Edinburgh. It was only when the wait was behind me that the possibility this might come my way occurred to me. My only real claim was that, until I reached the rank of Brigadier, I had served exclusively in or with Scottish regiments.

Scottish Command in the 1950s was something of a military backwater as the Field Army was in the South of England, Germany or other places abroad. The ten regimental depots, however, were still in existence because National Service was still running. From a personal point of view, however, the appointment gave me the opportunity to renew many of the friendships I had formed during the War while serving with the Highland Division. The Command was unusual because we had access on the civil side, which was the equivalent of government level, although it was not often issues arose, apart from civil defence where close discussion was called for.

There were two districts, the 51st (Highland Division) (and District) and the 52nd (Lowland Division) (and District), each commanded by a Major General. The role of the Commander-in-Chief rather bore out a remark made to me once by a well-known Guards officer, who said that it seemed to him that it was reserved for some 'deserving officer, keen on fishing, shooting or golf or some combination of them, as a form of three years' terminal leave'.

The holder of the appointment was given a charming house, set in spacious grounds at Gogar Bank, just off the road from Edinburgh to Glasgow, and within a couple of miles of Turnhouse aerodrome. The new incumbent was always given considerable latitude when it came to decorating the house and this was dealt with by the Ministry of Works, who were very generous in giving Beatrice's professional eye considerable scope; she even added a delicate mural to help the proportions of a rather cumbersome-shaped drawing room.

A burning question in the spring of 1955 was the actual location of the Headquarters. Before the war it had been housed in a group of houses in Drumsheugh Gardens, but with the expansion brought about by the War, it was moved into a public school in Edinburgh. When the War was over the school got its premises back again and the first Commander-in-Chief after the war, General Sir Neil Ritchie, decided to take the whole of the Headquarters into the Castle itself. I was not in Edinburgh Castle very long before I became convinced that it was quite unsuitable as a Headquarters and in the event of war would have to be evacuated, leading to complete disruption in a time of emergency. Parties of tourists were continually being conducted over the Castle throughout the year and so the guides became desperate, as every two or three minutes they found themselves saying, 'Oh, would you please stand aside for a minute,' as some vehicle or other lumbered past. So I agreed a decision to move. Beatrice was most indignant and said, 'You will always be remembered as the Commander-in-Chief who took Scottish Command Headquarters out of the Castle.' Whether my 'image' suffered at all must remain a matter of speculation (the Headquarters had only been in the Castle for about seven years during the century). The Governor retained a suite of rooms, which was a great boon, and Beatrice painted some more murals in these rooms, which were much admired.

In the summer of 1955 I was installed as the Governor of Edinburgh Castle. This appointment had been resurrected about twenty years before; it carried no special duties with it but naturally could not be regarded as anything other than a high honour. The troops taking part in this ceremony were chosen by the Army Commander himself and were normally taken from regiments in which he had himself served. It was a delightful coincidence that the 1st Battalion the Gordon Highlanders, the battalion I had commanded at Alamein, was stationed in Redford Barracks and commanded by one of my Company Commanders of those days, Lieutenant Colonel J.E.G. Hay DSO ('Scrappy'). It was also easy to have representation from the Cameronians (Scottish Rifles) from Lanark and the Cameron Highlanders from Inverness. After the usual exchange of courtesies and salutes the Lord Lyon (Sir Thomas Innes of Lierney), with his court, moved forward and commenced the ceremony. As he moved into position a soldier in Highland dress appeared on the ramparts and shouted, 'Who goes there?' Back came the high piercing voice of the Lord Lyon, 'I come in the name of Her Majesty Queen Elizabeth the Second', and read out the whole proclamation nominating me as Governor, who was now authorised to take up residence. He concluded his address with 'and you will fail at your highest peril'. This imperious summons was terrifying in its awfulness and I think the sentry nearly fell off the ramparts with fright.

Each year the General Assembly of the Church of Scotland took place at St Giles' Cathedral. In our third year the Moderator of the Church of Scotland was (the Very Reverend) Robert Scott, who had done so much for the Church in Pont Street, London and who was about to hand over to a successor, the Reverend George Macleod, who was well-known and a somewhat controversial figure. The retiring Moderator gave an address at the end of which he put the question to the Assembly, 'Have I your permission to have inducted into this Assembly the Reverend George Macleod as my successor?' After this question there was a slight pause in which a general assent became apparent, only to be terminated when a young minister rose from the centre of the Hall, immediately in front of the Moderator and High Commissioner, and with great calmness and deliberation, opposed the motion on the grounds that in his opinion the Reverend George (Macleod) was in no way suitable. It was apparent that Robert Scott was unprepared for this objection, the speaker having given no warning of his intended action. There was a considerable pause after the opening remarks of the speaker from the floor and for an appreciable period of time the two stared at each other, wondering what the next move might be. The Very Reverend Robert hung on gamely to the front edge of the lectern, vainly trying to voice a suitable courteous retort – swallowing hard, he reminded the speaker that the Assembly would be in session for nearly two weeks and time would be set aside during that period for the point he raised to be fully debated. I gather the debate, which was arranged for a later date, was nothing if not frank, but the nomination stood. After this exciting interlude it was the turn of the Lord High Commissioner to address the Assembly. He knew only too well the background of the previous interruption and in his speech he said, 'Some are born moderate, some achieve moderation and others have moderation thrust upon them.'

Since the Second World War there had been an Edinburgh Festival in which the Military Tattoo had always played a prominent part. The production of it was in the hands of a former officer in the Queen's Own Cameron Highlanders, Brigadier Alasdair Maclean. He had an exceptional touch for this kind of military display. On one occasion the Queen, Prince Phillip and the Princess Margaret came on for the second part of the Tattoo, from the opera. When it was over, we left the box and on the landing outside I presented Alasdair Maclean and his wife; we then continued down the staircase towards the entrance. This flight of stairs cut us off from the rest of the Royal party before we turned the corner at the bottom, where the leaders of the various detachments were lined up to be presented in their turn. On our way down we were separated from all the others and while we were on our way the Queen's gown caught one of the flowerpots and turned it over. She looked back, bent down and put the flowerpot back in its place before going on down. A small thing, but an incident only the two of us shared.

The Tattoo was the most strenuous time of the year, and was quite exhausting; the guests included Sir Malcolm Sargent, the chief Music Critic of *The Times*, Professor Frank Howes, and Maclean, who was very anxious to have a *Times* critique of the Pipes and Drums at the Tattoo; the Professor made allowance for a visit to the Tattoo before he left. The Pipe Bands gave their usual high-class performance, but to our dismay Frank Howes informed us that he was unable to give them a notice because they had not played classical music, namely the pibroch, which alone could qualify for a notice. However, the situation was saved when he conceded that the drums of the Gurkhas could qualify in the field of classical music and a notice duly appeared.

On another occasion we were honoured by a visit from Field Marshal Montgomery who came to take the salute during our last year and stayed for three nights. On the first evening we took him to the opera where Maria Callas was singing in *La Sonnambula*. He arrived in time for tea which gave him time to lecture Beatrice and I on the problem of advancing age, and how to deal with the 'Twilight' of old age. We went on to the opera, which was a great success, in spite of the fact that Maria Callas was out of voice; it appeared that she had just completed a rigorous slimming course. We had arranged to send a bouquet of flowers around to her dressing room consisting of red carnations from the Field Marshal and were rewarded when we saw that she had placed one of them in her corsage when she appeared. The following night we had a dinner party prior to going off to the Tattoo where Monty was to take the salute. We went in convoy, as usual, to the Castle and the Tattoo was excellent. Monty had always referred to the Pipes as 'Savage Music' but he enjoyed it just the same.

Amongst our guests Prince Philip always provided a challenge. On our first meeting it was played in a minor key, when we stood together behind the Queen at the top of the steps of the Royal Scottish National Gallery in Princes Street when the Pipers playing at the Tattoo paraded past. 'What Regiments are these?' said he. There were quite a number but it was possible to discern from a distance the various kilts and provide an answer. He looked at me and appeared to be a little uncertain at my answer, but the Pipers swept past and beyond recall. Our second meeting was the occasion of the presentation of a new guidon [pennant] to the Royal Scots Greys, of which Her Majesty was Colonel-in-Chief, and which was to take place in the grounds of Holyrood Palace. I was to have been present with no particular role to play, when I was rung up from Buckingham Palace and invited to accompany the Queen on this occasion. I was required to remain on the saluting base with the Duke of Edinburgh, who also had no part to play on a parade which was a purely regimental affair to do with the Queen.

The sun was shining, but there was a very high wind and the officer holding the guidon had the greatest difficulty keeping his feet. The Queen was received with a Royal Salute and moved away, leaving me with the Duke of Edinburgh on the saluting base. At an early stage he asked, 'Oh tell me, General, why is it that the Royal Scots are being presented with this guidon?' Outwardly this would have appeared to be a glimpse of the obvious, in that the guidon which the Regiment had carried for some years was to be laid up in the Scottish National War Museum in Edinburgh Castle, and the purpose of the parade was to present them with a new one. This I explained. 'Oh yes,' he replied, 'but why is it that my Regiment, the 8th Hussars, have no guidon?' I had not really given the matter a great deal of thought, but on reflection I realised that the Royal Scots Greys were, or had been, heavy cavalry, whose function in the days of the horse was shock action, and after a charge (which might be quite short in distance), needed a guidon upon which to rally. Hussars were to do with the fluid battle, skirmishing, and needed no such aid. In the time available on the saluting base, that was as far as I got. The Prince listened attentively and appeared satisfied with what was no more than an impromptu performance. To what extent the Prince was personally involved with this matter I do not know, but soon afterwards all Cavalry Regiments had their guidons, including the 8th Royal Hussars.

On another occasion the Queen and the Duke came ashore from the Royal Yacht at Leith in order to go to St Giles Cathedral preceding the opening of the Edinburgh Festival. Drawn up was a guard of honour provided by the 9th Battalion the Royal Scots, always known as the 'Dandy Ninth'. This gave the Duke the opportunity to ask me why the guard was dressed in the kilt, as he had been under the impression that the Royal Scots was a Lowland Regiment. Well, of course, he was absolutely right, and the circumstances which led to a Territorial battalion in a Lowland Regiment wearing the kilt is part of history, consequently all I could say was that they were the exception that proved the rule. It went to show that the Duke missed very little.

In the meantime the War Office was busy considering how to streamline the Regular Army and the intention was to reduce the infantry by a fifth. So far as Scotland was concerned the aim was to reduce the number of infantry battalions from ten to eight. It was interesting to be reminded that the Highland Regiments outnumbered the Lowland by six regiments to four. In 1957 ten Colonels of the Scottish Regiments came to Craigiehall in order to consider how best the reductions called for could be carried out. The six Highland Colonels were closeted together in one room and the four Lowland Colonels got together in another. They spent the morning debating the matter and then they all came back to Gogar House for lunch. They knew each other extremely well and although not one of them would make any concession likely to weaken the position of their own Regiment they were always on the best of terms. I had a personal interest in the Cameronians in the Lowland Brigade and the Queen's Own Cameron Highlanders in the Highland Brigade, and the less I had to do with it the better.

After a considerable pause I was summoned to the War Office for a discussion with the CIGS, Field Marshal Sir Gerald Templer. I discovered that he was not proposing to discuss the whole problem, but wanted to ask me one or two questions regarding the Cameronians. The first question was whether, in my opinion, there would be an outcry from the Church of Scotland if this famous old Covenanting Regiment were amalgamated with somebody else? He then mentioned another Regiment and asked if any strong feelings would be aroused if the Cameronians were amalgamated with them. I replied that I did not think so and when I left the War Office I felt that the Cameronians were bound to be affected.

Some time later, all Colonels of Regiments and Commanders-in-Chief were invited to a meeting in London when the whole plan would be made known. I went in with Douglas Graham, the Colonel of the Cameronians, and as we did so I noticed that several Colonels were given a letter for them to read, but we did not get one. Field Marshal Montgomery was there and stressed that an equitable solution had been reached. The CIGS then uncovered an enormous chart showing the shape of the infantry in the years immediately ahead. Of course our eyes flashed to the Lowland Brigade and to our great relief there were the Cameronians.

This had been brought about by amalgamating the Seaforth and Cameron Highlanders, and taking the Highland Light Infantry out of the Highland Brigade, and putting it into the Lowland Brigade, amalgamating them with the Royal Scots Fusiliers. This aroused a storm of protest in Scotland, particularly in Glasgow, and a petition was drawn up by the local MPs in conjunction with the Lord Provost of Glasgow and submitted to the Prime Minister, Mr Macmillan. The latter refused to intervene and the amalgamation stood. The Highland Light Infantry was more concerned in leaving the Highland Brigade than in actually being amalgamated, but the combination of the two was almost insupportable.

*   *   *

Edinburgh is a very useful stopping-off place for Scotland and occasionally we were apt to become a sort of hotel. The social effort during the Festival was on a large scale and left us completely burnt out at the end of it. One year we decided that, instead of having relatively small, formal dinners, we would have buffets, thereby increasing the scope. At the end of three weeks we discovered that, during the three weeks, we had entertained nearly 1,000 guests, so we did not repeat the experiment. We were also invited to many public dinners and often had to reply to the toast of 'Her Majesty's Forces'. The standard of speech-making in Scotland was very high and some of the after-dinner speeches were outstanding. It meant that it was not always easy to enjoy the dinner, being much too concerned with the aftermath, which one took for granted at one's peril.

While we were in Edinburgh my wife had the opportunity of putting into practice her belief in art therapy and on most Thursday nights she would disappear into Saughton Prison, with some of my best gramophone records, and would work throughout the evening with an experimental class of first offenders. She would give a talk on some aspect of painting or drawing, then, to the accompaniment of classical music, they would draw or paint. It was quite astonishing to see the quality of the work done and I am sure that many of them kept it up when they were finally released.

The Commander-in-Chief Scotland is ex officio the chairman of the Board of Governors of the Queen Victoria School Dunblane. The big day of the year was known as 'Grand Day' when the Headmaster would give his annual report, a parade would be held and then there would be a number of displays and exhibitions. The last 'Grand Day' I attended was marred by tragedy. We all went down to the school, moved onto the platform in the room where the prize-giving was to take place and the Headmaster then made his report. The report was quite a lengthy one but it was noticeable that as he proceeded, his words were becoming a little blurred and as he went on he seemed to bend more and more over the script. I was sitting on his right and I suddenly realised that he was collapsing. I half rose to my feet and as I did so he slid in my direction; all I could do was lower him to the ground. He gave a sigh, said, 'Thank you Sir,' and died. We drew the curtains across the stage, went out into the sunshine to the Parade and the rest of the proceedings went on uninterrupted.

The Governor of Edinburgh Castle has his own pew in Canongate Church and we attended morning service there on Sundays whenever we were in Edinburgh. The Minister was the Reverend Ronnie Selby Wright and he had held the appointment since 1937. Canongate Church dates back to the seventeenth century and had simplicity, almost austerity, altogether in keeping with the Church of Scotland. We found the services there particularly satisfying and we always enjoyed them. There was a powerful boys' choir, the volume of which was glorious and they sang with a degree of abandon unequalled in my memory. They were banded together in a club, which had been formed in 1927, and it was as a team that they sang. It took many years and all the inspirational leadership and drive of Ronnie Selby Wright to get possession of Panmure House, in which Adam Smith spent the last few years of his life, to secure for them premises in keeping with the purpose.

In the New Year of 1958 I was informed that I was to go as Commander-in-Chief Northern Europe, a NATO command that included Norway, Denmark and Schleswig Holstein. This came as something of a surprise as Scottish Command was normally a form of 'signature tune' to be followed by retirement, but it was not for me to argue about it. So it was that in March, Beatrice and I were invited by the then Commander, Cuthbert Sugden, to go over and discover the 'form'. The appointment carried with it a private aeroplane (a Dakota) which landed at Turnhouse and we departed forthwith for Copenhagen. There was Cuthbert, without a hat, with his ADC standing in the most piercing cold wind I have ever experienced, coming as it did straight off the Baltic. We looked around the 'property' and found that the Danish Government had been more than generous. As the 'residence' of the Commander-in-Chief they provided a most beautiful eighteenth-century flat in the Sokvesthuset, and also a suite of offices in the Castellat. The flat was palatial and in the nineteenth century had been the home of a famous Danish actress. It had a lovely dining room, suitably furnished for at least thirty persons to dine, and with some delightful naval pictures from the Academy. There were also two drawing rooms. After two days in Copenhagen meeting the Heads of Services and other authorities, I then flew on to Oslo and the Headquarters.

On my return the announcement was made that George Collingwood, a fellow Cameronian, who had joined the Regiment on the same day as I did thirty-five years before, would succeed me in Edinburgh, which gave all of us in the Regiment tremendous pleasure. This was followed almost at once by my appointment as Colonel of the Regiment in succession to Major General Douglas Graham, who had reached the age limit for the appointment, which was 65. This latter appointment led to a certain amount of speculation at the time because our Colonel-in-Chief was His Majesty the King of Sweden and the timing of my appointment to NATO, and at the same time Colonel of the Regiment, with Sweden a neutral country, raised the possibility of Sweden changing its political attitude. In the circumstances it was agreed that it would be impolitic for me to call on our Colonel-in-Chief, the King in Stockholm so long as I was Commander-in-Chief of Northern Europe, and I never went to Sweden at all. It was not until 1961 that we had a regimental dinner in London over which he presided, and 1964 before we had a proper parade, which was held in Edinburgh.

The last few weeks of my command in Scotland were spent in hospital, as my right hand, which had been badly damaged at El Alamein and had given me no trouble at all for fifteen years, turned septic. It was not until we were about to leave in 1958 that I escaped hospital, made my farewell address to the Headquarters and departed. We spent a couple of weeks in the Lake District; Beatrice then went north to paint a mural in the ballroom at Gleneagles and I went to Lanark to pick up some of the threads of my first regiment. We did not leave for Scandinavia until early July.

Chapter Twenty-two

Scandinavia

The scene of our departure from 30 Cornwall Gardens was one of chaos. Beatrice had lived there since the War and had handed it over to her son Lyon when we went to Gogar Bank House in 1955, and he lived there for about three years. It happened that the Rent Restriction Act had been repealed and the rise in the rent was such that he decided he would live elsewhere; his move coincided with our departure for Scandinavia.

We arrived early in Norway on the morning of the third day and sailed up the Oslo Fjord, which gave me the opportunity of seeing for myself the same scene as the Germans saw when they invaded in 1940 and were surprised by the fort astride the fjord. In 1940 it was only manned by cooks and sanitary men who sank a cruiser to the bottom of the fjord, where it still lies.

My Chief of Staff, Major General George Cooper, who had served in the Royal Tank Regiment, was there to meet us. He had already served two years in the appointment. Cuthbert and Pim Sugden had left in the ship which had brought us over, so we went straight off to the house in the Holmenvei where we had stayed the previous spring. The house had been taken by the Sugdens almost in despair about a year previously, having been in Norway for a year and a half without having found anything suitable. We met the agents and agreed that we would occupy it anyway for three months and would give them three months' notice of any intention to leave. The ground floor included two small drawing rooms, the dining room and the kitchen. The dining room was small and narrow and during a dinner party, which would not exceed about sixteen, the noise of the conversation was quite deafening. In view of the size of the command and outside commitments, this dining room imposed considerable limitations. There was a side entrance, which led into a passage, which ran through the basement the full length of the house, finishing with a few rooms in which the staff lived. There was something eerie about the whole set-up and we were not surprised to hear that it had been used by the Gestapo during the German Occupation.

The soldiers loathed it and one of them admitted that he slept with a loaded pistol under his pillow. Our bedrooms were on the first floor above the drawing rooms, where the cook also slept. The central heating was most efficient, but in cold weather it caused the wooden panels to creak or sometimes groan. At night little imagination was required to draw conclusions, which might not be founded on fact. There was a folding partition separating the two drawing rooms on the ground floor and on one night I thought I distinctly heard this partition being run back so I went down to investigate. So far as I could see it was in exactly the same position that it had been in when I went to bed, but I remained quite convinced that, by some agency or another, that partition had been rolled. My experience reflected the feeling of the staff and they were clearly determined to get us out of the place at the earliest opportunity.

The appointment of Commander-in-Chief Northern Europe (CINCNORTH) covered Norway, Denmark and Schleswig Holstein, and embraced all three services. The Command had great strategic importance as it covered the exits into the North Sea from the Barents Sea and the Baltic. The frontier was much reduced as a result of the neutrality of Sweden, which covered nearly 1,000 miles of Norway's eastern boundary and left only 200 miles of frontier with Finland and a short frontier of 50 to 60 miles with Russia (at Kirkenes). There was another land frontier between Schleswig Holstein and East Germany. The problems involved were mainly to do with the sea and the air, and when I said so, eyebrows were raised in surprise that a soldier should nevertheless hold the appointment. On the whole it was better so, as both of the other two services would have found it difficult to be as impartial as a soldier could be. The Headquarters was situated about 8 miles outside of Oslo at Kolsos. The operational Headquarters, which was only fully manned in emergency or during exercises, was dug into an enormous rock-shaped hill. The working Headquarters consisted of a number of attractive wooden huts for offices, and included restaurants and a large lecture room, which could also be used for social occasions.

The Air Force had a separate headquarters at the bottom of the hill which was contained in a separate compound. I do not know how this arrangement came to be made, but it was a psychological mistake to have part of the Headquarters isolated in this way. It led to a way of thinking in the minds of the Air Force officers of assuming the war would probably be settled by air power, and it took most of the remainder of my time in Norway to correct this. The operational Headquarters, being carved out of solid rock, was assumed to be proof against any form of aerial attack, including nuclear. It was hundreds of feet underground, was approached through a guarded gate and this led on down a long passage to offices at different levels, operation rooms and map rooms. The plan was for the staff to work in relays and be housed outside, but there were ample facilities for living and feeding inside on a short-term basis.

My staff was about 1,000 strong and included 600 officers. These were one third British, one third American and one third Scandinavian. We also had two Canadian officers to start with, but these were later replaced by German officers. Cuthbert Sugden had had an unpleasant experience in 1957 when he flew back from Paris with the Commander-in-Chief Centre, General Valley, and his Chief of Staff, General Speidel. Although the War was already over ten years away, the memories of the German Occupation were still fresh, consequently when the Sugdens' aeroplane touched down the occupants were pelted with stones by men who darted out from some of the buildings on the airfield. Cuthbert walked through this barrage to the control tower and diverted the following aircraft to another airfield further down the fjord, as his guests (German officers) did not happen to be with him. The latter drove on up the road to Oslo in some form of disguise, but it showed that it was premature to admit German officers into the country. Going around the Headquarters later on it was instructive to see how officers from different countries got along so well, although the Danes never shook off their antipathy, mainly because it went back over the centuries.

My first official duty was to call on the Chief of the Defence Staff, who was General Øen, an airman. I was received by a guard of honour (while I was in Norway that country continued to have conscription, the men were picked from all over the country and looked magnificent). They had a disarmingly frank expression on their faces and were availing themselves of the opportunity of having a good look at me whilst I was inspecting them. After the inspection, I was surprised to hear that my predecessors had never been prepared to provide the Chiefs of Defence with a full appreciation of the overall problem confronting the Northern Region and I promised to look into it. My staff did not appear to be too keen on providing this, but the following year we did so.

General Oen was a delightful person to work with, having a clear brain, a splendid sense of humour, and a very quiet and modest approach. He was still in the job three years later, which was a great help to me.

I think it would be appropriate here to make a few comments on NATO as I saw it at the time. When it was created in 1949 under General Eisenhower, it had two main objects:

- to stem the advance westwards of the Russians;
- to provide a political and military shield for the economic recovery of Europe.

Even in those days there was some doubt in the minds of many whether, after ten years of its existence, these aims had not already been achieved. Norway was particularly sensitive, having the only frontier with Russia, and whereas they were prepared to accept the 'Honest John', a form of nuclear weapon, they were not prepared to take the warhead, which the weapon needed in Norway. The National Forces in Norway, Denmark and Schleswig Holstein remained under national command and control, only coming under command of CINCNORTH in emergency. But exercises showed that this could work perfectly well and I had free access to all formations, units, headquarters and installations at all times. In any case our plans were drawn up in the closest cooperation with the national Staff in all three countries.

Within a couple of weeks of our arrival, Field Marshal Montgomery, who was Deputy to General Norstad (SACEUR) turned up in Oslo on a farewell visit. It had always been his determination to serve on until he was 70 and this birthday fell in 1958, when he had completed fifty years' service. Field Marshals remain on the Active List until they die, but in this century have seldom been actively employed beyond the age of 60 and, needless to say, the purpose of the Field Marshal was to be the exception that proved the rule. He was duly met at the airfield by myself and the heads of service, and then swept off to stay with the British Ambassador in Norway, Sir Peter Scarlett and Lady Scarlett. It transpired that this was normal custom and we were relieved to hear it because the accommodation we could provide in the Holmenvei was hopelessly unsuitable. That evening Beatrice and I were invited to the Embassy to a quiet dinner party which we very much enjoyed. (The Embassy is built on an almost palatial scale, and it appeared that when King Edward VII went over to see his daughter married to the King of Norway, King Haakon, he was most unimpressed by the British Embassy then being used, and insisted that better provision should be made.)

We sat about after dinner, when Beatrice, having talked to the Field Marshal for some time, became aware of the fact that the conversation continued to revert to the question of going to bed, however much it might be switched to another topic. I knew the 'form' and when the minute hand crept up to 10 o'clock I caught Beatrice's eye, instead of the other way round, and we rose to take our departure before the possibility that Monty might anticipate us.

The following day the King of Norway gave a luncheon party in his private house above the Oslo Fjord. This house had been presented to him by the Norwegian people on the occasion of his marriage and the setting was quite perfect. It was the first time I had met the King of Norway, but I well remembered him when he was in the United Kingdom during the War and how impressed we had been by him. He spoke, needless to say, perfect English. On these occasions there would normally be an all-male company, with his then unmarried daughter acting as hostess. It was a private party and there were no speeches.

Norway is very democratic and they have no aristocracy. Having been a province of Denmark for centuries, they came under the suzerainty of Sweden in the time of Napoleon, when the Marshal Bernadotte became King of Sweden, and so remained until they finally broke away from Sweden at the beginning of the present century. It was a great boon that the King of Norway was a strong supporter of NATO and gave us all the support we could have wished for. When NATO came into existence ten years previously, King Haakon ensured that Norway became a Member State, but he found the presence of foreign troops on Norwegian soil irksome and we never flew flags when travelling in Norway by road. King Olav took a different view and we had the privilege of entertaining him on at least two occasions at Kolsos.

After lunch we took the Field Marshal off to my Headquarters where he addressed the officers on his task and what he thought of the future. As usual he made great play regarding the conflicting needs of NATO and some of the Member States, but he had brought a couple of slides with him, which were shown on a screen and which depicted a view, facing west from Moscow, of the water-ways leading away into the Atlantic. One was of the Barents Sea and the Baltic, and the second leading out through the Black Sea into the Mediterranean and on into the Atlantic. Of course it was almost a glimpse of the obvious and had been the dominating idea in the mind of Peter the Great 300 years earlier, but what surprised me was that Monty, at this stage in his career, should be so startlingly aware of the sea. In the last ten years it had become increasingly apparent that Russia was becoming more and more aware of the urgent need to share the seven seas, without which her ability to intervene in other people's affairs would be negligible.

That evening the Norwegian Government gave a dinner in honour of Monty at the Dronningen Hotel which is perched out on the end of a jetty sticking out into the Oslo Fjord, on a lovely summer evening, with salt water lapping all around and very Norwegian. This was a complete 'stag' party, over which the King presided in person. I suppose there must have been over sixty guests there and as they included the leading political and military leaders, it gave me an excellent opportunity of meeting all those with whom I should be working during the years ahead. At the end of dinner the King made an excellent speech paying tribute to the splendid job Monty had done as Deputy SACEUR and wishing him all happiness on his retirement. Monty then replied and naturally gave a survey of his years in NATO and sketched some of the problems involved. He went on to say 'you have no idea the difficulties I have had in welding NATO into a proper military machine. It took me seven years, seven years to bring Germany into the Alliance, incredible, quite incredible.' I found it quite difficult not to laugh because those who had ensured that it would take all that time were the very audience he was addressing. They, however, were very warm in their applause because despite his lack of political sense, they acknowledged him as an outstanding soldier. It is customary in Norway, when dinner is over, to adjourn to neighbouring rooms for coffee, cigars and liqueurs and this we proceeded to do. This, however, formed no part of Monty's way of life and as the clock was already moving towards 10 o'clock he made his apologies to the King and bowed himself out. The King was well aware of the form and took no exception to it, however odd it may have appeared to others.

The following day we went down to Copenhagen for the second part of Monty's farewell visit. It was important to fly ahead instead of going along with him, otherwise things were likely to get out of control. I arrived on the International Airfield at Copenhagen and was greeted by Admiral Qvistgaard, who was the Chief of the Danish Defence Staff. He did not appear to be in a very good humour, and it was only later that I discovered that he and Monty did not get on that well. The story may be apocryphal but it went as follows: A previous NATO commander had, apparently, suggested to Monty that the Admiral was not up to the job. Monty subsequently had an interview with the King and doubt was cast upon the Admiral's ability. If reports of this interview are to be believed, it went very badly. It was astonishing that those concerned were not aware that the King, as Crown Prince during the War, was held by the Germans in house arrest and his companion during these years was no less a person than Admiral Qvistgaard. The upshot was that very soon afterwards, the Admiral, who had at that stage been a Vice Admiral, found himself a full Admiral and continued to enjoy the full confidence of the King and the Royal Danish Government. So the demeanour of the Admiral on this morning was understandable.

We flew out in Monty's aircraft with the Admiral and Monty sitting opposite each other on the other side of the gangway. The trip did a great deal of good, because at the end of a conversation (which would not have lasted less than an hour), they were on very good terms. It was customary for the Danish Royal Family to spend some weeks in their country house in Jutland, on the border with Schleswig Holstein, which may have been a custom of long standing for political reasons. We arrived at an airfield in the south of Jutland and went by car to the Royal Lodge. Monty was still a public figure in Denmark and a group of people assembled at the entrance to cheer him.

We were presented both to the King and the Queen and to the three princesses, who at this time were relatively young and un-married. Without any further preliminaries we went in to lunch and sat down at a very large oval table with about forty others. Looking around I saw that the company was composed of both the elderly and the very young (it was a country house luncheon party where all five members of the Royal Family invited their own guests). In Scandinavia it is customary for the principal male guest to sit on the left hand of the hostess, and I was surprised to find myself in this position on the left of the Queen with Monty on the other side. On my left I had the Princess Marguerite, the eldest of the three princesses and next in line to the throne. This was the first occasion that I had been present during a Danish lunch and the Queen soon spotted this and could not have been more helpful and gracious. It was, for instance, my first introduction to Aquavit, which was served in very small glasses, interspersed amongst the other wine glasses. These were automatically filled and refilled if needs be with great speed. The Queen told me that it was customary to drink the Aquavit in one gulp, but it was strong and a little went a long way. At a suitable moment I picked up the glass, emptied it as directed and was conscious of a burning liquid coursing down my throat which left a pleasant glow behind. I then saw Monty suddenly jump to his feet with a glass in his hand. A footman bent over him and whispered something in his ear, and then the King, seated at the far end of the table raised his glass. It is customary to 'Schol' important guests, and Monty and the King first of all raised their glasses, drank to each other and the toast was over. The King was strictly teetotal and presumably was drinking lemonade, so I could not help wondering whether, on such a special occasion, Monty had broken his own strict rules in the matter. This little ceremony came as a warning to me and a few minutes later I found myself on my feet in turn exchanging a 'Schol' with His Majesty, and ensuring that I got the technique right. (The rules relating to who should 'schol' whom, and in what order are very strict. For instance it is not done to 'schol' the hostess except in very exceptional circumstances, presumably because a series of well-intentioned 'schols' might be too much for her.)

The lunch was enjoyed enormously by everybody and was completely informal. When it was over we moved outside and were photographed with the whole of the Royal Family on the terrace. The princesses were intrigued with the mass of medal ribbons on Monty's chest; there were so many that he had had to have the breast pockets of his jacket lowered to make room for them. There was one medal ribbon to which he drew their attention, which was the Russian Order of Suvorov, and which had been presented to him by Stalin. He assured them that this Order entitled him to travel free on all buses in Russia. Whether this was true, I never discovered, but the princesses were suitably impressed.

We flew back later in the afternoon to Copenhagen and the Field Marshal came back with us to the Sokvesthuset for tea. Although we were only to be in Copenhagen for two or three days we never-theless had to bring down the nucleus of the staff. It was fun to stay in this palatial flat if only for a short time, and we were most grateful that the Danish Government had made it available to the C-in-C. The troops were thrilled to have this opportunity of seeing the Field Marshal at close quarters. During the course of conver-sation the question of his retirement came up, and the publication of his Memoirs. Apparently they were far advanced and would be published only after he retired from NATO that autumn. 'The danger with Memoirs,' he said, 'is that you must be careful not to be critical about your friends, because you are bound to lose them. As you get older you cannot afford to lose friends, as you cannot replace them. Look at Brookie; he was much too outspoken about Winston and their friendship finished.' So Monty was not going to make that sort of mistake apparently, but when we discussed the matter further he added, 'But I must speak the truth.' The truth, thought I, what will the truth turn out to be? And my heart sank. Sure enough, when his Memoirs came out there were some pretty caustic remarks in them regarding Ike Eisenhower's generalship during the Normandy Campaign in 1944. Ike was just reaching the end of his second term as President of the United States and it is not difficult to visualise his feelings and the feelings of thousands of Americans when these strictures were published. I am not concerned with the truth or otherwise of these criticisms, but the fact that Monty lost a great deal of regard in which he was held, there can be no doubt whatsoever.

That evening the Field Marshal was dined by the Danish Government. At the end of the evening Monty was presented with a handsome silver casket, which appeared to be designed as a cigar box, but I never discovered what other use Monty made of it. The following day we said farewell to him as he flew back to Paris and retirement. His very long and distinguished career was coming to a close, and a few days later he handed over to General Sir Richard Gale and left for England and his Mill.

We returned to Norway in my Dakota as soon as we could as the summer was beginning to slip away. In Norway it is all too short. We were in August and it was time to explore Norway before the winter set in. We packed into two Mercedes Benz cars from the Headquarters and set off up Route 50. On the first day we travelled through Lillehammer to Dombas, and thence to Andelsnes. I was particularly anxious to travel down the roads traversed by British forces when they made their abortive efforts in 1940 – nearly twenty years away. The main operation in the south had been to try and 'pinch out' Trondheim by two converging attacks based on Andelsnes to the south and Namsos in the north.

Lillehammer was on the main north road and it was here that some Territorials had been surprised and captured. Today there is only a railway museum to attract the tourist. As we went north so we found the hills closing in on both sides, the road and the railway running along side by side. We stopped for lunch on the side of the road some miles south of Dombas and found there a memorial, written both in Norwegian and English, commemorating a battle which took place nearby in the early seventeenth century. Reading the superscription it emerged that in about 1620 a group of Scottish mercenaries, under a Captain Sinclair, had landed at Andelsnes and were in the process of making their way to Sweden, in whose pay they were to be. Norway at this time was a province of Denmark, and the local Norwegian farmers decided to destroy this force before it could join the Swedes. They waited up in the hills until the force reached the point where the memorial was erected and then ambushed them by rolling rocks down the hill both in front and in rear of the column. A battle ensued in which the Captain and many others were killed and the rest taken prisoner and were then taken off to work on the farms.

We went on and then turned off to the west at Dombas and made for Andelsnes. It was up this road that the Regular 15th Infantry Brigade had marched in order to link up with the other column, but they did not get far because the Germans anticipated them at Dombas and in the presence of superior German air forces, were forced to go back the way they came. This withdrawal was not easy and often they had to lie up during the daytime in railway tunnels. Nevertheless, it culminated in a masterly evacuation with remarkably few casualties, which was not surprising because the column commander was Bernard Paget.

We stayed in Andelsnes for the night and I held a press conference. It became clear at an early stage that the press were somewhat sceptical regarding the ability of NATO to come to the rescue of Norway if attacked by Russia. Their memories of 1940 and the subsequent occupation by Germany were a little too fresh. I could show that NATO was a closely-knit confederation of powerful states, with their motto: 'One for all and all for one.' I went on to point out that Norway, a relatively small country with limited forces, was astride two of the three exits to the open sea for Russia, therefore vital in any major 'confrontation'.

At this stage it was obvious that they attached importance only to what they could see on the ground in the form of soldiers. This was a matter to which we gave increasing attention and, by 1960, we had infantry brigades, composed of several nations, available to be flown in at short notice from the centre. It was a delicate encounter with the Norwegian journalists, who were, in the politest possible way, seeking some positive proof that 1940 would not be repeated, leaving me in no doubt that much as they appreciated the interview, doubts still remained.

The following day we set out for Namsos, where General Carton de Wiart had landed, being the other wing of the pincer movement against Trondheim. He met with no greater success, his difficulty being to work his way down the side of the Trondheim Fjord in the face of enemy warships. He had to retrace his footsteps and it must have been a very long time since ground troops had found themselves attacked by enemy naval gunfire. From then onwards we went north and finally arrived at a large air station in the north, commanded by General Tufte Jonson. We spent the night there and the next day went on ferries to Narvik and Bardofoss. When we arrived at Bardofoss we sent the cars back to Oslo and flew on to Kirkenes, the most northerly point of Norway and adjoining Russia.

The interesting thing was to drive out to the frontier and visit some of the frontier posts. These observation posts were built in exactly the same way as those on the DMZ in Korea, which I had seen four years before – I suppose few people had witnessed the extreme east and the extreme west of the Communist enclave in this way. These posts had their Russian counterparts and it was obvious that there must have been long stretches of time, particularly during the winter, when neither side could see a thing, but what mattered was to keep the posts occupied. Apparently the Laplanders moved through this sort of no man's land with total indifference to the two garrisons, complete with their reindeer. Whether it was Finland, Russia, Sweden or Norway, they remained a law unto themselves.

We then boarded a ship and commenced the long crawl back by sea, visiting Varda, Hammerfest, Tromso, Harstad, Trondheim again and finally Bergen, from where we returned to Oslo by train. The whole trip took nearly three weeks, but I came away with a clear picture of the rivers and mountains, roads and railways, ferries and islands. Norway is very long and very narrow. Its length is demonstrated by the fact that if Norway was pivoted on its most southerly point, Kristiansund, Kirkenes would come to rest in North Africa. Along its coasts are a quarter of a million islands of all sizes and the population of this enormous country was at this time less than four million, or half the size of Greater London. This wide dispersion led to the permanent stationing of a Brigade Group in North Norway.

When we got back to Oslo we were well into September and there seemed to be a lot to do. We had an excellent Public Relations officer in Klaus Koren and he suggested that we should have an 'Open Evening' at Koleas and invite as many local Norwegians in to show them how we lived. The first part of the evening included some excellent playing of the Hardanger violin by a very skilled Norwegian player, some Norwegian country dancing, our own piper and some Highland dancing. Our piper, Mackeown, was very popular and when a certain part of the concert was reached, he turned to the audience, who understood English perfectly, and in broad Scots announced that he would translate into English what had transpired. The earlier, rather frigid atmosphere was broken when we had our own eightsome reel in which Beatrice, myself, Sergeant Thurlow and Corporal Kean took part. This latter was a tour de force as we danced with rare abandon, finally to the accompaniment of shouts from the Norwegians themselves who had never seen anything like it, and probably never would do so again. It was a memorable evening for all of us and achieved the aim of assuring the Norwegians that we were only human.

In October we commenced preparations to stay in Copenhagen but before we went we had to make up our minds whether we wanted to stay in the Holmenvei. The mood of the staff after the first three months hadn't changed; they said that it was a risk they were prepared to take if it only meant living in Kolsos whilst we lived in a hotel. So the die was cast and we departed for Denmark. This visit, being the first, entailed a lot of visiting of commanders and establishments. I started off in Zetland and had amongst other things an interesting day with the Royal Danish Navy which included a run down the coast in a motor torpedo boat. Denmark is very flat and the highest point is over in Jutland where there is a hill about 400 feet high, called the Mountain of Heaven. Running down the coast the lowness of the cliffs demonstrated what little height there was anywhere and the contrast with Norway could not have been greater. The Army is the number one service both in Denmark and Norway, in the same way as the Royal Navy was with us, and the Army Commander, General Hjalf found it difficult to believe that I thought the problems of the Northern Region were more to do with the air and the sea rather than the land.

The urgent need, from an operational point of view, was to create a suitable command for the Baltic. This sea was one of the only two exits into the Atlantic open to the Russians, and the Germans in Schleswig Holstein were not linked up in any way with the Danes who dominated the channel between them and Sweden.

The Danes throughout were lukewarm regarding the whole project, whereas the Germans were enthusiastic and were prepared to make considerable concessions in respect of command in order to bring it about. In order to give some idea how strongly the Danes felt, a conversation took place between the Danish Minister of Defence with the then German Minister of Defence, Herr Strauss. The latter, in pressing the agreement of Denmark to the formation of what was called Combaltap (Command Baltic Approaches), said that they quite understood Danish reservations in the matter as the occupation of Denmark in the War must have been most painful to them. 'Oh,' replied the Danish Minister, 'we were not thinking of that war but of the Prussian-Danish War of 1864.' This took the wind out of the sails of Herr Strauss who had not realised that the Danish hatred of Germany was already a century old. The Danes realised that it was not possible to ignore the overriding need of NATO indefinitely, but time was still required to overcome the political difficulties.

Copenhagen is quite a different capital to Oslo and everything is so much more concentrated in this lovely city with its ballet, theatres, art galleries and other places of interest. The lovely flat, which we inherited, was put to good and continuous use during the time we were there, and it also gave us the opportunity of meeting some of the leading Danish figures, such as Professor Nils Bohr, the famous physicist and scientist, and Mr Schaufuss, the leader of the Royal Danish Ballet.

We moved on to Kiel where the Commander was a German sailor, Rear Admiral Rogge, who had commanded a raider during the War, in the South Atlantic and Indian Ocean, until he was finally sunk somewhere near St Helena. The cruiser which sank him did not stay, as there was a German submarine in the vicinity and this resulted in the Captain and the crew taking to their open boats and navigating their way back to Europe, which they reached intact. That was the measure of this very interesting man. He wrote a book called *Ship 16* or *Under Ten Flags*, the later title indicating the measures forced upon them to remain afloat. He was married to a most charming wife. He was prepared to go to any length to bring about the Baltic Command and he had made a number of approaches on his level to help to bring this about. He was quite happy to see the overall commander a Dane, with the Headquarters located (as it would need to be) in Jutland. The enthusiasm of the Admiral was quite infectious and was one of the deciding factors which led to this command coming into existence before I left. On this trip although I took two or three Danish 'aides', the Danes generally were still somewhat difficult. We arrived in Kiel with the 'home' team, which, needless to say, included the Piper. We gave a large dinner party at the Club for about forty guests, but I think the Piper rather stole the show, as the entertainment he provided must have been unique. I think Admiral Rogge was amused at this display and to a certain extent envious that, as late as 1958, such a thing was still possible. We were in Kiel for no more than ten days, but during that time we travelled around and visited many regiments, airfields and naval establishments. The Admiral always carried with him a portfolio containing complete details regarding the units we visited, with thumbnail sketches of commanders, state of equipment and training and building projects. Nothing was left to chance, with typical German thoroughness.

It was at a later stage that I discovered that the Lüneburger Heide, where I did my attachment to the German Army in 1937, over twenty years previously, was within the bounds of Schleswig Holstein. Our reception in Germany was warm and generous and it was an atmosphere which I knew and in which I felt at ease. This did not apply either to Beatrice or the Piper, both of whom found the situation and the people difficult. It was not until the beginning of December that we flew out to Oslo, and it was a measure of the size of the command that it had taken nearly six months to acquaint myself with the overall military and political problems.

By December the immediate problem was to pick up our Dalmatian which had been left with some friends of ours, Wing Commander and Mrs Evan. There had never been any difficulty about taking a dog into Denmark, provided the necessary formalities were observed, but Germany was quite another matter. I think rabies was so rife that it was permissible for anyone to shoot a loose dog and this was apt to be generously interpreted. In conversation it emerged that we had given notice to quit our house in the Holmenvei and that if we failed to find a suitable alternative house we would be moving into a hotel. 'Oh,' said the Wing Commander, 'have you not had a look at the house we call the

Commander-in-Chief's house?' It emerged that a well-known Norwegian shipping owner had built a house on the fringe of Oslo Fjord, although he and his family were based in Tromso. So we went out to have a look. The house was perched high up on the bank of small fjord leading into the main Oslo Fjord. We walked around, and it was surprising how big the dining room was, but the ceiling was low. I asked the Piper whether the ceiling was not too low for piping, but he assured me that there was plenty of clearance. Actually I do not think there were more than a couple of inches in it. The house was almost exactly what we wanted and once the decision had been taken the staff lost no time in giving effect to it. Nevertheless, we only just managed to be installed before Christmas, but did very little entertaining until the New Year. The Christmases we spent in Oslo were all punishing. With such an international Headquarters it was natural for each department to wish to excel the others in the hospitality they dispensed. It was automatic to attend each one of them, but one could only do justice to the excellent fare provided in the time available. And so we moved into 1959.

That year proved to be quite exceptional. I had heard that the Queen Mother was paying a Royal visit to Kenya in February and as Colonels of Regiments were allowed one free trip abroad to visit Regular battalions, I thought this would be a good opportunity to go.

The Mau Mau rising had been put down by this time and Kenyatta was in house arrest up country. I flew out from Heathrow, stopping at Rome and Khartoum, arriving late one afternoon. I was met by Charles MacKinnon who was commanding the Battalion at this time, and also Major General Nigel Tapp, the District Commander, with whom I would be staying for most of the time. Nairobi is 6,000 feet up, so it was important not to attempt too much too quickly. This was the first time I had been with the 1st Battalion since I left it in India twenty-six years before. It was a very different atmosphere from the one I remembered.

Much of the accommodation was temporary. Being practically on the equator, heavy rains were of frequent occurrence and turned the whole camp into a quagmire. The troops were in good order nevertheless. They had only recently arrived from Bahrain where they had been operational and had not yet had time to get bored. It was normal to do most of the training up country, which would provide a further break from normal routine, and as Nairobi was reasonably sophisticated the danger of boredom had not yet arisen.

On the following Sunday the Queen Mother attended Divine Service and then came on to the barracks to visit the Battalion. The Royal car was to drive around the barracks, the troops grouping themselves outside their company lines to give her a cheer as she passed. I had stayed the previous night with Charles MacKinnon and we drove together from his house up to the barracks. We were about to enter when he gave a gasp and said that he had left his uniform behind. He could hardly proceed without it, so I went on and took his part at the Battalion early service while he rushed back to the house. The service was held in a tent and when it was over we went off and got dressed for the Royal visit. The reception party assembled outside the Officers' Mess, consisting of the Commanding Officer, his wife, myself, the Adjutant and a small girl, beautifully turned out, who was to present a bouquet to the Queen Mother when she arrived. It was now close on to the arrival time when we would get some sort of warning of the arrival of the Royal car, but the silence was broken by the small voice of the little girl: 'But where is the bouquet?' There was a moment of stunned horror when it was realised that there was, in fact, no bouquet at all. The Adjutant wasted no further time, snatched the ribbon, which was luckily available, and dashed to the Mess, demonstrating a burst of speed of which I had not deemed him capable. Bursting upon the assembled wives like a tornado, the company exploded around the room pulling out every variety of flower from the many vases which stood arranged, and just as a long hoot from the Royal car announced the arrival of the Queen Mother, an imposing bouquet was thrust into the hands of the calm little girl, who rewarded this tremendous effort with a quiet and contented smile.

The Queen Mother swept around the barracks, came to rest at the Mess and thereafter everything went according to plan. She had a word with everybody and could not have been more charming. I stayed a couple of nights with Bill Henning and his wife Mavin. His son-in-law was Hugh Worthington Wilmer, who had carried the key of Edinburgh Castle when I was installed as Governor, and who had since retired and was farming next door. The whole thing was somewhat depressing, because there were many signs of the long tenure of the British, with churches and clubs soon to be demolished.

I flew back to London and thence to Oslo again. We went down to Denmark for a couple of weeks and then on to Paris for the spring NATO meeting, which was attended not only by NATO commanders and their staffs, but also the Chiefs of Defence and Heads of Services of all the nations composing the NATO Alliance. It was a colourful meeting and lasted about a week. One of the subjects discussed was the weakness of the Northern Flank and what was necessary to strengthen it.

There was one field where an improvement could be effected, which was to bring Denmark and Germany much closer together and form the Baltic Command. General Laurie Norstad, SACEUR, invited me to consider the problem and to report to him the following year. A great deal had been done in the previous years to make the north more effective: the Norwegian Navy had been redeployed away from the Oslo Fjord and was now largely based on the Atlantic ports; two modern airfields had been built at Bodo and Bardofoss and a complete infantry brigade was now permanently stationed in the north with Headquarters at Harstad. The Danish Navy had previously been largely concentrated at Copenhagen, but was now deployed in a number of ports and was therefore much less vulnerable.

We flew to England and on to Scotland in the summer of 1959. Later I went to the Army Golf Meeting at St Andrews, for the General's Cup, [**Editor's Note:** which he won, characteristically not mentioned] while Beatrice went on up to Dornoch to work on some murals she had painted there some years before. We then flew back to Norway and Midsummer's Day. I could not remember a better summer since 1921. The celebration for Midsummer's Day in Norway goes back over the centuries and is more to do with paganism than anything else. It looked as if it was going to be an exceptional year so we pushed the boat out. We had the usual drinks and buffet, followed by Highland dancing and Norwegian folk dancing, all of it interspersed with trips into the fjord on the barge of the Commander-in-Chief Home Fleet who happened to be visiting Oslo at this time. Normally there were huge bonfires on all the hills, but the summer was so dry, even in Norway, that this was stopped. I think the party finally broke up at about four in the morning, but it was difficult to say, as it remained fairly light throughout.

After a few weeks here we went back to Denmark for a month, which enabled me to commence some of the planning necessary for the creation of the Baltic Command, and also on into Schleswig Holstein to see some training there. I went to the Munster Lager, where I had carried out training with the German Army twenty years before and rather astonished some of the officers with my knowledge of the country which I remembered clearly from 1937.

From there we went to call on Sir Christopher Steele, British Ambassador. It was the first time that I had a German Guard of Honour, and it was embarrassing to find oneself followed by hundreds of eyes because it was the custom to look at the inspecting officer throughout. I was interested to discover that strong measures were being taken to ensure that never again would the German General Staff be allowed to move back into the position they occupied before Hitler's day.

It was soon the autumn when I flew out to the United States with Captain van Gorder of the US Navy. It had always been considered desirable that CINCNORTH should fly out to Washington, primarily in order to meet the Standing Group, who had overall responsibility for the NATO Alliance as a whole (including SACLANT). On such occasions the Americans do not do things by halves. We flew into Washington early one morning and our first trip was a visit to George Washington's home at Mount Vernon – a very comfortable old colonial estate it proved to be with every-thing left exactly as it was in his time. The following day we drove out to Yorktown, where Cornwallis had surrendered to Washington in the American War of Independence. It was notice-able that the history of the United States is of such recent origin that great care is taken to preserve everything of historical impor-tance years. So when we visited Yorktown the battlefield was well preserved with flags stuck in the ground to show where the British positions were at the time. These flags interested me in that they were supposed to be Union Jacks and yet had an unfamiliar look. Then I realised that the Union with Ireland had taken place in 1801, about thirty years later, and therefore it was the national flag of the day without the Irish.

At a later stage we went on to Gettysburg where the South sustained a defeat from which they were never to recover. This battle was not very well fought and demonstrated that, without that tactical genius Stonewall Jackson, Lee's strategy was bound to founder. The final deployment, shaped like a horseshoe and extending over many miles, is today a National Memorial to all those who fought there because every regiment and battalion had erected in the area a memorial of their own. The attack by Pickett's Brigade, which was utterly destroyed, was composed of men for the most part well under 20 years of age. Their memorial shows a leader pointing towards the enemy, with mere youths as his audience, but the artist was worthy of this scene and the look of eagerness and determination which shines in their faces made the whole trip to Gettysburg worthwhile. Talking to many Americans after the 1939–1945 War it was an experience to discover that the thing that remained in their minds was the fact that 'class mates' at West Point found themselves engaged in battle against each other during the Civil War.

We then flew down to Fort Benning, which is the American School of Infantry, and the organisation there had to be seen to be believed. The War with Vietnam had yet to come but this machine was running in high gear. I particularly remember being present at a demonstration laid on for some National Guards by the Rangers, a specialist infantry formation, which approximated to our own Commandos during the War. Their training had reached a very high standard. Thence to Norfolk and the Headquarters of SACLANT (Supreme Allied Commander Atlantic). This is one of the most important Headquarters of the Western Alliance, and is sumptuous. I was given a complete quarter to myself in a VIP compound, and then had a series of discussions with the senior sailors.

SACLANT would have liked to have had the Norwegian Fleet closely integrated into the Atlantic Fleet, but our feeling was that the fleet was particularly well suited for work closer inshore and could serve SACLANT better from there. We felt that this applied just as much to the naval effort as to the air and ground forces. The sailors were very understanding, even if they were not convinced, and allowed the matter to drop because the forces we were discussing comprised only a fraction of the whole. This was our last port of call and we then returned to Washington to attend a meeting with the Standing Committee in the Pentagon. There had been considerable discussion as to whether it was sound to have the political heads of the Alliance in Paris, with the military heads in Washington on the other side of the Atlantic. To me it appeared unavoidable as by far the greatest contribution to NATO came from the United States and the simplest place from which to control the whole machine was Washington. In any case it was to the Pentagon that we went, and plunged down into the basement to confront the serried ranks of the Committee which was led by Air Chief Marshal Sir George Mills and who was supported by high-ranking officers from all the member countries, together with a powerful supporting cast of a great number of staff officers.

One of the main issues was the question of the Baltic Command structure. Here a great measure of agreement was reached and they were glad to hear that it would be raised at the NATO Conference the following spring, and that action would proceed rapidly thereafter. There was another question which worried them and that was why Norway had accepted atomic weapons (in the form of the Honest John) but declined to accept the missiles they fired. The Norwegians, with their common frontier with the Russians, were very sensitive regarding Russian reactions and had argued that in an emergency the missiles could easily be flown in, whereas to keep them on Norwegian soil could be interpreted by the Russians as a veiled threat which they wished to avoid. The Committee suggested that I should discuss this issue with the Norwegians when I returned, as they would far prefer to see them in Norway. This I promised to do, but I made no impression on the Norwegians who steadfastly refused to accept them, however illogical it might appear from the viewpoint of Washington. With the conclusion of this discussion our mission to the United States was complete.

When I got back there was a piece of news for me which gave me intense pleasure: I had been promoted to full General which set the seal on 1959 as a really vintage year. We managed to get across to Glasgow for the Armistice Sunday service of the Regiment and then we finally came to rest in Oslo for the Christmas and New Year, with the usual round of drink parties, lunches and dinners.

*   *   *

In the early spring of 1960 we went off on a protracted tour in the Mediterranean as a consequence of a plan which Richard Gale had introduced whereby the commanders should be at home in turn to each other. This particular plan included visits to the Commander-in-Chief Mediterranean, Admiral Sir Alexander Bingley, and the Commander-in-Chief South, the American Admiral Brown, known as 'Cat' Brown. This provided us with a splendid alibi for something of a 'swan' which the aircrew were avid to exploit. We departed in the middle of March and first of all flew to Rome, where we spent three days, then to Athens and a long drive out to Corinth and on the canal.

We spent half a day at the Acropolis and saw the gaps there created by the removal of the Elgin Marbles to the British Museum over 100 years ago (which always irritated Beatrice that such vandalism had not yet been put right). Then we left for Malta and the beginning of the business of the trip. We arrived in Malta late in the morning, and the following morning I called on the Governor, Admiral Sir Guy Grantham. It was just ten years since I had been in Malta and I always enjoyed staying there. We operated separately during the day, with Beatrice going off to have a bathe and later attending a presentation given by the Commander-in-Chief Mediterranean.

This command was entirely naval and included the fleets of the United States, Great Britain, Italy, Turkey and Greece. France had withdrawn her fleet from this command. The combined strength of these fleets was impressive, and the importance of having a separate Naval Command in the Mediterranean was clearly demonstrated, and which added substance for the need of a similar organisation in the Baltic. That evening the Governor, Admiral Sir Guy Grantham, gave a mammoth cocktail party. The following day was free, enabling me to go to one or two of the places I knew in the 1940s, and in the evening Admiral and Lady Bingham gave a large dinner party at Admiralty House. The last time I had dined there was ten years before when the Commander-in-Chief Mediterranean was Admiral Sir John Edelsten, and I had sat on the left of his wife, Frances. I always considered this house to be quite outstanding for a Commander-in-Chief and was surprised to discover that plans were under way to put him somewhere else.

Apart from anything else it was exciting to discover that the floor came from the deck of a famous old battleship in the time of Nelson. I thought that that should have been sufficient reason for staying, but the decision had been taken. A very colourful evening when I dined 'in state' with the Royal Navy for the last time, and it was fun to share it with Beatrice.

The following morning we all departed for Naples and the Headquarters South, of which 'Cat' Brown was the Commander. Again the arrangements were somewhat elaborate and led to me flying off with Laurie Norstad in his palatial aircraft, with Beatrice and the rest of our party tagging along later in the Dakota. It was ten years since I had been in the Mediterranean, but this spring day in April 1960 was exceptionally lovely and the flight was over all too soon. We were met at the airport by 'Cat' Brown and moved into the cars lined up there while he left by helicopter so as to get to the other end ahead of us, thence on to the Headquarters and a beaming 'Cat' to receive us.

The Admiral led off with Laurie Norstad, followed by General Valley and followed in turn by Admiral Bingley and myself. It was a very large parade made up of contingents of Italians, Greeks and Turks. Along a high embankment behind the parade was a row of Carabinieri mounted on horses. It was very colourful and a remarkable achievement for a sailor. We all marched around the parade, keeping more or less in step, returned to the saluting base and the troops marched past very creditably. There was little doubt that 'Cat' Brown was a very popular commander, enjoying the confidence in particular of the Greeks and the Turks. On one occasion, when carrying out an inspection in Greece, he turned up wearing Greek national costume and did so very convincingly.

We left the parade and moved over to his offices, which were quite close. In the anteroom there was a photograph with the caption 'I like those who like me'. Looking closer one saw that there was a group of men standing on either side of 'Cat', all of whom had had his face superimposed upon their own. We had lunch and then went on to the presentation. It was very impressive to find such a high degree of cooperation within a command of widely different nations such as the Greeks and the Turks, who had been natural enemies for centuries. We all stayed at the Admiral's House and were royally entertained for two or three days, with a dance in the evening. On the Saturday, Admiral Brown laid on a trip to Capri, which included also Desmond Vigors, my Personal Assistant at this time, and Pip, his wife. It was a brilliantly sunny day and the sun's rays were reflecting through the entrance to provide a different sort of light inside which was quite enchanting.

The following month we were back in Paris again in order to deliver an address on the creation of a Baltic Command to the assembled company of NATO senior officers. It was well received and was followed by an open discussion in which Admiral Qvistgaard played an important part. At the end of the session it was accepted in principle that such a command must be set up and it was left to the countries concerned to decide how best this could be achieved. By this time a great deal of preparatory work had been carried out and the framework was in being before the end of the year. The Headquarters was to be set up in Jutland, near Aarhus, and the commander would be a Dane. The Naval Command would alternate between Germany and Denmark, with a German to start with. The Air Headquarters were to be at Karup. During the remainder of my tour in command we steadily built this Headquarters up and a long-felt need was met. I sympathised with the inborn hostility of the Danes towards the Germans, but the latter's efforts to make the plan work were beyond praise.

In June we went north again as I was particularly anxious to see whether it would be practicable to create an airfield at Banak. This was a temporary airfield built by the Germans during the War to help them to operate against our convoys to Russia. It was crude by modern standards and the runway was made of sleepers. The Norwegians were anxious that it should be made operational and be paid for out of infrastructure. Obviously the matter needed to be examined in detail by the air experts, but the site was excellent. We stayed locally for the two or three days involved and it was the only occasion during my tour that I stayed for any length of time in the north in summer when the sun never set. The midnight sun apparently is associated with a red sun peeping just over the horizon, but ours was well above the horizon all night and it was difficult to go to sleep. As I lay in the bedroom with the blinds drawn, I could not help recalling those amusing lines of Lewis Carroll from the *Walrus and the Carpenter*.

'*The sun was shining mightily, shining with all its might,
And this was strange because it was the middle of the night.*'

It came as something of a surprise to find that the place was swarming with the most enormous mosquitoes; how they managed to survive the winter I would not know. I do not think they were malarial, but they certainly knew how to bite.

Later that summer we received permission to visit Bornholm. This island is situated in the heart of the Baltic and is Danish. When I first arrived I was asked not to visit the island, as the Russians were very sensitive about it. The island is about 200 miles west of Denmark and therefore deep behind the frontier separating West and East Germany. Of course it is an asset to NATO because of the radar establishments installed there. The Governor was a great character and had played a big part in inducing the Russians to leave in 1945.

That autumn there was a large-scale exercise in the north with the British Parachute Regiment taking part. Norway is not the best country for exercises of this sort and the area was strewn with boulders of varying sizes in the middle of a swamp. We watched this take place, General Sir Richard Gale having flown up from Paris to be present. When the troops had landed they moved past us on their way to their forming-up place (and it was marvellous to see their faces shining with the satisfaction of achievement). The paratroopers then took to the hills and came down across the forward routes of the defending Norwegians in much the same way as the Germans had done in 1940 and the Chinese later on in Korea. The Norwegian General Staff were well pleased, as all the lessons which had been learnt in 1940 were shown still to apply.

After the usual hectic Christmas and New Year we moved into 1961 and the last year of my career as a soldier. In February we were invited to dinner by their Majesties the King and Queen of Denmark at the Amelienburg Palace in Copenhagen. The invitation included our Piper, now Maclean from South Uist, and my ADC, Johnnie Langlands. The Piper had been provided by the Queen's Own Cameron Highlanders (now the Queen's Own Highlanders after the amalgamation with the Seaforths) and he was not only an excellent Piper, but also had a magnificent physique, and in full dress looked tremendous. We duly presented ourselves and later went in to dinner, the King escorting Beatrice, while I accompanied the Queen. The King sat at one end of the table with Beatrice on his left. There must have been about forty guests.

The King was anxious for the Piper to play in exactly the same way as he would do on a guest night but wanted me to be responsible for the procedure. We had arranged a programme beforehand, the first part to consist of a Slow March, a March, a Strathspey and a Reel, the latter being played behind my chair. At the conclusion of this part of the programme the Piper would stop, be offered a dram of whisky and then play off with another march and leave the room. He was to come back later for the rest of the programme.

Dinner came to an end, the table was cleared and the stage set for the Piper. The doors (leading through towards the kitchen) were thrown open and in trooped practically the whole of the Royal staff. This little army moved around behind the Queen and took up position to hear and see the Piper. Then the doors on the other side of the room were opened and we heard Maclean tune up and start the first tune. Maclean swept into view like a ship with all its sails set, moved majestically behind the King and around the far end of the table. It was only then that he became aware of the assembled party and was clearly disconcerted as his eyes at once shot towards the ceiling and he turned pink in the face. From then onwards he took no chances and played as if his life depended on it. He played splendidly, duly got his dram and withdrew, returning later to complete the programme. When dinner was over we first of all had a series of reels and other Highland dances. The first of these was an eightsome reel and when this was over the Queen said that she would like to have a word with the Piper so we moved over to where he was still standing. Her Majesty put Maclean completely at his ease and they had a pleasant chat lasting quite a few minutes. Soon afterwards he was joined by Johnnie Langlands to discuss the next dance. After a few moments the taciturn Maclean said, 'Oh, excuse me Sir, who was that very nice lady I was just talking to?' The evening passed rapidly, culminating in some Danish country dances in which the King excelled, but which we could only watch. A memorable evening.

*   *   *

We had a very big exercise in the early spring involving large troop movements, covering Schleswig Holstein. It became unreal when we were again forced to have the airdrops in broad daylight, with the defending troops 'cheating' and trying to exploit a situation, which had nothing to do with war. It was fun to see Rear Admiral Rogge playing the part of the Land Commander, which he thoroughly enjoyed.

In May we went down to Paris for the last time and my last NATO Conference where Admiral Sir Alexander Bingley and myself, as retiring NATO Commanders, were presented with commemorative citations for our work for NATO. After we had wound up our affairs in Copenhagen, it was very flattering that all the Heads of Service, led by Admiral Qvistgaard, were at the aerodrome to bid us farewell.

We finally left as we had come, by sea. When the ship pulled clear and moved down the fjord, all the little boats of the Headquarters sailed alongside and escorted us towards the open sea for some miles before turning away back to the shore. I had had aspirations to join the Royal Navy so it was appropriate that my career should have finished at sea.

Chapter Twenty-three

Envoi

When I retired in September 1961, it was almost exactly forty years since I had arrived, somewhat apprehensively, at Sandhurst in 1921. My active thirty-eight years as a soldier included thirty in which I was either a regimental soldier or in command, the other eight being spent either at the Staff College or on the Staff. The last seventeen years of my service were spent in the rank of Major General or above, and this, combined with a last appointment overseas of three years, meant that when the time came to retire I had no contacts with the outside world in civilian life. The Army Council appreciated this and offered me the appointment of Governor of the Royal Hospital, Chelsea. This was very generous as it provided the means of bridging the gap for a period of upwards of five years with a roof over our heads and a small salary in addition. I felt, however, that if I had anything to offer it should be placed at the service of the young and therefore I declined it. In retrospect it would have served as a 'firm base' from which Beatrice could have picked up the many contacts in London which she had garnered over the years, but whereas I was concerned in starting her off as an artist, she was equally determined to set me up in civil life in a proper home.

We first of all rented a flat in Queen's Gate and soon after we were settled there I was offered a lucrative job in the Fiji Islands to do with trading between the islands and Australia. It seemed to be yet another way of prolonging profitability without much personal satisfaction. That was to be the end of efforts to keep me in circulation.

It was rather exciting to be informed at the end of 1961 that I had been created a Knight Grand Cross of the Order of the Bath, which set the seal on my career as a soldier and was very acceptable. In March 1962 we finally bought a manor house in Inveresk, which was situated about 6 miles out of Edinburgh. It was a lovely house, having been built in 1760, and included two cottages enclosed in five acres. I was still Colonel of the Cameronians (Scottish Rifles) and from there it was possible to carry out the duties involved with Regimental Headquarters at Lanark.

We were in the process of trying to come to terms with the new situation when a regimental crisis of some dimensions arose. In April 1962, our 1st Battalion, stationed in Minden, Germany, had had a monumental fracas with the bargees on the River Weser, 'which washes its walls on the southern side'. It had started in the usual way with far too much drink taken and in the early hours of the morning a cafe was wrecked and much other damage was done. This incident had been widely reported in the Scottish press but was completely ignored by Fleet Street as being 'news unworthy'.

It was in June that Mrs Bessie Braddock put a question to the Minister for War, Mr Profumo, in respect of a court martial held in Germany of two or three soldiers of a regiment in her constituency who were charged with 'Incitement to Mutiny'. These men were found guilty and the sentence was very heavy indeed. Fleet Street had its representatives in Germany but, somehow or other, the trial of these men escaped notice. The debate became increasingly heated, with the Minister for War insisting that the normal procedure had been followed, but with the Opposition suggesting that the Army had something to hide. If this affair had been played down there might well have been an end to it, but unfortunately, the Minister for War 'trailed his coat' and suggested that, perhaps, on this occasion, the press had missed a trick. 'Missed a trick, have we indeed?' said Fleet Street, being aware of certain other matters to do with his private life and at once Fleet Street was emptied of reporters, whose orders were to go to Germany and rake up whatever was available to besmirch the reputation of the Army, and indirectly the reputation of the Minister for War.

On arrival these reporters found far too little for their purpose until they stumbled upon the Cameronians, whose guardroom was packed with soldiers awaiting trial for the affray of two months before. This was heaven sent and they gorged themselves on this unexpected prey. It was therefore from Minden that the press launched their attack on the hapless Secretary of State for War and their virulence knew no bounds. The cafe proprietor described the soldiers as 'Poisoned Dwarfs' and although the interpretation of this word is 'Damned Nuisances', the Regiment was confronted with an appellation which continued until they finally bowed themselves out some years later. The London press leapt upon this with glee and the headlines were plastered for days afterwards with it.

So it was that I found myself flying out to Germany to do what I could to repair some of the damage. It happened that the Battalion had had a particularly good year both in training, where they carried out some very exacting tests in the winter, combined with considerable success in the sporting world, and they were furious at the treatment that had been meted out to them by their own fellow countrymen. I called on the Mayor of Minden, Herr Pohle, and he found the whole thing quite incomprehensible as the citizens of the town continued to remain on the best possible terms with the soldiers. The Battalion was fortunate to have at this time as its Commanding Officer, Reggie Kettles, who proved to be completely 'unflappable' and tribute was paid to him and his 'unflappability' by a Labour MP in the House of Commons, which was well deserved. My visit was not without value, as I think they were happy to meet somebody whose purpose was to be helpful, but it was also possible to be aware of other problems which needed to be anticipated.

I reported back to the Secretary of State and he could not have been more helpful in trying to offset the predicament in which we were. The attack by the press upon a defenceless battalion, which bordered upon frenzy, was despicable because they knew that no retort was possible. They cared little what damage they did in order to achieve the object of getting rid of a politician and this kind of irresponsibility cannot fail to undermine the loyalty of the services; no regiment, no army could long survive treatment of this sort. (At a later stage, when their hysteria had faded a little, I think they realised that in order to have some viability they would need to be a little more temperate.)

The winter of 1962/1963 was one of the worst in living memory. It was a great pity but Beatrice became more and more absorbed in the business of being the chatelaine instead of moving back into her own field of painting. We were getting nowhere and it was necessary to break the deadlock in some way. It came by virtue of the arrival in Delhi of Lyon and Elizabeth Roussel, Beatrice's son and daughter-in-law. The fact that Beatrice had never travelled out of Europe seemed to be a heaven-sent opportunity to see this part of the world of which she had only dreamed. So it was that in December 1963 we embarked in the *Caledonia* for India, arriving at Port Said at the beginning of the second week of December.

It was a delightful and typical winter's day in Egypt, with the sun warm to hot and a cool breeze coming in from the desert. It enabled Beatrice to sketch all day. First of all she installed herself in the rigging of the ship, but was 'moved on' by a ship's officer, and then took up position on one of the hatches. It was a very exciting and colourful day for Beatrice and she revelled in its warmth

Thence to Bombay, where we arrived on December 21st and were met by representatives of the British Council and swept straight through the famous or infamous Customs of 1931 in record time. By this time I had made up my mind that having got as far as India we would be foolish not to go on to Australia, and we booked passages that day for Perth in Western Australia, in a cargo boat sailing in early February 1964. We arrived in Delhi on the evening of the 23rd and there were Lyon and Elizabeth Roussel to meet us. We were then swept into the Christmas festivities of Delhi for some days. It culminated in the New Year's Day parade which was taken by the President, and at which the Prime Minister, Mr Nehru, was present. It was to be one of his last public appearances as he died that year. The parade was watched by hundreds of thousands and the day was sunny but sharp, although it got a little warmer later.

The Army organised visits which were of real interest to us, but a keen and industrious staff officer saw to it that every minute of the day was completely filled in to our embarrassment and disappointment. One of the conducting officers had been captured the previous autumn by the Chinese when the latter crossed the existing frontier from Tibet, but apparently had been quite well treated and released as soon as the war was over. The Indian Army had long since pointed out to the Minister for Defence, Krishna Menon, that the Indian Forces on this front were dangerously weak and that one or more additional mountain brigades were needed up there. When the attack finally came in from Tibet, at a height of 14,000 feet, it was irresistible because the Chinese were organised and trained for operations at this real height, whereas the Indian reinforcements had to be rushed up from the plains, in the heat of the summer, un-acclimatised and unsuitably clad. Apart from that the roads up through the foothills towards the top were quite inadequate to support operations on any scale and much had to be done by airlifts with a depleted Transport Command. The Chinese fought the campaign on ground of their own choosing and the outcome was a foregone conclusion.

I believe that the Chinese were satisfied that operations on 'the roof of the world' had achieved their effect, and for which they were well-equipped and trained. Had they succumbed to the temptation of pursuing the Indian Army on down onto the plains they would have overreached themselves and gradually the Indian Army would have gained the initiative, even possibly reversing the situation. The Chinese set out to do two things: first was to move forward and establish themselves on a frontier which they had always maintained was legitimately theirs; and second was to establish China as the foremost Asiatic power. She had achieved both of these aims and was not going to prejudice either of them in seeking some spectacular victory on ground selected by India.

Delhi occupies a splendidly central position to the north-west, and so it was that we decided to travel up to Dehra Dun, a well-known hill station in the days of the Raj, and the home of the Indian Military College, which had been opened by the then Commander-in-Chief India, Field Marshal Sir Philip Chetwode, about thirty years before when I was there as a junior officer. The reason for this trip was to meet a retired Indian Army General (living there), Major General Rudra, who was amongst the first of the Indian Army officers to be promoted to the rank of General when India gained its independence in 1947, and under whom Lyon Roussel had served towards the end of the War. He had been commissioned from Sandhurst before 1914 and his stories of the reactionary British Army of those days were fascinating. One involved his sitting in a first-class carriage (having a ticket to do so) and the only occupant ordering him out. He declined to move, suddenly the other apologised and they became quite friendly for the rest of the trip. He saw a lot of fighting on the Western Front in 1914–1915, but when he returned to India was quite appalled at the handling of the Amritsar affair where hundreds of Indians were mown down. He wondered what he had been doing fighting in Europe if this sort of thing could happen in his own country.

The main interests in this six-week stay in India were to renew an association (which I had not expected to do) and to see the India of the 1960s through the eyes of Beatrice. Beatrice was entranced with the warmth, the colour and the people, and also had a deep respect for Indian religion and the Indian way of life. India had had independence for nearly twenty years when we were there, although strong British influences were still apparent; the India of thirty years before was fading away.

Since I had a number of friends in Australia, this also justified spreading our wings a bit, and led to us booking passages in the *Galileo*, an Italian ship of Lloyd Trestino. We sailed off from Freemantle towards the south and finally east along the south coast. The weather was miserable and the sea most uninviting, but our fellow passengers were practically all Italian immigrants and there must have been nearly 1,000 of them. They were either skilled or semi-skilled workers and I was later informed that the basic and secondary industries of Australia, which were just springing up, depended in large measure on these people. Apart from British immigrants, the most powerful influxes came from Italy, Yugoslavia and Greece. Not only were they essential to the growth of Australian industry, but they also made a considerable impact on Australian social life. When I had passed through Australia ten years previously on my way back from Korea, it was difficult to avoid mutton, or possibly beef, at most meals. Breakfast might easily consist of a steak crowned by two fried eggs and so on through the day. The arrival of these Europeans in great numbers led to a much more sophisticated approach to food. In the hotels and restaurants the menus had become much more wide-ranging, and even in small townships delicatessen shops abounded. It was the Italians who introduced English football to add to both types of rugger and their own game of Australian Football (rudely referred to as aerial ping-pong). Until then it had hardly been played at all. The Italian is very tenacious when it comes to speaking Italian and they tried to make the teaching of Italian compulsory in the schools. This the Australian Government could not permit as the only official language had to continue to be English. Immigrants from non-European countries were permitted to attend courses at Universities, but were required to leave the country when these courses had been completed. Talking to Australians the feeling was that the policy in the 1960s was the correct one and that it should be followed as long as it was practicable to do so. (They realised that Australia was a power vacuum, although immigrants from Europe helped to make it less obviously so; but they pointed to the difficulties now obtaining in the United States which were a result of having a 'free for all' right up to 1921.)

Before we left the ship the local press cornered me and I gave them an interview. They were particularly interested to hear that I had been alongside the 9th Australian Division at Alamein and had commanded Australians in the Commonwealth Division in Korea. In answer to a further question to do with readiness for war, I said that it was a matter for Australia, but the trouble with democracies was that they were apt to be overtaken by events, and at the outset of a war were normally at a disadvantage.

The following day a call came through from Canberra from a staff officer of the British High Commissioner inviting me to give no more press interviews, which was a form of effrontery as I was in Australia as a private citizen and at liberty to say what I thought. I met the High Commissioner later in Melbourne when we got there and apparently the Prime Minister, Mr Menzies, had gone up in smoke on reading the newspaper reports of the interview I gave, which appeared pretty innocuous to me. On the other hand there was sufficient fuel there for an Opposition spokesman (Mr Whitlam) to want to have an interview with me, which was quite another matter as I had not come to Australia to rock the boat. At the same time it was a sharp reminder how incredibly sensitive the Australians are to outside criticism of their affairs, however constructive it might appear to be. During this time Beatrice got really concerned with the possibility of settling in Australia and so a dilemma arose – to stay or not to stay? In this period I saw much of the Governor, General Sir Douglas Kendrew, and we played quite a bit of golf together; he was delighted with his job and the people with whom he worked, and was very much inclined to stay on after he retired. At this time, however, Beatrice got letters from home indicating that her daughter was more than interested in a young man and it seemed to be wrong to ignore the signals and with little further debate I booked passages back to England by air, events having proved to be too strong to remain in Australia.

Back in the UK, I was casting about to see if there was anything I could do with youth clubs but, as usual, they were looking for much younger people. It was in September that I ran into Dick Villiers who was the Secretary of the Royal Hospital and Home for Incurables in Putney, who asked me if I would like to join the Board with the possibility of becoming its Chairman. I went down and had a look at the Hospital and also met some members of the Board. The previous Chairman, General Sir Douglas Grace, had died suddenly in the summer from a heart attack and they were having difficulty in finding a successor. This was not the sort of work I was seeking. The hospital and home had been in existence for over a century and cared for patients who suffer from a wide range of rheumatic diseases for which there was no known cure. All the patients were completely immobile and get about either in chairs, or on stretchers. At that time there were 250 patients and they were tucked into every available space, making the nursing problem very heavy indeed. I could see that a great deal needed to be done in the way of modernisation, but when I heard that part of the property had been sold for over £300,000 and this sum would be available for reconstruction, I decided that here was something worthwhile to do and I accepted.

It was always understood that Beatrice would not be involved in the affairs of the Chairman, and did not wish to be considered for the day-to-day work. She decided that the best contribution she could make to the Hospital would be through her art. In 1965 she painted a mural in the men's dining room depicting St George and the Dragon, which she still considers the best of her works here. The ladies, who outnumbered the men by four to one, made it clear that they hoped that Beatrice would carry out some other work in their dining room and in 1967 she produced her impression of the fountains in Kensington Gardens, two figures in alcoves depicting Fortitude and Courage, and a third of Pan. The far wall was painted with the coat of arms of the Duke of Devonshire, our President, and a reproduction of an angel flying in through the window; it had the effect of transforming a very ordinary and uninteresting room into one that mattered. The rooms on the other side of the passage were lovely Adam rooms and these murals helped to offset the great disparity when she painted a series of equestrian and yachting murals in the men's rest room. It looks very much like a men's retreat today and they derive great pleasure from drawings of the more famous horses from the stables of the Queen, the Queen Mother and the Duke of Devonshire. With the completion of these murals her main contribution to the Hospital was completed.

In October 1967 we went up to Scotland by train, the occasion being a special gathering of the Highland Division on the North Inch of Perth. This famous old Division was about to be broken up, like so many of the others, and this was to be its swan song. We arrived in Edinburgh sufficiently early to take breakfast with Dorothy Simpson, and then we were on the road to Leila and Douglas Graham, who were now living in Brechin. I had not realised that Douglas was beginning to suffer from loss of memory, otherwise we would have made other arrangements, but as soon as the Grahams heard that we would be attending this reunion they insisted that we should stay with them. I suppose it was inevitable as I had commanded the 1st Gordons in his Brigade at El Alamein, and had succeeded him as Brigade Commander when he went off to command the 56th (London) Division. The following morning we all piled into the Daimler and set off for Perth, where we arrived in good time. It was an occasion to be remembered, and it was touching to meet so many of the commanders of twenty-five years before, even if we did all look quite ancient. Douglas Wimberley was of course the central figure, we all duly paid our respects to him and gathered together to be photographed with him and Field Marshal Montgomery.

After lunch we moved about meeting the others until Monty went out with James Oliver to take the parade. The rest of the afternoon was taken up with various displays, the most impressive of which was a parachute drop from about 4,000 feet by some experts who handled their parachutes so cleverly that they landed like daisies just in front of the saluting base. The Beating of Retreat by massed pipe bands concluded the day and, as these were pulled in from all over Scotland, included the pipe band of the Cameronians then stationed in Edinburgh. Needless to say it gave Douglas Graham and I tremendous pleasure. Even Douglas Wimberley thought that as the Regiment was to be disbanded the following year, it was poetic justice. Monty sat out on the saluting base with myself on his right and Lieutenant General Sir George Gordon Lennox on his left.

Monty gave good value this day, as he always did and did not depart until the early evening. We ran back to Brechin and spent the weekend there before returning to Cupar, Angus to stay for a couple of nights with the Riddell Websters. We stopped off for a night with Dorothy Simpson in Edinburgh and then ran through to Coventry to see the Cuthberts, finally arriving in Farnham well after midnight. So ended my last glimpse of a famous old Territorial division.

When we next returned to Scotland it was to be present at the disbandment parade of my first Regiment, the Cameronians (Scottish Rifles) at Castle Douglas in Lanarkshire. We were the only Rifle Regiment in the Lowland Brigade and all our rifle customs were almost certain to disappear. That evening there was a regimental dinner in the Queen's Hotel, attended by all serving and retired officers and their wives. The speeches were excellent and the evening very long. It could be the last one I shall ever attend. I have never subscribed to the inclusion of women, however much they lend colour to these parties. I do not think they have any place in such gatherings.

The following day we picked up Robin Money and drove out to the Tinto Hotel where we were the guests, along with a great number of others, of George Collingwood and the Lord Lieutenant of Lanarkshire, Lord Clydesmuir. It was a grey blustery day on the 279th Anniversary of the raising of the Regiment, and there was a huge attendance. The occasion was very moving and it seemed symbolical that as soon as the troops finally marched off without their drums beating, the skies opened as if in sympathy with this sad occasion.

1970 proved to be a much more active year than I had expected; in the autumn we needed to resolve who was going to be my successor as Chairman of the Hospital as it was over six years since I had been appointed and eventually Sir Leslie Tyler was chosen. In the meantime dear old Lisle Watson, the Warden of the Pitt Street

Settlement since he had formed it in 1911 had died. I had come into contact with him as a result of his service in the 1914–1918 war in the Cameronians, and we met at regimental dinners. In 1965 he asked me to join the Board of Control of the Settlement. It was concerned initially with the spiritual and physical development of young men, particularly between the wars, and had as its outlet the Boy Scout movement. The Settlement did a marvellous job over the years, although Lisle Watson became increasingly out of touch with the young of today and tended more and more to live in the past and after three or four years, he felt that I was not in sympathy with his efforts, and would I please resign. I refused to do this as I felt that the Settlement still had an important function to fulfil.

When he died he left his personal estate to the Settlement and expressed the wish that the Settlement should be continued, but without stipulating what form activities should take. There were still a few active members of the Board available and when we met we agreed that we should convert the Settlement into a community centre, a badly-needed requirement in Peckham where a full-scale plan was about to be launched to rehouse thousands of the inhabitants with all the social dislocation this entailed. At a later stage it was agreed that the Settlement should be continued on its existing site, and that it should gradually be transformed into a community centre. We also agreed to advertise for a new Warden in the hope that he would be able to assume the duties by early June. In the meantime several of the old Board of Control had either died or wished to retire and the need to build up a new Board was an issue of some importance. We managed to get the Reverend Clifford Wright to join, but we had to collect a few more if the Board was to have the solid basis it urgently needed. The pity of it was that Lisle could have provided this framework when he was still alive, but I realised then he was in no mood during the last few years of his life to do any such thing.

Reflections

These pages have set out the course of my life covering a period of seventy years, commencing with life in Winchester and my school days there, until I went to Sandhurst and embarked upon a career in the Army. Thereafter a stream of events followed, over which I seldom had control.

It was probably the presence in Winchester of the Depot of the Greenjackets which made me aware of the Army and the glamour it then had. My uncle, on my mother's side, had, in the last century enlisted as a soldier, which was considered a great disgrace to the family and 'no stone was left unturned' to scrape together the money necessary to buy him out. He would have made a splendid soldier, but the reputation of the Army precluded the member of any 'respectable' family from going in through the ranks. The fact remains that the colour and dash of those Riflemen before the First World War left an impression on me that I carry to this day.

I knew that a career in the Army would enable me to lead an open-air life and an opportunity to travel, both of which I wanted. At the end of the two-year course I was fortunate enough to be commissioned into a Regiment in which you were encouraged to take your profession seriously and, of all things, also a Rifle Regiment.

The Staff College started to loom up on my horizon when I had been serving for only six years and in 1929 I went off to Germany for three months to study German, become an interpreter, and thus have a strong 'optional' subject when the time came to take the examination. It may have been over-optimistic to run for the Staff College Examination in the spring of 1933 within a matter of weeks of relinquishing the Adjutancy, but I nearly passed in and would have done so but for one paper which I failed by ten marks to reach the qualifying minimum. It was a great disappointment, but on balance there was much to be said for going to the Staff College later, because everything came along so much more easily.

All this meant that I was a subaltern for twelve years, which I think was rather a long time, but life was so varied that somehow this long period in the lowest rank failed to blunt the enthusiasm.

I was interested in sports. I was a bad shot, probably because I moved into this field at a very late stage, and lacked real practice. This was probably accentuated by the fact that the birds were lovely to look at and that I lacked the killer instinct. I never had much opportunity to learn to fish and although fishing is regarded as a good form of relaxation in pleasant surroundings, I found it inexpressibly dull. The fact was that throughout my life I was far more interested in hitting a ball of whatever nature, or running or jumping.

I remained on the Staff for four years, until 1942, and then spent the remainder of my service in command. This latter period in the rank of Lieutenant Colonel and above more than offset the long apprenticeship I had served as a subaltern. In fact that apprentice-ship stood me in good stead throughout my service. I remember visiting a famous cavalry regiment and on entering a barrack room made a few criticisms, and one or two commendations. I suppose I moved through the room in a matter of only a few minutes. I stayed on for lunch and later a squadron commander came up to me and said, 'General, how do you do it? You spotted at once all the things that mattered.' I replied, 'It was not General Murray who carried out that inspection, it was Mr Murray who had gazed upon such a scene in years gone by, sufficiently often not to have to think about it.'

When I got command of the 1st Battalion the Gordon Highlanders in May 1942, I could not fail to have doubts as to my ability to command adequately an infantry battalion in war. Apart from three months with the Cameron Highlanders in Catterick in 1938, I had seen no regimental life since I left Lucknow in 1934, where our transport consisted of carts drawn by bullocks, or AT carts drawn by mules. I was fortunate that the Gordon Highlanders were about to go abroad with the possibility of going on active service. In fact, within a few days of my arrival, the transport set out by road for Liverpool. I took a very close look at the Battalion in the weeks remaining before we followed the transport, and it was most reassuring. I knew we would make a proper job of it.

I did nothing to 'manipulate' my career except in 1943 when I pulled strings to avoid going on a hospital ship to South Africa. By the spring of 1943 I was sufficiently recovered to arrange my return (without authority) to the 51st Highland Division. The War anyway moved so fast that the main thing was to keep your head above water. We were approaching Cape Town: it emerged that our destination was Suez and the Western Desert; it could well have been Burma or India. It was on my 40th birthday in 1943 that I 'cadged' a lift in an RAF plane taking off from Cairo, and the same evening I landed at Sfax within a few miles of the Highland Division which had taken nearly six months to get there. The Division was already planning the invasion of Sicily and, possibly because I was immediately available, I was given command of the infantry brigade in which I had served, consequent to the promotion of the then Commander, Douglas Graham, to command the 56th London Division. The campaign in North Africa was over by mid May and early in July we embarked upon the invasion of Sicily. The Sicilian Campaign (on which I wrote a paper in 1943) was over in a matter of weeks and to my subsequent surprise we were then shipped back to England to prepare for the Normandy invasions.

After the interlude in the UK which included the pre-Normandy conferences at St Paul's School and other venues, some four months in all, the Division was off again in June 1944 to renew the fight against the Germans, this time in Normandy.

After Normandy I took command of the 6th Armoured Division in August 1944 near Florence in Italy and this third command in the space of just over two years carried with it promotion to the Acting rank of Major General. Again I found the prospect of commanding a new formation composed of Cavalry, Yeomanry, Guardsmen and Greenjackets somewhat daunting. As usual anticipation proved more frightening than realisation. It was late August when I landed in Rome from Algiers, and it was reassuring to find several of the key staff officers of the Division taking leave there. The Division had gone into action that May in the Liri Valley near Cassino and thereafter took part in the pursuit up Italy being now on the outskirts of Florence. Italy is not well suited for armoured operations and the pursuit, inevitably, was somewhat clumsy. Nevertheless, the Division did well. When I went around the Regiments it was obvious that some Regiments were very tired, which was not surprising after the long-drawn-out operation of the summer, and that summer in Italy was very hot indeed. When I looked at the ground I saw that armoured action was clearly not on. I then heard that XIII Corps, in which we were, had come under command of the American Fifth Army and the Eighth Army had moved east down to the coast and was to attack from there. The plan was for them to attack late in August up the coastal strip and, when they had drawn off the German reserves, the Fifth Army under Mark Clark would thrust through the Apennines towards Bologna. In the event the Fifth Army did not attack until the middle of September.

In the early spring we rejoined the Eighth Army down on the coast. We then had two months of intensive training and it was a great relief to discover that the Division had not lost its edge as a result of its experiences during the winter.

The spring offensive of 1945 was extremely well planned with the Eighth Army attacking first, followed later by the American Fifth Army. The only Division in reserve in the spring of 1945 was mine, the 6th Armoured. The battle started early in April with some subsidiary operations. Although progress appeared to be slow it was astonishing how easy it was to be left behind. On the 18th of April (my 42nd birthday) we passed through the forward troops and took over the front in the area of Argenta. We deployed on a wide front and at once ran into trouble. We then regrouped, found another hole, went through it and redeployed on the other side. Again a hold-up, but resistance was getting weaker. A further regrouping, another hole, and this time we deployed on the other side on a 40-mile front, and went hard until we finally reached the River Po on the 23rd, five days after we had started. So we swept through across the Brenta, then the Adige and on into Austria through Tarvisio, Villach and Klagenfurt until we finally came to a halt on meeting the Russians at Judenburg when in full cry to Vienna.

Sitting in the Schloss Tentschach above Klagenfurt in the summer of 1945 it was possible to relax and think through all these happenings. I started my career in an 'unfashionable' Regiment in 1923, as an impecunious subaltern, and found myself twenty-one years later commanding an armoured (or one could almost say, cavalry) Division in a pursuit battle across the northern plain of Italy into the heart of Austria. The interesting thing was that the pursuit was largely in the hands of those same Greenjackets who had captured my imagination over thirty years before.

I married Beatrice in 1953 and we played an impressive hand both in Scotland and Scandinavia as a team. I provided the background and she provided the depth of colour to these appointments. She may well be better remembered in these places than I. Consequently I was far more concerned in ensuring that, as far as it was possible, when we retired she should move back into the field which was her life. Had I known more of the problems here the transition would have been effective much earlier than was the case.

It was fun sorting out some of the affairs of the Royal Hospital and Home for Incurables, and ironic that I found myself involved with the preservation of the old, instead of fostering the young. Since then, consequent upon the death of Major Lisle Watson, I got involved in the restoration of a community centre (better called a settlement) in Peckham, one of the hotter spots in the East End of London. Events had taken over control yet again. It was a situation which simply could not be ignored.

The 'Twilight of Life', an expression which Monty loved to use when he was much younger, was basically misconceived.

I feel that my life has gone full cycle, and this was confirmed by the facts that the 51st Highland Division folded in 1967 and my first Regiment, The Cameronians (Scottish Rifles) disbanded the following year.

Beatrice has always felt that there was always something around the corner demanding my attention. I, on the other hand, am quite convinced that my life has gone full circle and I no longer seek challenges, which is an indication of a changed approach to life.

It was interesting to discover that, at the relatively early age of 58, one was regarded as unemployable. I continue to have the greatest confidence in the oncoming generations, however much they try to disguise their quality. I saw enough of the teenagers of the 1930s, who played a major part in winning World War Two, to be quite convinced that the young of today, given proper challenges, will be just as good. They are more honest and frank and in any event, whether they like it or not, tomorrow is in their hands and not ours. The wind is set fair and they should be given all encouragement.

[**Editor's Note:** Nap Murray died in the DGAA, Vicarage Gate, South Kensington, in July 1989. Whilst there he preferred to have no television; only books, visitors and a half-bottle of claret each day (to keep him going). Nap Murray wrote these memoirs in the 1970s on an old Imperial typewriter without assistance. His recall was excellent and he had kept many of the original papers and letters to draw from. He knew the memoirs were not going to be published in his lifetime, although he hoped they would be one day. At that time he said 'I have my dreams and memories to keep me company' and they were a sufficient distraction.]

Bibliography

Blaxland, G., *Alexander's Generals* (William Kimber, London)

Delaforce, P., *Monty's Highlanders* (Chancellor Press/Octopus Publishing Group Ltd.)

Doherty, R., *None Bolder* (Spellmount)

Lyndsey, M., *So Few Got Through* (Pen & Sword)

McGregor, J., *The Spirit of Angus* (Phillimore)

Salmond, J.B., *51st Highland Division* (Blackwoods, 1953)

Index